Foreign Accent

To what extent do our accents determine the way we are perceived by others? Is foreign accent inevitably associated with social stigma? Accent is a matter of great public interest given the impact of migration on national and global affairs, but, until now, applied linguistics research has treated accent largely as a theoretical puzzle. In this fascinating account, Alene Moyer examines the social, psychological, educational, and legal ramifications of sounding 'foreign.' She explores how accent operates contextually through analysis of issues such as: the neuro-cognitive constraints on phonological acquisition, individual factors that contribute to the 'intractability' of accent, foreign accent as a criterion for workplace discrimination, and the efficacy of instruction for improving pronunciation. This holistic treatment of second language accent is an essential resource for graduate students and researchers interested in applied linguistics, bilingualism, and foreign language education.

ALENE MOYER is Associate Professor in the School of Languages, Literatures and Cultures, and Associate Dean in the College of Arts and Humanities, at the University of Maryland.

Foreign Accent

The Phenomenon of Non-native Speech

Alene Moyer

CAMBRIDGE
UNIVERSITY PRESS

University Printing House, Cambridge CB2 8BS, United Kingdom

Published in the United States of America by Cambridge University Press, New York

Cambridge University Press is part of the University of Cambridge.

It furthers the University's mission by disseminating knowledge in the pursuit of education, learning and research at the highest international levels of excellence.

www.cambridge.org
Information on this title: www.cambridge.org/9781107005815

© Alene Moyer 2013

This publication is in copyright. Subject to statutory exception and to the provisions of relevant collective licensing agreements, no reproduction of any part may take place without the written permission of Cambridge University Press.

First published 2013
Reprinted 2014

Printed in the United Kingdom by Print on Demand, World Wide

A catalogue record for this publication is available from the British Library

Library of Congress Cataloguing in Publication data
Moyer, Alene, 1961– author.
Foreign accent : the phenomenon of non-native speech / Alene Moyer.
pages cm
ISBN 978-1-107-00581-5 (hardback)
1. English language – Pronunciation by foreign speakers. 2. Second language acquisition – Social aspects. 3. Languages in contact. I. Title.
PE1137.M83   2013
305.7–dc23

2012036028

ISBN 978-1-107-00581-5 Hardback

Cambridge University Press has no responsibility for the persistence or accuracy of URLs for external or third-party internet websites referred to in this publication, and does not guarantee that any content on such websites is, or will remain, accurate or appropriate.

In memory of Frank E. Donahue

Contents

List of tables   *page* x
Acknowledgments   xi

Introduction   1

1 The scope and relevance of accent   9
    1.1 A definition of accent   10
    1.2 Challenges for the L2 user   12
        1.2.1 Phonological style and fluency   13
        1.2.2 Attitudes toward non-native accents   14
        1.2.3 L1–L2 phonological contrasts   15
    1.3 Ultimate attainment in L2 phonology   18
    1.4 Conclusion: the salience of accent in a second language   19

2 Accent and age   21
    2.1 Age effects research in L2 phonology   21
    2.2 A critical look at the critical period for phonology   25
    2.3 Neural organization and the question of plasticity   27
    2.4 L2 phonological knowledge and cognitive processes   30
        2.4.1 Categorical perception   31
        2.4.2 Transfer   37
        2.4.3 Universal processes and markedness   39
    2.5 Possible advantages of early bilingualism   42
        2.5.1 Metalinguistic and phonological awareness   42
        2.5.2 Underlying phonological representations   43
        2.5.3 Uniqueness of bilingual language processing   44
        2.5.4 Early passive exposure to L2   45
    2.6 Conclusion: reframing the age debate for L2 accent   46

3 Accent and the individual   49
    3.1 Intrinsic individual differences   51
        3.1.1 Aptitude   52
        3.1.2 Memory   53
        3.1.3 Hemispheric preference, musical 'talent,' and experience   54
        3.1.4 Learning styles and strategies   56
        3.1.5 Gender differences   58

	3.2	Socio-psychological factors	62
		3.2.1 Identity, acculturation, and the 'linguistic ego'	62
		3.2.2 Motivation	67
		3.2.3 Attitudes and learner investment	70
	3.3	Experience and input	72
		3.3.1 Length of residence	73
		3.3.2 L2 use	75
		3.3.3 Language dominance	76
		3.3.4 L1 attrition	78
	3.4	Exceptional language learners	80
	3.5	Conclusion: gaps in theory and method	82
4	**Accent and society**	85
	4.1	Historical perspectives on a standard accent in English	87
	4.2	Communicative effects of a non-native accent	92
		4.2.1 Comprehensibility, intelligibility, and accentedness	93
		4.2.2 Phonological accommodation	99
	4.3	Reactions to non-native speech	102
		4.3.1 Prestige, prejudice, and familiarity	102
		4.3.2 Linguistic and contextual factors	105
		4.3.3 Demographic factors	106
		4.3.4 Communicative consequences	107
		4.3.5 Critical summary	108
	4.4	Strongholds of accent stereotypes	109
		4.4.1 Media portrayals of non-native speakers	111
		4.4.2 Call centers	113
		4.4.3 The international teaching assistant controversy	116
	4.5	Conclusion: accent and assimilation	121
5	**Accent and the law**	125
	5.1	Linguistic profiling	126
	5.2	Accent, employability, and earnings	128
	5.3	Challenges to accent in the workplace	131
	5.4	Accent bias in the courtroom	140
	5.5	Conclusion: future empirical and legal challenges	143
6	**Accent and instruction**	146
	6.1	Phonology's place in the FL classroom	147
	6.2	Classroom approaches to phonological instruction: past and present	148
	6.3	The basis for instructional efficacy in L2 phonology	152
		6.3.1 Explicit practice, attention, and awareness	152
		6.3.2 Self-monitoring	154
		6.3.3 The role of feedback	156
	6.4	Computer-assisted pronunciation training	158
	6.5	Effects of orthographic input	161
	6.6	Accent within current standards models	163
	6.7	Conclusions: the potential of phonological instruction	167

7	Conclusions	171
	7.1 Accent in a second language: viewpoints and expectations	171
	7.2 Remaining questions and methodological recommendations	172
	7.3 The unique challenge of L2 accent	177

Glossary 179
References 184
Index 217

Tables

3.1 Intrinsic and extrinsic factors relevant to L2 accent   *page* 83
6.1 Phonological control – CEF descriptors per proficiency level   165
6.2 ILR descriptions of speaking ability   166

Acknowledgments

I owe much to the anonymous readers whose suggestions were invaluable in strengthening the final manuscript. Special thanks go to Roy Major and Thorsten Piske, whose unflagging encouragement kept me going throughout the research and writing process. I also gratefully acknowledge my home institution, The University of Maryland, which granted me a generous research leave to complete this book. Finally, I am most thankful for the loving support of my remarkable family – Aviel, Martin, and Joseph – who carried me through, as always.

Introduction

Research in second language acquisition (SLA) has long tended toward a 'deficit' view of second language (L2) learners, focusing on what they fundamentally do not know compared to native speakers. For phonology, cognitively oriented studies examine the ability to perceive L2 phonological contrasts accurately, and measure degree of foreign accent for speaking skills. Age of first exposure to L2 is commonly cited as the primary (neurobiological) predictor of success in phonological attainment. Yet studies on ostensibly universal developmental errors like phonemic/phonetic substitution show that individual variation is ubiquitous (Beebe 1984; Major 2001; Osburne 2003). And although an early start appears to be advantageous over the long term, a host of interrelated variables is at play, having to do with learner orientation and experience (see Birdsong 2005; Moyer 2004, 2007a; Scovel 2000). One valuable contribution of sociolinguistic work in SLA has been to call attention to social, cultural, and psychological circumstances relevant to individual L2 users – a reminder to take a more nuanced look at what underlies age effects in SLA.

This book brings together various strands of research from competing theoretical paradigms, both cognitive and sociolinguistic, with an emphasis on accent as critical to "the entire act of speech communication ... [as] an integral part of meaning, discourse, context and situation" (Morley 1996a: 146). As Miller has written, L2 users face a huge challenge; they must find a way to participate in the 'dominant discourse' if they are to renegotiate their identities and successfully integrate into the wider society (2003). Accent affects this negotiation in no small part, because only by being 'audible,' i.e., acknowledged in the second language, can L2 users fully participate in society (ibid.). *Intelligibility* is central to this threshold.

Second language users face a difficult task: They must learn to perceive fine phonemic differences and establish a new system of phonological rules; produce sounds and sound sequences that often contradict the rules of their native languages; and replicate the patterns of stress, rhythm, and intonation that carry implicit as well as explicit meaning. If accent is an especially difficult skill to acquire, much depends on it from the standpoint of communication.

By definition, accent encompasses all the layers of phonetic and prosodic precision required to convey and negotiate meaning.

Although there is increasing interest in second language accent of late, this interest is characterized by disparate theoretical agendas rather than any overarching appreciation for the importance of accent. For example, accent is at the center of the cognitive debate on *nativeness* as the proving ground for the *Critical Period Hypothesis* – the idea that certain language functions can only be fully acquired within a specific window of time, typically by puberty if not well before. And even if some advanced learners perform like natives for various aspects of L2 grammar, phonological *authenticity* is out of reach for most. Nativeness is a sociocultural hot potato as well, seen as a hegemonic vestige of the 'monolingual speaker ideal'. These generalizations perpetuate mutual exclusivity; rarely does one paradigm recognize the relevance of the other. The cognitive paradigm is limited by a lack of contextualization, and its sociocultural counterpart is all but disinterested in how acquisition proceeds. Both end up with a limited appreciation for how accent evolves as such an important aspect of linguistic knowledge and performance.

Acquiring a new system of sounds is predicated on a balance of cognitive, social, and psychological factors. Someone whose future career success depends on sounding native or near native may initiate strategies to improve his accent (Moyer 2004, 2007a), while others manipulate accent for effect, approximating a native sound (or not) according to context (Piller 2002). Accent in a second language is thus more fluid and permeable than is often assumed.

The understanding reflected in this book is that, by its nature, L2 phonological acquisition lies at the intersection of ability, inclination, and reception. The aim is therefore to bridge competing theoretical paradigms to appreciate the immediate, as well as the overarching, significance of sounding foreign. Guiding questions include:

- To what extent can accent be acquired beyond a certain age? Specifically, which mechanisms predict the difficulty of phonological acquisition relative to other language skills like grammar and lexicon?
- How much of a role do individual factors like motivation, identity, and target-language experience play vis-à-vis age at first exposure to the language?
- Is intelligibility a more reasonable goal for late learners than 'near-nativeness,' and, if so, what criteria influence perceptions of intelligibility?
- What are the consequences of sounding foreign in public domains? Will these consequences likely shift with increasing immigration and mobility for non-native populations?
- Can overt instruction effectively improve a foreign accent, or is naturalistic experience in the target-language environment necessary to attain real authenticity?

Beginning with a comprehensive definition of accent (Chapter 1), we consider neurobiological and articulatory constraints on phonological acquisition (Chapter 2); the cognitive, psychological, and experiential predictors of long-term phonological attainment (Chapter 3); accent's communicative impact and the perpetuation of its negative reception through stereotypes (Chapter 4); the reception of accent in the public sphere, specifically, as a potentially actionable aspect of workplace performance (Chapter 5); and the history and efficacy of formal instruction directed at improving accent (Chapter 6). Whereas applied linguistics research has largely treated L2 phonology as a theoretical puzzle, this work takes an inclusive approach in the hopes of integrating theoretical and practical perspectives on sounding 'foreign'.

Chapter 1: The scope and relevance of accent

This first chapter lays the groundwork for understanding accent as a salient aspect of communicative *fluency*. We first define it in linguistic terms, as encompassing phonetic and phonemic aspects of speech alongside intonation, pitch, rhythm, length, juncture, and stress. Together these features convey both literal and implicit meanings, and in that sense they greatly affect intelligibility and pragmatic appropriateness. Chapter 1 also describes accent as communicatively dynamic, in L2 as it is in L1. Not only does accent shift over time in response to one's experience with, and orientation toward, the target language, it also fluctuates more immediately at the situational level, as seen in phenomena such as *style-shifting* and *accommodation*.

Finally, the reader is introduced to the L2 learner/user[1] as the expectations and conditions for SLA are contrasted with those of the first. Several important theoretical concepts are introduced, including the critical period, ultimate attainment, and nativeness. With an inclusive definition of accent in hand, the remaining chapters detail problems in the theory and practice of second language phonology.

Chapter 2: Accent and age

Phonology is unique compared to other language realms because it relies on both motor-based and cognitive skills for perception and production, and thus involves multiple *processing* centers, any of which could be subject to a decline in capacity or function over the individual's lifetime. At the same time, the nature of such declines has remained elusive. Do they represent a motor-based or conceptual loss of function, such as a decline in categorical perception?

---

[1] *L2 learner* and *L2 user* appear interchangeably throughout the book. Although the terms may be distinguished for various reasons (see Cook 2002), no social or political distinction is intended here.

Or are they due instead to an increase in certain capacities or processes, specifically: Do higher-order analytical abilities interfere with innate language-learning faculties?

Because it relies on articulatory precision, auditory–perceptual processing, and higher-order analysis, phonology may be especially prone to age effects in the neurocognitive realm. On the other hand, some scholars assert that neurobiological age is an unsatisfactory explanation for non-native-like outcomes in L2 phonology because it is inherently tied to external conditions and the learner's socio-psychological orientation.

To clarify the role of age, Chapter 2 examines the processes believed to underlie phonological skills, with an eye toward how these may shift over time. The neurological foundations of phonology are outlined first, followed by a discussion of the critical period, neural processing differences between early and late bilinguals, and the universal mechanisms presumed to guide L2 phonological acquisition. We also compare theories about the influence of L1 on L2 accent before reviewing a few persistent quandaries, e.g.:

- whether the critical period 'window' for phonology truly closes at all, or whether it closes much earlier than puberty;
- whether the ability to perceive, but not produce, L2 phonetic contrasts (or vice versa) means that these two skill sets are somehow separate;
- whether early childhood exposure to a given language, even if passive, confers any advantage on phonological acquisition later in life.

The conclusion summarizes the importance of intrinsic factors in light of: (a) the differences between L1 and L2 phonological knowledge; (b) the prevalence of individual variation in phonological abilities.

Chapter 3: Accent and the individual

Socio-psychological research, and even some age effects research, suggests that accent hinges in no small part on learner orientation, and on certain aspects of L2 experience such as social contact and friendships with native speakers (Moyer 2004, 2011). Where immigration occurs before adolescence, both formal and informal avenues for language contact are normally available. Adult language learners, by contrast, must bridge potential cognitive constraints and social barriers to assimilate linguistically and socially to their new environment, usually without the advantage of formal instruction. By comparison, they must work much harder to forge new relationships and learn new ways of self-expression – unlikely achievements unless opportunities for interaction in the target language are plentiful.

In light of all this, Chapter 3 takes a detailed look at individual differences, beginning with aptitude, working memory, and strategy use, as well as possible differences in how males and females acquire, and aspire to, phonological accuracy. While most studies treat factors in relative isolation, there is no doubt that cognitive, social, psychological, and experiential variables interact. We therefore highlight research that speaks to their interconnectedness, paying special attention to identity, motivation, and attitudes as essential to the long-term process of language learning.

An appreciation for the significance of one's opportunities to engage with native speakers is now gaining traction in the L2 phonology literature. Chapter 3 therefore brings together what we know about learner orientation and learning circumstances as essential to *ultimate attainment* in accent. Discussions of *passing* and exceptional outcomes underscore the personal nature of individual differences, and set the stage for Chapter 4's treatment of accent in the broader social context.

Chapter 4: Accent and society

Chapter 4 begins with a historical treatment of *prescriptivism* as the driving force behind language codification in general, and notions of phonological correctness, specifically. Norms for pronunciation in English, set forth in early dictionaries and historical essays, reflect a desire for linguistic purity and social unity alongside a thinly veiled fear of diversity. This is particularly relevant for non-native speakers who must negotiate a way to be heard for *what* they say rather than *how* they say it.

Accent in a second language is often problematized as a matter of intelligibility rather than absolute accuracy. On the practical side, many scholars and teachers assert that this is a more realistic and fair expectation of L2 learners. In terms of theory, *intelligibility* and *comprehensibility* speak to the immediate, communicative impact of sounding foreign. By implication, they also call to question the less-explored issue of acceptability (Derwing and Munro 1997; Seidlhofer 2004). Put another way: What is really in question when an accented speaker is deemed 'hard to understand'? This is a question that must be asked given that a foreign accent – even a strong one – does not necessarily render a speaker incomprehensible. Beyond segmental or prosodic precision, what other linguistic and non-linguistic factors are salient in the listener's mind?

With an emphasis on the social reception of accent, Chapter 4 considers discourse phenomena like intelligibility and accommodation as well as broader attitudes connecting accent to intelligence, status, ethnicity, and so forth. A major challenge for future research is to dig deeper, going beyond the documentation of such attitudes in order to clarify the linguistic, demographic, and contextual criteria that underlie them. Two current controversies – overseas call center workers and international teaching assistants – practically illustrate how multiple factors, some linguistic and others purely social, influence native speakers' willingness to 'hear' and thus accommodate those who sound foreign.

Chapter 5: Accent and the law

Accent-related notions of acceptability shift as attitudes toward specific foreign and/or ethnic groups change. For example, L2 users of Hispanic background may endure more problems in the US today given the heated national debate over immigration, and anyone perceived to have a Middle Eastern background likely suffers greater discrimination since the terrorist attacks on September 11, 2001. Scholarly and popular sources up to now have dealt almost exclusively with the negative effects of sounding foreign, though it must be noted that some accents are prized, and therefore result in advantages rather than difficulties.

Bias toward accent is predicated on listener attitudes vis-à-vis the familiar categories associated with language variation: *social class*, race and ethnicity, age, education, regional background, gender, religion, etc. It has often been said that accent is a proxy for discrimination on those grounds. These biases play out in the workplace, and in our schools and neighborhoods, with real consequences. A new term has emerged in this context – *linguistic profiling* – relevant for both housing and employment decisions as landlords determine how they will treat potential occupants, and employers decide whether to interview and hire those with a foreign accent. We therefore look at the promise and limits of the law as it provides recourse to those who experience accent-based discrimination.

While it is true that some non-native speakers are more difficult to understand than others, the adjudication of formal claims against them must be fair. Title VII of the US Civil Rights Act (1964) prohibits discrimination based on national origin, including "cultural or linguistic characteristics" but this protection has been extremely limited in practice. The argument that an employee's accent negatively impacts his ability to communicate effectively has thus far been considered a bona fide defense against discrimination complaints, as seen in cases such as *Carion* v. *University of Oklahoma Board of Regents* (1984); *Fragante* v. *City and County of Honolulu* (1987); *Kahakua* v. *Friday* (1989). Yet there is no consistency in the substantiation of such claims; each case seems to be decided ad hoc, absent any external validation of the plaintiff's language proficiency.

Chapter 5's discussion underscores how muddled the issue of accent is in the legal sphere. Perhaps most surprising is the common assumption by the courts that anyone can readily change or improve his accent – a contradiction of everything the research tells us. More unsettling are the stereotypes that continue to prevail, even in this high-stakes, yet purportedly unbiased, context. Because discrimination cases related to language/national origin are on the rise in the US and elsewhere, some general guidelines are given for evaluating accent more fairly.

Chapter 6: Accent and instruction

If foreign-accented individuals wish to change the way they sound for personal or professional reasons, they may seek out instruction on how to do so. The kinds of activities they are likely to encounter through either classroom-based or online programs have not changed appreciably for decades, but little is known about how effective they are. There is some evidence that formal training leads to short-term gains in perception and production, as well as greater authenticity over the long term if based on discourse-level practice that includes attention to suprasegmentals (Akita 2006; Derwing and Rossiter 2003; Moyer 1999).

Current pedagogical emphases on oral proficiency and communicative competence, and most models for foreign language (FL) standards, treat accent only cursorily; it is mentioned as a barrier to comprehensibility at the very earliest stages of learning, and as an aspect of fluency that is suddenly quite meaningful at the very advanced/superior levels. What of the gap in between? Interested scholars and teachers have long advocated an integrated, discourse-level treatment of phonology (e.g., Pennington, Levis, and others), but this call has gained little traction among FL teachers in the US, and no particular program has been proposed to develop phonological fluency over the long term.

In this chapter, we trace the history of accent as a pedagogical priority, and examine the efficacy of various approaches and techniques, including: corrective feedback types, cross-modal practice, technological innovations, self-monitoring, and awareness-raising tasks. This discussion underscores the paucity of empirical evidence in this area, while highlighting the need to address accent as central to discursive fluency – the clear priority of current FL instructional approaches.

Given that few teachers receive formal training in phonology themselves these days, and few FL textbook packages include sufficient resources, accent has not been given its due in the post-methods era. In the absence of any national program that speaks to its importance, much less specific guidelines on how to address it in the classroom, teachers in the US in particular must decide for themselves whether to prioritize or disregard accent. Some may de-emphasize it on principle, as a way to favor intelligibility over the nativeness principle (Levis 2006), but are students then left unaware of how they sound, much less how to make any desired improvements?

Chapter 6 proposes that students be taught techniques to 'notice the gap' between their own accents and those of native speakers. At the same time, they should learn about regional, social, and individual variation so that the broader relevance of accent is appreciated. In this way, they will be better positioned to make their own decisions about how to pursue this aspect of L2 fluency.

Chapter 7: Conclusions

The final chapter reiterates the need to integrate multiple understandings of accent – neurobiological, cognitive, social, psychological, and communicative – to appreciate why it presents such a challenge for late language learners. Empirical research has a long way to go in this regard, as does the field of FL pedagogy.

On a broader level, we also take a more critical look at accent, asking whether (or where) it still matters in this age of globalization, multiculturalism and 'expanding circles' of L2 users (Kachru and Nelson 1996). Many argue that accent is relatively unimportant compared to other aspects of linguistic fluency, or that it should receive less emphasis because the 'standard' ideal is outdated, at best. But the salience of accent is both immediate and real; it is the means by which we make ourselves understood, and the yardstick by which others judge us, whether we like it or not. This is particularly relevant where second language users have few linguistic resources at their disposal to adjust and accommodate to other speakers, phonologically.

With an appreciation of accent as both individually constructed and as externally salient, researchers can move beyond what Atkinson (2010) has called 'radically internalist' perspectives to better understand how learners structure and process phonological input – cognitively and socially – throughout the course of the acquisition process.

Note: Terms which appear in italic are defined in the Glossary at the end of the book.

1 The scope and relevance of accent

> This voice I speak with these days, this English voice with its rounded vowels and consonants in more or less the right place – this is not the voice of my childhood. I picked it up in college, along with the unabridged *Clarissa* and a taste for port ... At the time I genuinely thought this was the voice of lettered people, and that if I didn't have the voice of lettered people I would never truly be lettered. A braver person, perhaps, would have stood firm, teaching her peers a useful lesson by example: not all lettered people need be of the same class, nor speak identically. I went the other way ... This voice I picked up along the way is no longer an exotic garment I put on like a college gown whenever I choose – now it is my only voice, whether I want it or not. I regret it; I should have kept both voices alive in my mouth. But how the culture warns against it!
>
> Smith 2009

By nature, humans distinguish themselves from one another along group lines, comparing physical or cognitive abilities, wealth, physique, and any other criteria deemed to have value (Giles 1979). Among these criteria, language is one of the most prominent, and salient. If it is the means by which we "construct and understand ourselves as individuals ... and also as members of a culture" (Lakoff 2001: 21), accent is at the forefront of this process; it can immediately identify us as either familiar or foreign, young or old, male or female, and so on. It is also the basis for intelligibility, affecting the extent to which others understand what we are trying to say.

Accent encompasses the sounds, rhythms, and melodies of speech. Beyond mere acoustics, however, it bears much symbolic value. Simply by speaking we convey much more than literal meaning, "sometimes by design and sometimes whether we like it or not" (Brown and Levinson 1979: 300). And because everyone has a unique accent in whichever language(s) he speaks, accent is as relative as it is ubiquitous.

The intention of this chapter is to address the scope and relevance of accent with an emphasis on the adult second language (L2) user. To that end, we first define accent, then briefly describe its communicative and social significance, and the special challenges of phonological acquisition beyond early childhood.

1.1 A definition of accent

Defining accent is no easy task. This is partly because of its inherent variability. How we sound has much to do with where we have been, and with whom we have affiliated. It provides clues about our age, gender, regional background, level of education, and even social class. At the same time, it is a moving target of sorts, meaning that while listeners easily pick up on features that sound 'southern,' 'educated,' and so on, no two members of the same *speech community* sound exactly alike, nor does any one person speak in acoustically identical ways across different situations, even if using the same words. When speaking with others, we continually adjust our pronunciation and alter our prosody to clarify meaning, punctuate important points, and signal distance vs. affiliation. In other words, we use accent to position ourselves vis-à-vis others. Thus, accent is a fluid, contextualized expression of our personal and social identity as well as our communicative stance.

Considering all of the information it conveys, and the deeper significance it carries – social, communicative, linguistic, and psychological – can accent be neatly defined? Let us first consider what accent is *not*.

Accent is distinct from *dialect*, though the terms are sometimes used interchangeably. For example, Cockney is both a dialect and an accent, but strictly speaking, *dialect* refers to a fully functioning language variety with its own vocabulary and grammar, as well as discursive style, in addition to a distinct accent. African American English, Southern Dialect, New England Dialect, etc. are all considered dialects of American English although each varies locally and socially. Thus, in common parlance, both *dialect* and *accent* refer to patterned language behavior within distinct regions, social classes, ethnic groups, even age groups, but *accent* refers only to speech sounds – the phonetics and phonology[1] of a given language variety.

Adding to the potential confusion, accent is also used interchangeably with *pronunciation*, but this is not a precise match either. Pronunciation typically refers to articulation; the place and position of speech organs (tongue, lips, teeth, uvula, larynx, nasal cavity, etc.) when producing specific speech sounds. Accent is a broader term that refers not only to the articulation of individual sounds, or *segments*, but to *suprasegmental* features as well: intonation, rhythm, pitch, segmental length, tempo, and loudness. These features distinguish semantic and

---

[1] In this book, the term *phonology* will be used more generally, to encompass both phonetics and phonology – a common practice in the SLA literature unless referring to specific learning phenomena, such as the acquisition of phonetic contrasts (e.g., /ɪ/–/ɛ/). Strictly defined, phonetics refers to the system of discrete speech sounds in a language – their articulatory, auditory, and acoustic properties and classification – while phonology refers more broadly to the rules governing the relationships between sounds. Phonological rules explain language-specific phenomena such as segmental assimilation, elision, deletion, coarticulation, etc., as well as phrasal rhythm and stress patterns.

A definition of accent

pragmatic meaning both within and beyond the word level. *Accent* is therefore narrower in scope than *dialect*, but denotes a fuller picture of speech fluency than does the term *pronunciation*.

A common situation illustrates the broad array of features inherent to accent: Consider how easily we understand the speech of a good friend, even in noisy and distracting surroundings. If we are unable to hear clearly articulated sounds, we still recognize her characteristic vowel length, intonational curves, pitch range, and rhythm. Ascertaining meaning is possible even in poor acoustic conditions because much of our interpretive work as listeners occurs on deeper levels of analysis, aided by a range of auditory stimuli beyond the segmental level (of course, numerous non-linguistic cues help as well).

If all visual cues were unavailable – if we could not see mouth shape, jaw movement, facial expressions, or gesture – could we still understand a speaker's message? Indeed, this is what we face when conversing on the telephone, where phonetic details are sometimes lost through a poor acoustic signal. Yet even a stranger's voice provides clues about age, gender, educational background, mood, and physical health, as well as the purpose for the call. These assumptions are based on complex acoustic features, many of which are suprasegmental in nature. The listener thus gleans a great deal of information from accent, acoustically; it delivers literal meaning, gives us insight into the speaker's background, and helps us to ascertain his communicative purpose.

Accent is a dynamic aspect of linguistic *fluency*. In practice, we adjust it to accommodate our listeners, or conversely, to establish social distance from them (details in Chapter 4). Furthermore, we mark important words and syllables with stress and pitch, we indicate that we want to hold the floor through rising or flat intonation, and we indicate points of thematic transition through syllable length, volume, and vowel quality (Couper-Kuhlen 2007). The ability to do so is an integral part of communicative fluency. While speaker personality and mood certainly play a part in such modulations, they are determined in great measure by convention. Much of our phonological performance reflects what is considered appropriate for the context and the relationship we have with our interlocutors.

All of these points underscore the salience of accent on multiple levels. In purely linguistic terms it delivers semantic content; at the level of discourse it controls the flow of interaction and signals our communicative intentions; socially and psychologically it situates the speaker in terms of group belonging and affirms personal identity and stance in an immediate way. The following definition reflects these complexities:

Accent is a set of dynamic segmental and suprasegmental habits that convey linguistic meaning along with social and situational affiliation.

It is understood that this definition applies to native and non-native speaker alike, even if there are differences in their respective abilities to convey all of these nuances. Individual variation in fluency will necessarily affect our ability to control the features mentioned, and thus affect how others 'hear' us. Indeed, our overall linguistic competence may be questioned on this basis.

To appreciate how this plays out in broader contexts, we briefly mention several fundamental concerns – style and fluency, and attitudes toward accent – noting that these are rarely addressed in foreign language (FL) classrooms; they are aspects of language practice typically acquired with naturalistic experience in the target-language community. We then outline several phonetic and phonological difficulties facing L2 learners, using English as a second language for our examples, and conclude with an overview of the contextual realities of sounding foreign.

1.2 Challenges for the L2 user

As noted, accent is a reflection of our past experiences: languages known, regional and social upbringing, educational background, and affiliations with various speech communities and social networks. This holds true for the second language as it does for the first. Perhaps this is where the similarity between L1 and L2 accent ends. The L2 learner begins from a radically different starting point; by early-to-mid childhood (possibly as early as age 4 years) a solid foundation in the mother tongue phonology is already in place and thus presents both a basis for metalinguistic awareness and a potential source of interference for any languages learned later on. Over time, the child also becomes socially and psychologically grounded in her mother tongue culture. These influences must be borne in mind in any account of L2 phonological acquisition.

It is an oft-repeated truism that children master their native language(s) while adult L2 learners fall short of full mastery, though this universal is increasingly coming under scrutiny (Spada 2011). The puzzle driving SLA research has been how to locate the source of this 'fundamental difference' (Bley-Vroman 1989). Do the relevant acquisitional processes change, or alternatively, do external circumstances, learner aptitudes, or differences in linguistic experience account for non-native outcomes in SLA? The essential question for phonology can be expressed in even more direct terms: *Why is a foreign accent in a second language so intractable?*

Much evidence suggests 'the earlier, the better' when it comes to acquiring a new sound system, and indeed, the relationship between age and accent is generally documented as a negative one. Other language skills appear less susceptible to age effects, perhaps because phonology – unlike any other aspect of language – involves more than analytical skills. The motor-skill basis of our speech apparatus appears subject to flexibility limits as early as 4–6 years of age.

Some scholars disregard evidence unsupportive of the *critical period*, yet the neurocognitive mechanisms presumed responsible for it are not directly observable. Moreover, age as a causal factor is difficult to disprove or falsify; it covaries with affective and experiential factors such as attitudes, identity, motivation, access to authentic input, and so on (explored at length in the next two chapters). These concerns 'ramp up' with puberty, at least through late adolescence and early adulthood, if not beyond. Researchers are challenged to disentangle this confluence of cognitive, psychological, social and neurobiological factors implicit in late language acquisition.

Beyond the pure mechanics of it, late learners also face constraints of an external nature. Among these challenges are negative attitudes toward accented speakers, which have the potential to constrain interaction, and thus exert detrimental effects on acquisition itself, for it is through interaction that we come to understand and apply the semantic and pragmatic nuances inherent to phonological fluency.

1.2.1 Phonological style and fluency

How we speak at any given time and place depends on myriad factors having to do with personal roles and relationships, the depth of our affiliations along certain categorical boundaries (age, gender, class, etc.), and numerous situational concerns as well. As native speakers, our linguistic repertoire is typically broad enough that we adjust our speech accordingly, and express some measure of individual style at the same time. This *style-shifting* – the ability to flexibly apply and adjust certain features for contextual effect – affirms identity and establishes communicative stance and intent. As an example, slurring and elision can indicate carelessness, informality, or a sullen attitude, just as careful enunciation can mark formality, urgency, or threat. In addition, pitch range, speech rate, and loudness can all be adjusted to obtain a certain effect, or perlocution. The utterance "*Why don't you get back to me if the situation changes?*" could be a sarcastic brush-off or a polite request, depending on pitch dynamics and rhythm. Context helps the listener figure out the intended meaning.

Phonological variation and style – a seemingly effortless practice in L1 – is undoubtedly a challenge in L2. For native speakers, this is acquired simultaneously with grammar and lexicon from earliest childhood (Kerswill and Shockey 2007). By contrast, many non-native speakers diligently study a target language in the classroom, only to discover that it sounds quite different on the street. The realities of variation present them with a real conundrum. Such *procedural knowledge* may not be addressed overtly, much less actually practiced, in the classroom. To acquire it one needs an interactive base, a social network in other words, and building up such a network is a predictably slow process for those joining the target-language community as adults. Furthermore, the relationship between language abilities and social networks is surely circular in nature. To achieve real fluency, one needs experience beyond the classroom, but fluency is often a precondition for forming deeper social bonds (see Moyer 2004).

Sociocultural approaches see interaction as the locus for creating identity and thus social meaning (LePage and Tabouret-Keller 1985). In fact, newer perspectives assert that linguistic markers are not so predictably tied to static categories like class, gender, etc. Instead, language behavior is more nuanced, reflecting degree of integration and attitudes toward specific social networks (Campbell-Kibler 2011; Chambers 2009). This accounts for members of the same class, gender, and age within a regional or social network who do not sound alike (see Labov 1963, cited in Chambers 2009). Yet many adult immigrants have limited contact with native speakers, at least initially, thus they struggle to build social networks in the target language, affecting the fluency needed to move fluidly along the style continuum. Where missteps or gaps are evident, language competence – and by extension, social acceptability – may be questioned.

1.2.2 Attitudes toward non-native accents

Tabouret-Keller (1997) stresses that style is not strictly a matter of volition. Some speakers are simply expected to talk a certain way because of who they are: "Group affiliation is hardly something that anyone can dispense with, but some groups one is part of willy-nilly, e.g., gender or age groups; some are imposed upon one, e.g., by social categorization" – working class, as one example, or "non-native" as another (ibid.: 321). Kang and Rubin (2009) have shown that even native speech in a *matched guise* is 'heard' differently as a function of how speakers are expected to sound (see Lambert 1967). If listeners expect to hear a foreign accent based on non-linguistic cues (e.g., physical attributes), they will indeed 'hear' it, and comprehension and recall can suffer as a result (discussed in Chapter 4).

As social beings, we inevitably size up one another according to perceived similarity–difference. Thus it is no real surprise that listeners rate their own accents positively, while foreign accents tend to be viewed negatively by comparison. At the same time, Hamers and Blanc's (2000) summary of language attitude studies shows that certain foreign accents get high marks for status and intelligence (e.g., Asian and European ones in English), so prestige is not only about sounding 'standard'. Personal affiliations and contextual factors further complicate the picture. Ryan et al. (1975) found that Anglo and Mexican-born Hispanic listeners rated Anglo speakers as more highly educated when the task represented classroom language, but both

Anglos and Hispanics preferred Spanish-accented speech for the home/family context. Simply put, prestige may be context dependent.

If accents considered less prestigious or less familiar are particularly susceptible to negative evaluation, this can have far-reaching consequences for the L2 speaker. In his essay, "Defining Who We Are in Society," David Troutt makes the following observation:

> Perhaps nothing defines us more than our linguistic skills; nothing determines as much about where we can and cannot go. How we talk may be the first – and last – clue about our intelligence, and whether we're trusted or feared, heard or ignored, admitted or excluded. (2005: 289)

To the extent that accent functions as a gatekeeper, opening the way to further communication with others, a disfavored accent can diminish the opportunity to be heard, or worse (more in Chapters 4 and 5). Which consequence obtains is largely a function of pre-existing attitudes and the willingness of one's interlocutor to share the communicative burden.

1.2.3 L1–L2 phonological contrasts

Miller (2003) frames the transition to communicative fluency in L2 as a question of 'audibility'; only those who speak clearly and proficiently, in a way that readily represents their sense of self, will be audible to mainstream groups (48). In her study of immigrant adolescents in an Australian high school, she details an interaction with 'John,' a native of Hong Kong whose English she describes as "very jerky" and "staccato, with long pauses" (ibid.: 91). An excerpt of their conversation about John's goals for university study illustrates the ensuing challenges when both he and Miller must overcome a miscommunication based on his faulty pronunciation of a basic phoneme (in this case, /n/ in the word *neighbor*). Miller's own frustration, even as a researcher intent on understanding John's message, underscores how a strong foreign accent can affect comprehensibility, and trigger a breakdown in communication.

John's speech typifies the early stages of L2 phonological development, where simplification strategies such as vowel insertion and consonant deletion are common. The source of these errors may be at the level of production only – an inability to articulate a specific sound – while others result from faulty perceptions of the phonemes and phonetic contrasts in question. Indeed, many scholars maintain that because the L1 system sets the perceptual framework for all subsequent language learning, it invariably constrains the ability to learn new sound categories and sound patterns later in life (Escudero 2007; Strange 1995).

In *Foreign Accent: The Ontogeny and Phylogeny of Second Language Phonology*, Roy Major (2001) catalogues potential difficulties for learners such as John, ranging from phonetic contrasts to broader patterns of phonology and prosody. The list below follows Major's discussion and examples, with a few additions:

(1) **Segments:** The individual characteristics of each distinct sound, or segment, in a language must be mastered in terms of tongue height and placement, lip movement, aspiration, etc. This means that even a seemingly straightforward phoneme like /t/ will vary. For example, the Spanish version is unaspirated, but the English version is aspirated in initial position (as in Spanish *tu* vs. English *two*). L2 learners may not actually notice the difference without overt feedback. *Voice onset time* – (VOT) the time that elapses between the release of airflow (or burst) from the lungs and the beginning of vocal cord vibration – is a common point of comparison between native and non-native speakers. The seemingly minute difference between the short VOT lag (less than 35 ms.) of a Spanish speaker pronouncing /t/ and the longer lag pattern of an English speaker (over 35 ms.) is easily detected by a listener. Experience makes a difference, however, with more fluent American learners pronouncing a French /t/ with a target-like, shorter VOT duration as compared with beginners (as in Flege 1987, cited in Zampini 2008). Other challenges arise with altogether new sounds. The learner must recognize contrastive features as well as their allophonic realizations (e.g., voiced vs. voiceless /s/ in *someone* vs. *shoes*). Other oft-noted problems in English include voiced and voiceless *th* /ð/–/θ/ contrast and the /æ/ of *lather* or *rat* – realized among some L2 learners as /ɛ/ so that *lather* sounds like *leather*.

(2) **Syllable structure**: Composed of at least one vowel as the nucleus (in the great majority of languages), the syllable is a unit of timing, but it operates under language-specific phonotactic constraints. L2 learners typically modify syllable structures to fit their L1 structures. For example, languages like Hawaiian and Japanese require CV (consonant–vowel) syllable structure, so that even direct adoptions like *Big Mac* end up as [bigumaku]. Along similar lines, German learners of English must learn to voice final stop consonants. (These do not occur in German, so a beginner might pronounce *log* as *lock* [lɔk].) Non-syllabic complex consonant clusters are another common difficulty. ***Splendid*** in word-initial position, but also ***stretch***, ***simplify***, ***excruciating*** in medial and final position can all be problematic for learners of English. Depending on influences from L1 and other universal processes, learners typically insert vowels to break apart the clusters, delete consonants to simplify them, or substitute a familiar consonant (see Hansen 2004).

(3) **Prosody**: Numerous suprasegmental features can present difficulties for L2 learners, including stress, length, intonation, rhythm, and timing.

    (a) ***Stress***, where the prominence of a syllable falls, tends to be transferred from the first language, so that a French speaker might say *proBLEM* instead of *PRObelm*.

(b) **_Segment length_**, or **_duration_**, varies since vowels and consonants can be short, long, or overlong. In English, vowels are short before voiceless consonants, and long elsewhere, e.g. the [i] in *see* and *seed* are about 50 percent longer than the [i] in *seat*. Learners may not notice this distinction, or the fact that long vowels in English tend to occur in stressed syllables.

(c) **_Intonation_** is significant at the syllable/word level and at the phrasal level to indicate intent, emotion, and utterance type. A declarative, as opposed to interrogative, intonation pattern can require very different rise/fall characteristics, depending on the language in question. For example, a variation of Brazilian Portuguese interrogative intonation uses a rise–fall pattern for *yes/no* questions, but to an American speaker, this can sound like implied doubt or disbelief (Major's example is, '*You like snails* ↘?').

(d) **_Pitch_**, where used to distinguish lexical meaning, as in tonal languages, can be particularly difficult for L2 learners to perceive if they come from a non-tonal language background. On the other hand, Burnham and Mattock (2007) present evidence that adults are better at perceiving this than are young L2 learners.

(e) **_Rhythm_** and **_timing_**, the repetitive patterns of stress and length, are identifying qualities of any language, Major notes. We recognize our own language and detect a foreign accent on this basis. English is a stress-timed language, and as such, stretches out the duration of stressed syllables relative to unstressed ones in order to preserve equal timing between stress groups. In Major's example, *THIS is the HOUSE that JACK BUILT* has the same rhythm as *THIS is the HOUSE that KENnedy BUILT*, even though the syllable count is not equal. Other languages (e.g., Spanish) preserve syllable timing so that syllables are of relatively equal length throughout. Others follow mora-timing (e.g. Japanese), so that a syllable with two morae is twice as long as a syllable with one mora. According to Nakamura (2011), Japanese learners of English tend to have inaccurate ratios of both lengthened syllables and shortened syllables.

(f) **_Tempo_** or **_speech rate_** is an especially salient criterion; speaking either too slowly or too fast can be detrimental to the listener's perception of accent and/or intelligibility (Anderson-Hsieh and Koehler 1988; Derwing and Munro 1997; Kang 2010; Munro and Derwing 1998; Trofimovich and Baker 2006) (more in Chapter 4).

These challenges underscore the fact that late language learners are bound to draw comparisons between L2 and L1. First, slight differences in quality, as in voice onset time or aspiration (e.g., the example of /t/, above) can be difficult to perceive. Second, distributional differences often mean that the learner must acquire a new sound category (as in /æ/ and /θ/, mentioned above), or apply it to an unexpected linguistic environment. A familiar L1 category might be substituted in the meantime, which might get the job done communicatively, but it clearly signals non-native status. Finally, it is not enough to master a new phonemic inventory. Kang (2010) shows that suprasegmentals such as pitch range, pause and stress patterns, as well as speech rate, contribute independently to perceptions of *accentedness*. And Major notes that the longer the speaking turn, the more easily a foreign accent is detected; one can only avoid a certain phoneme or intonation pattern for so long. Discursive and semantic gaps can be disguised more easily, by comparison.

1.3 Ultimate attainment in L2 phonology

Much of the research on L2 is oriented toward *ultimate attainment* – the purported 'end-state' of learning. One main objective is to compare the performance abilities and underlying knowledge or intuitions of native speakers and advanced L2 users. This premise is not without its problems. Let us first consider so-called 'exceptional' learners. Are those who sound native expected to "fool some of the people some of the time, all of the people some of the time, or all of the people all of the time?" (Major 2001: 12). (The issue of which tasks constitute a valid test is another matter.) Second, we might question the practical purpose of the native–non-native dichotomy in light of so many L2 users who are fully functional in the target language. As noted, some scholars decry the nativeness construct as privileging the 'ideal monolingual native speaker' when in reality most native speakers are neither linguistically ideal nor monolingual. We must also remember that not all L2 learners strive for native-like-ness. Some see it as an unrealistic target, or prefer to hold onto their discernibly foreign accent for its symbolic value (Moyer 2004 and 2008). Another issue is the inherent circularity of phonological fluency: L2 users with a more authentic accent report feeling more comfortable in the second language and thus seek out contact with native speakers, thereby increasing language use and reinforcing phonological fluency (Moyer 2004 and 2007a). The flipside of that coin is that a strong foreign accent can be a barrier if it discourages L2 users from seeking out such contact.

There is a growing chorus among L2 phonology researchers that, developmental and universal processes notwithstanding, ultimate attainment is likely a function of the quantity and quality of language experience. Quantitative factors like length of residence in the target-language country, and especially L2 use relative to L1, correlate significantly to gains in phonological production and perception. Thus, acquisitional constraints long attributed to age may have much to do with the consistency of language use (see MacLeod and Stoehl-Gammon 2010). In terms of the quality of L2 input and use, accent has been shown to correlate significantly to the consistency of one's contact with native speakers and L2 use across multiple domains (family, home, school, work, etc.) (Moyer 2011). Many socio-psychological factors are significant as well, including concern for pronunciation accuracy, sense of identity in L2, motivation, and positive attitudes toward the target-language culture. New insights from the empirical research highlight these relationships between age, affect, and linguistic experience, signaling a welcome shift in the critical period paradigm.

1.4 Conclusion: the salience of accent in a second language

The importance of accent for the L2 learner extends far beyond segmental accuracy. Intonation, loudness, pitch, rhythm, length, juncture, and stress are among accent's many features, all of which clarify speaker intent as they encode semantic and discursive meaning. On the whole, accent is fundamental to communication, for without a reasonable degree of phonological fluency, spoken interaction will falter. At the same time, accent is a medium through which we project individual style and signal our relationship to interlocutors. Even more broadly, it reflects social identity along various categorical lines.

We have emphasized from the outset the importance of context – a crucial reference point for any comprehensive account of accent. Here, the operative context is second language acquisition, with all that that implies socially, cognitively, and linguistically. Second language users, particularly those living in the target-language country, are under considerable pressure to fit in, yet their ability to acquire a native-like accent hinges on a complex interplay of internal and external factors. Empirical research in SLA has brought to light many relevant concerns for phonological acquisition, chief among them the availability of high quality target-language input, and the opportunity to build strong social networks. Surrounded by a host of friends, acquaintances, and teachers, children living in an L2 environment typically have no problem doing so. This is not the case for their older counterparts. In addition to these challenges, various neurocognitive and affective concerns may exert a disproportionately negative influence on accent compared to other language skills. This does not imply an automatic disadvantage, but in L2 contexts, linguistic shortcomings are typically compounded by any negative perceptions a particular accent evokes.

As already stated, accent is one of the primary means by which others judge us; it is not just interpreted as a signal of linguistic competence, but also of attributes like status, trustworthiness, reliability, etc. There are echoes of such associations even in the FL classroom, where teachers can also harbor negative attitudes toward heavily accented students (Robinson 1979). In much higher-stakes contexts, Honey reminds us that accent can enhance the credibility of a defendant or witness in a court case, be crucial to the outcome of a job interview, or affect the diagnosis a patient receives from a doctor (1997: 105). Sounding foreign has far-reaching consequences, in other words. These points are addressed at length in the forthcoming chapters.

Even if the 'myth of non-accent' prevails, everyone has an accent, whether native or non-native speaker (Lippi-Green 1997). If so, why does accent constitute a compelling object of study? This chapter has briefly outlined some of the reasons, beginning with its significance for the negotiation of meaning in an immediate way, and the challenge it can pose for social integration over the long term. Having set the stage, we now address what is often called the 'intractability' of foreign accent, taking a closer look at the neurobiological and cognitive conditions of late language learning.

2 Accent and age

> Two decades after emigrating from Taiwan, Sean Chang's accent was a barrier to friendships with Americans. Native English speakers found it too much work when conversation went beyond small talk, said the electrical engineer from San Jose. Luis Ramirez, a home inspector born in El Salvador, developed a case of the mumbles when speaking English because of the insecurity he felt during inspections for Anglos. But when he spoke to Asian real estate agents with strong accents [he] would catch himself wondering, "Did they pass the licensing test?" before feeling a pang of guilt about stereotyping someone else.
>
> "How Accents Define Us," *San Jose Mercury News*, April 21, 2007

Anecdotally and empirically, we know that the experiences of Chang and Ramirez are not uncommon. Many older language learners retain an identifiable accent despite living many years in the target-language environment. Even in a city like San Jose where half of all adult residents are non-native speakers of English, this can lead to diminished opportunities for social integration. SLA scholars have long sought to explain why adults like Chang and Ramirez seem to be stuck, phonologically speaking, despite their long exposure to English. Many are convinced that age is the culprit, for the children of Chang or Ramirez would surely not face the same hurdles.

While children invariably master their first language, second language learning after early childhood is a far less reliable undertaking. The search for the cause of this age-related disparity has driven the empirical agenda in SLA since its inception as a unique branch of applied linguistics more than three decades ago. In this chapter, we outline arguments for and against *age of onset* with the target language as the determining factor in phonological acquisition, focusing on evidence from the neurocognitive realm.

2.1 Age effects research in L2 phonology

It is widely acknowledged that older learners outperform younger learners in the short term, as they are quick to learn new patterns initially, including phonological ones. A distinction is often made between *rate* and *route* of learning; the idea being that older learners approach language learning differently, leading to possible advantages initially, but poorer outcomes over time – especially for phonology (Krashen et al. 1982; cf. Muñoz 2008). Yet in Hyltenstam and Abrahamsson's (2001) view, the research is not conclusive on this point, because "even late learners can reach almost nativelike proficiency in a variety of aspects of the L2 ... or actually nativelike behavior on individual tasks, structures, or domains" (157). Indeed, much evidence confirms that adults can excel at certain aspects, such as morphology, lexicon and syntax, possibly because of a superior ability to recognize patterns in language (ibid.).

Phonology, by all accounts, constitutes the greatest challenge for late learners. Popular explanations for this challenge include memory, aptitude, and/or processing differences, and possibly a reduced access to some innate *language acquisition device*. To appreciate why the age debate has fueled so much interest, we take a closer look at evidence from L2 phonology research that compares younger and older learners' abilities.

In a broad analysis of 200 children learning English in the US, Fathman (1975) compared 6–10-year-olds with 11–15-year-olds and adults on a range of tasks. The younger group was most accurate for phonological tasks, and 11–15-year-olds were most accurate for morphological and syntactic tasks, even in the absence of any instruction. By contrast, Snow and Hoefnagel-Höhle (1982) tested 80 native English speakers in Holland learning Dutch without any formal instruction. Over the course of 18 months they measured pronunciation, vocabulary, and grammar skills, as well as phonemic discrimination among five age groups: 3–5-year-olds, 6–7-year-olds, 8–10-year-olds, 12–15-year-olds, and adults (exact age range not given). Teenage and adult participants initially outperformed the two youngest groups for most task types, yet within ten months the younger participants scored just as well for imitative abilities. Accuracy on a spontaneous speaking task was comparable across age groups. (NB: All participants repeated after a native speaker model – arguably not a robust test of phonological skill, but common to many studies in this vein.) Snow and Hoefnagel-Höhle rejected age as an explanation for the observed variance, mainly because the older learners quickly learned new phonological and grammatical features. Bohn (2005), however, notes that only rate of learning, not *ultimate attainment*, was at issue here.

A classic comparison pits age at first exposure with the target language (hereafter, *age of onset*, or AO) against length of residence in the target-language environment as influential for degree of foreign accent, also called *accentedness*. In a 1976 study, Oyama asked 60 Italian ESL learners in the US to complete read-aloud and semi-controlled narration tasks. Native speakers then rated their speech. Statistical analyses revealed a strong effect for age of arrival, but not for length of residence (cf. Asher and Garcia 1969). Interestingly, the extemporaneous speech elicited a more *authentic*, native-like accent than the formal recitations, as in the Snow and Hoefnagel-Höhle study mentioned above.

In a study of numerous potential factors in phonological attainment, Purcell and Suter (1980) found no significant correlations between accent and AO, but other factors were significant, including: aptitude for oral mimicry (based on self-report); length of residence in the target-language country, especially if living with a native speaker; degree of concern for pronunciation accuracy; and the mother tongue itself (for these L2 English speakers, those with Persian or Arabic as L1 fared better than native speakers of Japanese and Thai). No participant learned English before puberty, so there was no basis for comparing early to late exposure. Nevertheless, several did rate at a native level for accent. As a somewhat ad hoc conclusion, the authors write that 'having a good ear' is a better predictor of phonological authenticity than either age of onset or years of residence in-country.

Tahta et al. (1981) deserves special mention here, as they documented a decline in phonetic imitation abilities among English schoolchildren learning French as early as age 5 years and continuing steadily on to the oldest learners, aged 15 years. A decline in the ability to mimic novel intonation patterns did not appear until age 8 years, and actually showed a slight uptick around 13–15 years old. The authors therefore conclude that learners at any age can replicate intonation successfully given enough exposure and practice. However, an asymmetry between segmental and suprasegmental abilities suggests that having a good ear is not a straightforward matter; segmental vs. prosodic features may be controlled by different mechanisms with different 'offset' points implied.

Garcia-Lecumberri and Gallardo (2003) found that 11-year-old Basque–Spanish bilinguals were judged more accurate and more intelligible on English speaking tasks, and also performed best on a vowel and consonant discrimination task compared to groups with an AO of 8 years and 4 years, respectively. This casts doubt on a strict interpretation of the *Critical Period Hypothesis* – the idea that complete acquisition is only possible within a strict neurobiological window (Lenneberg 1967, discussed at length below). Looking at Basque–Spanish learners of English, Fullana (2006) found that once formal instruction reached a certain number of hours, there was little difference between age groups on a vowel and consonant discrimination task. The 11- and 14-year-old learners and adults started out with higher scores, but 8-year-olds caught up to them after extensive amounts of instruction. For the imitation tasks, where participants read isolated words aloud after hearing a native speaker model, there were no such effects of instruction. Overall these results underscore the need to test age effects longitudinally, at the various stages of learning, and to carefully take extrinsic factors like instruction into account.

Instruction is just one of many important influences that have been 'glossed over' in age effects research, as Muñoz and Singleton (2011) put it, making comparability between studies tenuous (see Muñoz 2006a). Even within a single study, participants sometimes represent vastly different amounts and types of instructional experience. Clearly, such factors must be carefully controlled if the aim is to verify main effects of AO. Several L2 phonology studies speak to this point. Muñoz (2011) found no independent age effects for phonetic discrimination among 162 Spanish learners of English, and Moyer's (2007a) study of 42 English learners in the US compared the effects of AO, length of residence, and factors such as desire to improve accent and reasons for learning the target language, with the psychological factors more significant than AO or length of residence (LOR) (see also Moyer 1999, 2004). A subsequent investigation confirmed the significance of specific contexts for L2 use for these same learners (Moyer 2011). Overall then, the age at which one begins acquiring a new language corresponds to a host of cognitive, affective, and experiential influences, meaning that AO could operate as a primarily indirect, rather than a direct, factor in L2 accent.

Empirical evidence increasingly suggests that age-related disparities do not apply in equal measure across learning stages. This begs the question whether different processing mechanisms are brought to bear at different points along the acquisitional continuum, i.e., according to different levels of proficiency. It is also noteworthy that some analyses find AO to be less statistically significant for accent than certain aspects of target-language experience. Finally, while phonology does seem to present a unique challenge compared to morphology and syntax, some late learners with a strong motivation and extensive experience in the target language *are* judged to sound native-like (Bongaerts et al. 1995, 1997; Ioup et al. 1994; Moyer 1999, 2004; Muñoz and Singleton 2007). A hard line insists that the *Critical Period Hypothesis* can only be falsified by such 'talented' individuals insofar as they perform at a native level 'in practically all ordinary communicative contexts' (Hyltenstam and Abrahamsson 2001: 158). Assuming such a benchmark could be operationalized, it is hard to imagine how any study could encompass it. Based on the evidence cited above, it is reasonable to assert that age does not provide a unitary explanation for L2 phonology outcomes.

With such questions about the nature of age effects in mind, we turn now to aspects of neurocognitive processing relevant to phonology, as well as research that juxtaposes age with environment, specifically, data from early bilingual language acquisition. The goal is to clarify what is known about any changes in the availability and functionality of the neurocognitive mechanisms needed to acquire a new sound system. What the learner then *does* with those abilities, i.e., whether or not he sets out to sound native-like, and how he brings to bear specific resources, is treated in the following chapter.

2.2 A critical look at the critical period for phonology

Considering the age-related disparities in long-term language acquisition, it is easy to see why a biologically based explanation for outcomes is appealing; its parameters are concrete and easily defined, and its predictions are inherently universal. More than any other single issue, the idea of a critical period has fascinated SLA scholars, particularly those interested in phonology.

Based on evidence of language recovery among aphasics, Lenneberg (1967) described a window for language learning, noting that if an injury to the left hemisphere occurred before the age of 9 or 10, full linguistic recovery was likely. He posited that language is acquired while cerebral growth is ongoing, but that "the critical period comes to a close at a time when 100% of the [growth] values are reached" (ibid.: 179), around the time of puberty, at which point cerebral *plasticity*, or flexibility, declines. Addressing phonology specifically, Lenneberg predicted that accent in a foreign language would be especially difficult to acquire beyond age 9 or 10 years.

Second language acquisition offers an optimal test for Lenneberg's *Critical Period Hypothesis* (CPH), and there has been a steady drumbeat of data that indicates some age-related window of opportunity for SLA. Johnson and Newport's (1989) examination of 46 Chinese and Korean learners of English graphed a linear decline in language-learning ability for various linguistic tasks, beginning with an AO of 7 years and ending at around 15–17. Thereafter, no age-related pattern was apparent; individual variation was the rule. Moyer's (2004) data on phonological attainment present a roughly parallel slope for late learners of German.

The Johnson and Newport results are challenged in Birdsong and Molis' (2001) replication, where this issue of linearity gets considerable focus. They specify that a dramatic offset point (which they did not find) would suggest the influence of maturation itself, while a gradual, continuous slope suggests some general age-related decline, possibly due to changes in processing speed or memory, although these are not typically attested before the age of 20 or later (see Birdsong 2006). The Munro and Mann (2005) data do present a continuous age-related decline in accent for their forty-two Mandarin speakers learning English, with no well-defined onset or offset. However, the latest AO for any participant was 16 years, allowing for no comparison with older learners.

A strictly interpreted CPH rules out true native-level attainment in adult language learning. Many scholars endorse this view, at least for phonology, because it seems to have an especially narrow critical period, closing as early as age 5–6 or earlier (see Bongaerts 2005; Perry and Harris 2002), and the probability of native-like attainment seems greatly reduced compared to other skills. Indeed a common assumption is that the neural functions associated with motor skill development mature earlier, and decline more quickly, than higher order processes associated with grammar and semantics (Singleton and Ryan 2004). Yet if maturation itself were the main cause for incomplete acquisition, it should apply to everyone in equal measure (Gregg 1996). We know that this is not the case, and that some late learners do manage to sound native-like. This raises several interesting possibilities. One is that the critical period is more fluid than previously thought – some refer instead to a 'sensitive' period to stress individual variation. Another theory holds that cognitive mechanisms take over to compensate for the loss of some endowed faculty, but that they are less effective, hence the presence of individual variation. Yet another possibility is that a critical period is only indirectly neurobiological – a logical hypothesis since invariably, young immigrants to a new country will attend school in the target language, make friends with native speakers, and develop a strong L2 identity, all of which predict a native-like accent. The conditions for early and late learning are not equivalent, in other words. To uncover the true nature of age effects, all such relevant influences must be examined and statistically compared, for participants that represent a range of AO. Only then can we appreciate how age corresponds to the availability of input and practice, which are essential for long-term attainment.

The CPH has its skeptics, and Lenneberg's much-lauded plasticity argument appears increasingly dubious. Martohardjono and Flynn (1995) long ago reasoned that lateralization, generally associated with a decline in plasticity, is present in very young infants, and therefore cannot explain a phenomenon that occurs much later in life. In fact, no one seems to know when plasticity definitively declines (Singleton and Ryan 2004), nor has a solid link been found between age-related neural changes and specific linguistic deficiencies. This cause–effect problem is a persistent intangible in the research. With all this in mind, Singleton (2005) launches a far-reaching critique of the CPH:

[The] CPH cannot plausibly be regarded as a scientific hypothesis, either in the strict Popperian sense of something which can be falsified ... nor indeed in the rather looser logical positivist sense of something that can be clearly confirmed or supported ... Nor does the option of reducing the various versions of the CPH to a single summary form get us very much further. Such a summary form would look something like this: "For some reason, the language acquiring capacity, or some aspects thereof, is operative only for a maturational period which ends some time between perinatality and puberty." This is not a hypothesis either; it is at best an extremely vague promissory note. (280)

Still others are just as strongly convinced that the CPH is on the right track. Long's (2005) position is that adults are only equal (or better) than younger learners according to short-term measures, i.e., not in terms of ultimate attainment. Munro and Mann (2005) also defend age as a reliable heuristic for ultimate attainment, stating that no model can specify: "before age X, a person is guaranteed to develop a native accent and, after age Y, a foreign accent is unavoidable" (337). Nevertheless, there are numerous unobservable phenomena to contend with, and there is no clear proof that actual competence, or underlying knowledge, is hampered by a late start.

According to Martohardjono and Flynn (1995), adults can "detect sounds pertinent to speech, and manipulate or integrate them into a systematic mental representation of the sound system for the language being acquired" (147). Simply put, the skills needed to build a sound system are still available and functional. Snow and Hoefnagel-Höhle (1982) clearly demonstrated that English speakers can learn new sounds in Dutch that are not distinctive in English (/x/ and the diphthong /uy/), and Flege et al. (1995a) have shown that Japanese late learners of English can produce the /ɹ/–/l/ distinction successfully. They therefore propose that a foreign accent results from any number of causes, among them: inadequate phonetic input, minimal motivation to sound like a native speaker, or interference from the first language phonological system (ibid.: 26), but these are not intractable barriers.

A final comment on the age-effects conundrum has to do with methodology. Some studies of L2 phonology include especially difficult tasks – important if the issue is ultimate attainment – meaning that they purposefully elicit phonetic, phonemic, and suprasegmental features known to be challenging for the L1–L2 pair in question. Other studies actually avoid difficult phonological contrasts. A second inconsistency has to do with task range. Some late learners are only expected to 'pull off' an authentic sound within an isolated task, yet they are far less convincing in real conversation where suprasegmentals and pragmatic skills come into play. Munro and Mann (2005) see extended speaking tasks as more representative of real communication, but of course lexical, suprasegmental, and morpho-syntactic features inherent in such tasks can influence listener ratings (334). The comparability of studies will continue to be an issue until tasks beyond the word level become standard, incorporating spontaneous speech to give a fuller picture of phonological fluency.

2.3   Neural organization and the question of plasticity

Perhaps the relevance of the CPH for phonology comes down to the neuromuscular basis for speech production and perception (Scovel 1988). This implies that an entrenched foreign accent is not the result of insufficient learning or practice, but that muscular constraints actually restrict the ability to form new articulatory patterns past a certain age. Let us therefore consider the flexibility of the neural substrates involved in phonological processing.

Phonology requires two levels of *processing*, the "mental activities involved in real-time [language] use," which for the native speaker are complex, effortless and very rapid (Herschensohn 2007: 193). These levels are: (a) perception, which invokes auditory and higher-order cognitive processing to connect sound to meaning; (b) production, which uniquely requires lower-order neuromuscular control of the articulatory organs (larynx, tongue, lips, uvula, etc.). These two levels are coordinated during speech, relying on a neural network of both specialized and general mechanisms (Chiarello 2003; Chiarello and Beeman 1998) located across several regions:

- *Wernicke's area* in the left posterior temporal lobe near the primary auditory cortex, largely responsible for acoustic processing and comprehension;
- *Broca's area* in the left inferior frontal cortex near the precentral motor cortex, involved with muscle control and sequential processing;
- the *inferior parietal lobule* located in the temporal cortex where the auditory, visual, and sensori-motor cortexes come together;
- the *auditory cortex*, responsible for the recognition of sounds;
- the *visual cortex* which processes written words and signs, as well as gestures and facial expressions (it may also come into play when a listener or speaker visualizes words while listening or speaking).

It is important to note that no specific region is believed to exclusively execute the processes for a given linguistic subdomain (e.g., syntax, morphology, phonology, etc.). Processing tasks are typically dispersed across multiple cerebral regions (Herschensohn 2007). At the same time, a fundamental aspect of neural organization is the division of labor between the left and right hemispheres, where certain functions are assigned to one or the other. This is referred to as *lateralization*, believed to be an evolutionary adaptation that economizes processing speed and space, thereby leading to more efficient skill development. Phonological processing relies on both hemispheres given that the left hemisphere (LH) performs most analytical, sequential language processes, while the right hemisphere (RH) is thought to process suprasegmentals like tone and pitch (Ross and Monnot 2008; Tokuhama-Espinosa 2003; Zatorre and Samson 1991) – at least for speakers of non-tonal languages (Burnham and Mattock 2007). Again, these are not rigid divisions. For most (right-handed) people, the LH is dominant during language processing because of audition, motor planning specific to speech, and rule-based decoding and encoding. On the other hand, flexibility and/or crossover in hemispheric processing are also evident, and LH language functions may be recovered by the RH after severe injury or insult, depending on age and individual processing tendencies (Dick et al. 2005; Schiffler 2001). Even under normal circumstances, processing allocations vary across individuals (Dabrowska 2004; Dick et al. 2005; Obler and Gjerlow 1999).

The relevant issue here is whether lateralization – a process thought to be completed very early in life – impedes *plasticity*, namely, whether neural cells involved in phonological acquisition and processing cease to adapt to new stimuli after early childhood. Abuhamdia (1987) claims that cells prevalent in the sensori-motor area lose their plasticity early in life, and that one or more languages can be acquired natively – without accent – only during this brief period (209).[1] Walsh and Diller (1981) similarly describe sensori-motor skills as minimally neuroplastic, yet Scovel points to great variation in language ability among children of the same age (1981: 35).

Declines in cellular plasticity have not yet been causally linked to language-learning problems, and strict lateralization is not well supported by the language–brain research. Walsh and Diller maintain that if motor skill development has biological limits, foreign accents are not insurmountable; they can be overcome "to a reasonably large extent with proper instruction or with an optimal natural environment" (1981: 14). In their estimation, later learning probably recruits different mechanisms, but this does not imply a disadvantage.

Researchers can now track electrical impulses and blood flow in the brain in response to incoming stimuli through event-related potentials (ERPs); functional magnetic resonance imaging (fMRI); and positron emission tomography (PET) (see Herschensohn 2007; Stowe and Sabourin 2005). These techniques depict the brain as dynamic and responsive rather than as rigid or linear (Dick et al. 2005). And, very recently, neurogenesis has been seen in adults, but the relevance of such neuronal growth for specific language skills is as yet unknown (Herschensohn 2007).

An important piece of evidence for hemispheric processing and plasticity is found in Sereno and Wang (2007). Focusing on the processing of tone, the authors compared the cortical activity of native Mandarin speakers and non-native speakers unfamiliar with the language. (Musical tone is associated with the RH, but linguistic tones make phonemic distinctions – a function associated with LH.) To assess hemispheric activity, the authors first employed dichotic listening techniques, in which the right ear or left ear receives stimuli and the listener identifies which ear 'heard' the tone. Previous research has shown that native speakers of some tonal languages have a right ear advantage during such tasks, indicating that tones were processed primarily in the LH.[2] In this study, 15 of 20 native speakers confirmed this pattern, but 20 American listeners unfamiliar with Mandarin showed no ear advantage, indicating a bilateral processing pattern. A group of Norwegian listeners behaved similarly, even though Norwegian has some tonal features.

The authors then examined a bilingual Mandarin–English group. Evidence has been mixed for hemispheric processing preferences among bilinguals, in some instances tied to age, with older learners being more left-lateralized, in other cases correlated to 'stage,' or proficiency level. The question is whether

---

[1] See discussion of myelination in reference to the CPH and phonology in Hyltenstam and Abrahamsson 2003.
[2] Right-ear stimuli connects to the LH via contralateral pathways.

more proficient L2 users process tones as native speakers do, i.e., with a LH preference. Indeed, this is what Sereno and Wang found.

To investigate plasticity, Sereno and Wang also tested the efficacy of a 2-week training procedure on a new group of non-native speakers and discovered a substantial improvement in the perception of tone. (The control group's performance did not change significantly from pre- to post-test.) This improvement was still apparent 6 months later, and was generalized to new talkers/new stimuli – an indication of real acquisition. To track cortical responses to training, the authors used fMRI to observe tonal processing for a small subset of participants, before and after. Slight changes were observed between the pre- and post-test, demonstrating an impact on neural activity in terms of both location and intensity. New areas were recruited to handle the processing tasks as a result of training, in other words, and in some areas this activity was intensified. Whether this intensity continues even after a high level of proficiency is attained is a question for future investigations.

Sereno and Wang's final experimental objective was to examine the connection between perception and production. They performed acoustic analyses on speech samples before and after perceptual training for a subset of eight American participants. Native speakers also rated the authenticity of tone for these production tasks. Great variability was evident among individuals before training, but afterwards, all trainees' performance had markedly improved compared to the control group. The perceptual training thus seemed to positively affect the production of tone, confirmed by pitch contour analyses. The findings suggest not just an interconnectedness between these processing realms, but also "a highly malleable speech learning system across both perception and production" (2007: 254). This result coincides nicely with recent evidence from neural imaging studies that portray the brain as (surprisingly) plastic, well into adulthood. Phonological processes may therefore be less constrained by specific neural substrates than previously assumed.[3]

2.4 L2 phonological knowledge and cognitive processes

Bever (1981) long ago proposed a non-neurological explanation of age effects, reasoning that by adolescence, one's capacity to learn language would either be 'filled up' by L1, or overtaken by "the superposition of an intellectualized, self-conscious way of learning everything" (182). His point is that SLA is not a *lesser version* of first language acquisition; it is a qualitatively different process. This section outlines the current thinking on how a second sound system is uniquely acquired, according to what distinguishes early from late learners cognitively.

---

[3] See Abutalebi (2008) for review of neural imaging research relevant to L1–L2 processing of morphosyntax.

A fundamental distinction between children and adults is that the latter have already experienced the transition to 'formal operations,' or abstract reasoning, which is commonly regarded as a turning point in an individual's way of thinking and learning. Linked to puberty, this increase in cognitive ability is sometimes blamed for interfering with innate language processes (Newport 1991). At the same time, adolescence brings a heightened self-consciousness, which is thought to be an additional hindrance to language acquisition (Krashen 1981). If so, this is especially relevant for accent given its connection to identity and cultural affiliations (more in Chapter 3).

For adults, language learning is highly conscious and effortful at the early stages (O'Malley and Chamot 1990), driven by processes such as attention, awareness, analysis, etc. (see Robinson 2003; Segalowitz 2003; more in Chapter 6). The foundation for acquiring any linguistic system is the ability to recognize new patterns, form appropriate categories, and systematically organize these in meaningful ways (Macken and Ferguson 1987; McLaughlin and Heredia 1996). Assuming enough interactive experience along the way, *declarative knowledge* of structures and forms is integrated with *procedural knowledge* – the 'how-to' aspect of using language meaningfully in context. Let us remember, however, that learning conditions – and thus the input received – are all but impossible to generalize across individuals. Furthermore, each learner is the actor in this process; he must acquire the linguistic code while adjusting "his own version of it to match that of the target language speakers" (Hammarberg 1993: 441).

The process of acquiring and restructuring L2 knowledge is therefore uniquely shaped, given the particulars of the input, opportunities for practice and use, and the learner's own cognitive and affective predilections. This inherent variability notwithstanding, there are common – if not universal – processes that typify the acquisition of a new sound system when at least one (L1) system is already in place. It is this interaction between the L1 and L2 systems that has sparked so much theoretical interest.

2.4.1 Categorical perception

As noted above, phonology relies on both conceptual mechanisms and muscular skills. The ability to perceive distinct sounds and categorize them in meaningful ways is part of our human language faculty. Already in utero the (hearing) child is exposed to the full range of prosodic and phonetic features of the mother's voice, and this exposure is thought to form the basis for perceptual preferences (Burnham et al. 2002). From birth, infants notice prosodic and phonetic interruptions in the speech stream that signal boundaries between linguistic units (Locke 1997), such as pauses or changes in pitch indicating the end of a phrase, vocal release of consonants signaling the end of a word, etc.

Nearly all vowel and consonant contrasts are also well perceived even at this early stage (Burnham et al. 2002).

Kuhl and Iverson (1995) characterize the early categorization process in terms of a Native Language Perceptual Magnet. The idea is that infants immediately begin to develop special sensitivity for the categories of sound in the language they are exposed to at birth. They establish prototypes of sound categories (e.g. /p/ vs. /b/) in response to frequently activated representations. This allows them to perceive similarity between instantiations of the same sound and to 'normalize' these sounds across talkers, i.e., to hear acoustically different representations as being members of the same category (ibid.). For example, in an English-speaking environment, infants learn to categorize a bilabial stop as either /p/ or /b/, depending on where it falls within the range of *voice onset time* – the measure in milliseconds of when phonation, or voicing, occurs for a specific segment. The range within each category varies, but the boundary itself becomes the salient point for comprehension.

Werker and Pegg (1992) observe that infants can initially discriminate nearly any phonetic contrast, including those not present in their language-learning environment (285). But because perception develops in response to available stimuli, phonetic and tonal properties not present in the input are effectively discarded as irrelevant (Wode 1992: 616). Reliable and relevant acoustic parameters are quickly given more 'weight' (Strange and Shafer 2008: 157), with perceptual biases solidifying as early as 7–11 months. The result is that phonological perception is strongly attuned to the mother tongue(s) within the first year of life, with phones taking on phonemic significance, and pitch taking on tonal significance for those raised in a tonal language environment (Burnham et al. 2002; Burnham and Mattock 2007; Polka and Werker 1994). Babbling behaviors also shift toward L1 sounds around the same age (Werker and Pegg 1992) since perceptual representations and vocal imitation are 'mapped' together through experience (Kuhl et al. 2008).

It is this early reorganization that is thought to minimize the ability to fully acquire new perceptual categories later on. The implications for SLA are that late L2 learners will not perceive, and likely not be able to produce, new sounds as completely or accurately as native speakers do. But exactly which developmental mechanisms change with time remains a mystery. Werker and Tees (2005) insist that training can mitigate age-related disadvantages so long as it builds on previous knowledge, offers frequent feedback and repetition, and is interactive in nature. After all, they write, "there is virtually no system for which some mechanism, at some level, cannot be found to allow further change" (2005: 242). This would seem to be good news, but they do not dismiss the age factor; neither naturalistic experience nor laboratory training can guarantee complete attainment past the optimal period.

To test second language perceptual accuracy, two main tasks have been employed: (a) identification, where the listener categorizes a stimulus (sound) by selecting or writing an orthographic symbol; (b) a discrimination task, where two contrasting sounds are presented and the listener decides whether they are the same or different. Reaction time may also be measured. Results across studies have produced mixed results. Flege, Munro, and Fox (1995, discussed in Flege 1995) found that experienced Spanish speakers of English had trouble discriminating certain contrasts, e.g., English /ɑ/ vs. Spanish /a / as well as /a/–/æ/ distinctions in English. Kuhl's (2007) American and Japanese adult listeners were able to identify phonemes from computer-generated sound sequences that varied by small, "physically equal" steps from one phonetic unit to another. The stimuli gradually proceeded from /ra/ to /la/. Americans consistently identified a point at which /ra/ became /la/ categorically, but Japanese listeners perceived only /ra/; for them, all sounds in the sequence were of the same category. Rojczyk (2011) used a similar discrimination task to present stimuli along a VOT continuum for beginning vs. advanced Polish learners of English. Although the advanced group did not overlap completely with native speakers, categorical perception according to VOT appears to be learnable given the obvious differences between their performance and that of beginners.

Leather and James (1996) write that L2 learners have a propensity to map new sounds onto their mother tongue phonemic system, doing so for prosody and tone as they do for segments (see also Broselow et al. 1987; cf. Grabe et al. 2003). But the likelihood of hearing new categories correctly seems to depend on whether they are associated with something familiar. Altogether new sounds may be approached differently. In their study of native English speakers learning French, Flege and Hillenbrand (1987) compared beginners' and advanced learners' ability to produce a familiar sound: /u/ (as in English *rude*, similar to French *trouve* – first person singular for *find*, though not identical). The advanced learners with 10+ years' experience most closely approximated a native-like VOT pattern. For a completely unique sound, /y/ (non-existent in English, but common in French, as in *tu* – second person singular pronoun), the beginners actually matched the accuracy of the advanced group. Accordingly, the authors argue that those sounds most similar to first language categories cause greater difficulty than do completely new ones. Supporting this result, Best et al. (1987) found that adult English speakers and infants in an English-speaking environment could accurately discriminate between African click sounds, suggesting that, absent any relevant L1 categories, listeners "concentrate their attention on purely auditory or articulatory properties of the stimuli" (275) (see also Polka 1995).

The relative availability of selective attention in discrimination tasks is a crucial issue. Strange and Shafer (2008) argue that adults can successfully perceive new sound categories when conditions are optimal, i.e., in quiet places with few distractions. Here they may operate according to a more careful processing mode, which accounts for greater accuracy (Strange 2002). Under conditions of natural interaction, however, learners must typically contend with noisy and distracting conditions so that, even with contextual cues, the discrimination of sounds is more effortful and mistakes are likely (ibid.: 250f.).

In her Feature Competition Model, Hancin-Bhatt (1994) characterizes L2 category development as more complex than simply matching new, unfamiliar sounds with the most proximate ones from the L1 inventory. Instead, a dynamic balance of language-specific and universal constraints affects the process. According to Hancin-Bhatt, L2 feature prominence is key. Those features that are salient are mapped onto L1 categories, affecting both perception and production. The nasal–oral contrast is an example of such a feature, generally more noticeable to the learner than place of articulation (e.g., anterior, high, back, etc.). For this reason, a complex consonant cluster containing a nasal sound may be acquired before one without that quality. Linguistic environment and the possible grammatical significance of a sound or sound sequence are also factors in salience, as noted by Hansen (2004). Until the learner is at the stage of acquiring past tense in English, she may not notice and accurately produce a word-final /t/ if it occurs in a complex cluster that is not allowed in L1 (e.g., walked as /wɔlkt/). A review of transfer effects on the perception of prosodic categories indicates a similar tendency to attend to features in the stimuli/input that are salient, i.e., meaningful, in L1 (Grabe et al. 2003). Thus, English listeners 'tune in' to amplitude cues when assessing syllable stress, while Estonian listeners are more sensitive to duration (Lehiste and Fox 1992, cited in Grabe et al. 2003). Not all phonological features are equally salient, so Hancin-Bhatt reasons they are not equally subject to interference from the mother tongue(s).

Several other theoretical models situate salience within the wider context of L2 learning, each with a slightly different focus:

- The Perceptual Assimilation Model, described in Best and Tyler (2007), focuses on non-native speech perception by naïve (monolingual) listeners. The model predicts that while listening to an unfamiliar, non-native phonetic segment, naïve listeners tend to perceptually assimilate it to the most 'articulatorily-similar' one in the native language. That is, it will be categorized as a good or poor exemplar of a similar native segment, or remain altogether uncategorized, or unassimilated (ibid.: 22f.). Best and Tyler assert that naïve listeners can nevertheless discriminate some phonetic and tonal contrasts at a native level, and further, that they show sensitivity to gradient-like, non-contrastive variation within categories, indicating that perception is not limited to L1-relevant features. This implies the presence of universal, not just experience-based, perceptual sensitivities. Also noteworthy is the fact that experienced L2 listeners appear to work along the same perceptual dimensions as native listeners, which means that increasing experience and fluency actually improve perception (ibid.: 20). This effect is greatest within the first year or so of immersion, they maintain, with less noticeable benefit thereafter.

- Flege's Speech Learning Model (1995) addresses the ability of L2 learners to accurately perceive and produce sounds they are in the process of acquiring. SLM's main hypothesis is that L2 sounds which are not contrastive in L1 are harder to perceive as age of onset increases. This is due to *equivalence classification*, whereby the L2 sound is presumed to belong to a familiar L1 category (despite dissimilarity), leading the learner to produce the two sounds in similar ways. An example is the difficulty some native Japanese learners have distinguishing and producing /r/ vs. /l/ in English. Not only does Japanese have just one liquid, the English /r/ and /l/ have different allophones as well. As a result, Japanese learners with this perceptual gap tend to produce *either* /r/ *or* /l/ in all environments. Some additional, important hypotheses include the following:
  - The greater the perceived *dis*similarity between an L2 sound and its closest L1 counterpart, the more likely it is that the learner will discern their phonetic differences.
  - The mechanisms and processes used in L1 phonological acquisition, including category formation, remain intact over the lifespan and can be applied to L2 learning.
  - Phonetic categories established in L1 are not static, but evolve to reflect properties of subsequent language learning.

On the positive side, the SLM states that experience does help learners accurately differentiate L1 and L2 sounds, be it based on formal instruction or naturalistic acquisition/learning. More direct testing of the perception–production link is needed to fully appreciate the implications of the model.

- The Optimality Theoretic Model for L2 phonological categorization recalls Hancin-Bhatt's focus on well-formedness constraints and the salience of auditory cues. Escudero and Boersma (2004) propose this model to explain how L2 learners' categorical perception shifts in response to increasing fluency. They investigated the perception of the English /i/–/ɪ/ contrast among native speakers of Spanish learning one of two varieties of English: Scottish Standard and Southern British. This feature was expected to be particularly challenging because it requires the accurate discrimination of both duration and spectrum (formant frequencies) – a more complex challenge than a simple 1:1 mapping. The two dialects were chosen because they differ in the acoustic dimensions of this /i/–/ɪ/ contrast in terms of height and duration. The authors were interested to see the extent to which participants across a range of AO and experience had become attuned to these acoustic features as a function of the available input. Sure enough, the more advanced L2 learners showed perceptual preferences toward either spectrum or duration, in line with the dialect they were acquiring. In other words, 'cue weighting' of specific features was increasingly influenced by L2 – not L1– as a function of distributional reliability. This eventually led learners to a stage of optimal categorization, on par with native speakers according to the authors, because while they started out with 'full transfer' from L1, learners have 'full access' to L1-like acquisition devices. This access is predicated on noticing L1–L2 mismatches, and being able to create altogether new categories where necessary (see Hancin-Bhatt 2008).

All of these models underscore the fact that, if the goal is to investigate older learners' capacity to form new categories, then those who are actively learning – namely, for the purpose of achieving fluency – should not be compared to naïve listeners with no experience in the target language. After all, L2 learners must reconcile the phonological significance of L2 phonetic contrasts, whereas naïve listeners merely distinguish acoustic properties in isolation, detached from meaning. For example, English-speaking learners of German must notice that German /ʀ/ represents a single phoneme equivalent to English /r/, even though it has at least four allophones – [ʀ, ɾ, ʁ, ʌ] – that vary phonotactically, not to mention dialectally. Best and Tyler (2007) argue that researchers should therefore differentiate between naïve listeners with no target-language experience, fluent bilinguals who started acquiring the second language as very young children, and late L2 learners who typically have a very different balance of L1–L2 usage. As they see it, linguistic and communicative knowledge and experience inevitably change one's perceptual abilities, so that older learners are not like infants, minus the age gap; their learning is significantly different (ibid.: 24) (see Strange 2007 for methodological critiques).

In her discussion of first language acquisition, Kuhl maintains that social interaction is essential for the establishment of perceptual categories; passive exposure to the sounds of language will not suffice. This makes sense given that social interaction stimulates attention as well as motivation, which in turn increases the amount of information that infants 'code' and remember (2007: 75). By her account, categorization is not simply a matter of neurobiological age. Her Native Language Neural Commitment Concept specifies that experience, not simply time (here: age), is the central force behind phonetic learning in L2. Put another way, acquiring the sound patterns of a new language is difficult by virtue of the fact that, with experience, the neural commitment to the first language increases and this precipitates a decline in neural flexibility (81). Assuming Kuhl is correct, corresponding L2 research must carefully document the details of target-language experience, delineating explicit training and informal passive exposure from meaningful interactive L2 experience.

If perceptual processes can be 're-educated with experience,' as Strange and Shafer have argued (2008: 170), success may come down to the availability of meaningful L2 interaction.

Finally, a compelling question is whether L2 sounds can be accurately produced if they are not first accurately perceived. Some research indicates that perception is the basis for production, but this is not consistent (Nowacka 2011). In the discussion above we noted that Flege's SLM views perception as primary, and the Sereno and Wang study indicates positive effects of perceptual training on production (see also Hirata 2004). That these two realms appear to develop 'asymmetrically' is fairly well attested in the empirical research; skill in one realm does not guarantee skill in the other. The general consensus is that they are partially independent, although integrated in some way. Dupoux (2003) has a unique take on this issue. He posits that perception is far less plastic than production, and that these two realms function more or less independently. Therefore, late learners can actually produce fine distinctions in L2 sounds even if they cannot accurately perceive these differences (cf. Baker et al. 2008). As of yet, the evidence is not conclusive.

2.4.2 Transfer

One goal of L2 phonological research is to model interlanguage development, to predict and explain the relative difficulty that learners will face as they acquire a new sound system (Colantoni and Steele 2008: 489). Those beyond childhood have the added challenge of needing to produce, not just perceive, relatively complex language from the outset. To do so they must acquire novel stress and intonation patterns, rhythmic patterns, constraints on allowable sound sequences and syllable structures, and various phonetic parameters such as aspiration, VOT, etc. in relatively short order (Archibald 1998). Having the first language as the point of departure for this process can be both a help and a hindrance.

The idea that L1 interferes with our ability to accurately hear, understand, and speak a second language was elaborated decades ago in Weinreich's 1953 work, *Languages in Contact*, which spelled out the various ways that L1 intrudes on L2 (cited in Major 2008). Weinreich's discussion of interference included a list of predictable phonetic and phonological errors, including sound substitutions, faulty categorization of sounds based on mismatches between L1–L2 inventories, and faulty interpretations of L2 distinctive features, both phonetic and prosodic (ibid.: 67f.). The common term for L1–L2 cross-referencing is *transfer*, and its accompanying theory of language development rose in popularity alongside a pedagogical approach called *contrastive analysis* in the 1960s, inspired by Lado's *Linguistics across Cultures* (1957).

According to the Contrastive Analysis Hypothesis, new languages are inevitably compared with those already known, and the only way to prevent false inferences and their accompanying errors is to overtly address the structural differences between L1 and L2. (A popular technique for phonological practice in this vein is the *minimal pair*, which presents two words side by side that vary by just one phone or phoneme, e.g., *cat*, *bat*; *true*, *tray*; *bug*, *bud*, etc. – see Lehtonen and Sajavaara 1984 for critique; more in Chapter 6.) The implication is that transfer is usually negative, and the term *interference* captures its detrimental effect.

Interference is presumed to operate at every level – lexical, grammatical, and of course, the segmental and suprasegmental levels of phonology. At the word level, Kaltenbacher (1994) attributes stress pattern inaccuracies to L1 interference for Egyptian learners of German, and Shen (1990) describes interference for her Chinese learners of French in terms of intonation. It is interesting, however, that Shen's participants accurately perceived and categorized French tonal patterns according to their meaningful contrasts. In other words, only the *production* of suprasegmentals was diminished; *perception* did not seem to be affected by transfer. This possibility of an asymmetrical impact on segmental vs. suprasegmental features is one of many puzzles for transfer research.

It is not clear exactly how L1 phonological knowledge affects sensitivity to new sound patterns. It has been argued that children are less prone to filter new sounds through mother tongue categories because their phonetic representations are only partially developed (Baker et al. 2008). Later on, adults are constrained by 'habitual attentional bias' more so than actual neurological change (Leather 1987: 61; see also Kuhl et al. 2008). Some evidence contradicts this premise, however. Burnham and Mattock (2007) report that Australian English-speaking children older than 10 years of age, as well as adults, can discriminate some tonal categories in Thai more effectively than do young children, implying a resurgence of perceptual ability with age. Transfer theory as it stands cannot explain such inconsistencies without more data on different age groups, and the relative salience of the L1–L2 features in question. What *is* certain is that on the level of production – phonetic, phonemic, prosodic – L1 interference can have far-reaching effects.

The appeal of transfer theory is fairly obvious, but in actuality, not all interlanguage errors can be traced back to the mother tongue, and some structures predicted to be difficult do not necessarily result in performance errors (Altenberg and Vago 1987; Broselow 1988; Jarvis and Pavlenko 2008; Piper 1987). Furthermore, ambiguities in the surface data obscure the source of a given error. Major provides an interesting illustration: A careful read-aloud item like *spy* for a Japanese learner of English can sound like [*supay*], yet in running speech it will likely sound accurate because of two natural processes that occur in spoken Japanese: vowel devoicing, and deletion between voiceless obstruents. In other words, transfer from Japanese could affect both slow and fast speech conditions, but transfer would only be immediately apparent for the surface form provided in slow, careful speech (2008: 69).

2.4.3 Universal processes and markedness

Perhaps the most vexing issue is the intrinsic overlap of transfer with other developmental, or universal processes. In an uninstructed learning environment, the learner is on her own to detect the boundaries between words, as these are key for tying meaning to sound. Over time, phonemes are discerned out of the phones (sounds) in the speech stream. Prosody, i.e., intonation, rhythm, tempo, loudness, and pause patterns also provide clues about pragmatic meaning (Wennerstrom 2001: 4). Gradually, a multilevel phonological grammar is constructed, whose nature and course are determined by universal tendencies, according to James (1987). In an instructed environment, the use of targeted input may speed up the acquisition process, but universal preferences are said to dominate the overall trajectory in any kind of environment. Let us therefore consider some specific universal phenomena relevant to L2 phonology.

Phonological universals seem to characterize both child and adult language learning. For example, Wode's (1983) study of the acquisition of German by young native speakers of Hindi, Arabic, Spanish, and French reveals parallel processes among all groups for vowel and consonant substitution, final devoicing, and overgeneralization. These are the same processes attested in the L1 literature, along with developmental strategies like deletion and assimilation.

At the level of the syllable, Tarone (1987) finds a universal preference for open (CV, or consonant–vowel) syllables based on her observations of consonant deletion and vowel insertion (e.g., [skuː] for school and [kəlæs] for class) among Cantonese, Korean, and Portuguese learners of English. This seems to be a preferred pattern even for syllable types common in a learner's native language. The basis for this preference could be simplification, or an adherence to the 'sonority sequencing constraint,' which holds that sonority should increase from onset to nucleus.[4] Benson (1988) also finds an open syllable preference among Vietnamese learners of English despite a preponderance of closed syllable types in Vietnamese.

Offering a cross-linguistic comparison of L2 syllable structure, Young-Scholten and Archibald (2000) indicate that the *route* of L2 syllable acquisition does not parallel that of L1; epenthesis appears far more frequently in early L2 learning and may increase with age of onset. This would seem to support the influence of both universals and transfer (see discussion in Zampini 2008). Task

---

[4] Thus, the word *stop* in English violates this by inserting an obstruent /t/ between the /s/ and /ɔ/, so it would be subject to consonant deletion or vowel epenthesis (discussed in Young-Scholten and Archibald 2000).

type is a possible influence as well, since this is especially noticeable on read-aloud tasks. The authors further speculate that instructed learners use epenthesis more frequently due to their inherent focus on written text, as compared to learners who acquire the language primarily through listening and speaking.

Language universals are closely tied to the theory of *markedness*, which posits that typologically infrequent, 'marked' features are more difficult to acquire than are unmarked features, i.e., those most common across the world's languages (open syllable structure is an example of an unmarked pattern). Eckman's *Markedness Differential Hypothesis* (1977) predicts that unmarked structures are more readily acquired in both first and second language acquisition. The quintessential example in the literature is the terminal devoicing rule: a native English speaker learning German will easily master the final devoicing of German obstruents since this pattern also occurs in English, but a German learner of English must work against markedness constraints – moving from an unmarked to a marked feature. He will thus experience difficulty or delayed learning (e.g., *mad* will first sound like *mat*, *bag* like *back*, etc.).

It is no easy task to disambiguate transfer, universals, and markedness. Consider Broselow's (1988) English speakers learning Arabic, who tend to mispronounce word-final consonants so that the phrase *mis ana* (*not I*) is misperceived and mispronounced as *mi sana* – a meaningless utterance, but one that appears to reflect English juncture patterns. Broselow blames L1 interference, while also acknowledging a universal preference for open syllable structure. Along similar lines, Anderson's (1987) Arabic and Chinese students of English appear to experience difficulty with consonant clusters, and the more complex the cluster, the greater the difficulty, even if similar clusters exist in L1. Consonant deletion is the most common strategy observed, which could reflect developmental preferences. Another strategy is to insert a vowel, as seen in the Tarone examples above. Hecht and Mulford (1987) further differentiate transfer effects according to segment type, with vowels susceptible to L1 influence but consonants and affricates subject to developmental processes. A rare longitudinal analysis is offered by Hansen (2001) whose data from L2 English learners of Mandarin background reveal several constraints: transfer, markedness, sonority principles, and other phonological processes (epenthesis, deletion, etc.) – all apparently operating on syllable codas. All of these studies attest to the influence of numerous strategies and constraints, operating simultaneously it seems.

The interplay of simultaneous learning mechanisms is illuminated in Major's *Ontogeny–Phylogeny Model* (OPM) (2001). Major schematizes the relative balance of transfer, markedness, and universal learning processes as they shift over time, with increasing fluency, and according to both individual and contextual factors, where stylistic variation comes into play. Major's OPM predicts that transfer is most prominent in the early stages of learning, and in casual tasks, while universal developmental processes emerge over time and eventually take the lead.

Importantly, Major contextualizes the OPM in light of bilingual and multilingual settings to explore how language use and language dominance affect the dynamic nature of these mechanisms. An example he gives is the fact that many Spanish–English bilinguals in the Southwest US have Spanish-accented English but also English-accented Spanish (e.g., they have a /b/–/v/ distinction but also merge /tʃ/ and /ʃ/) (143), showing the mutual, bi-directional influence of transfer (see also Beebe 1984). Mennen (2004) has also shown that Dutch learners of Greek exhibit Greek intonation patterns in their spoken Dutch, as compared to monolingual native speakers of Dutch reading the same passages (so-called "reverse transfer") (cited in Jarvis and Pavlenko 2008). This is likely related to the balance of L1–L2 use, and recalls Flege's SLM characterization of L1 phonology as pliable in the face of subsequent language learning.

Transfer, universal patterns, and markedness could well explain specific trouble spots, but does any one theory fully capture phonological acquisition? Broselow et al. (1998) maintain that markedness does. Their Mandarin ESL learners' preference for devoiced final stops – not motivated by patterns in either L1 or L2 – supports their hypothesis that all learners revert to an 'initial state' where markedness rules the day (see Carlisle 2001). This lines up nicely with the Optimality Theoretic Model, which argues for full access to *universal grammar* principles regardless of the learner's age. So while transfer is thought to dominate the early stages, a full access model covers the whole process, from beginning to end-state (elaborated in Hancin-Bhatt 2008). This hypothesis does not account for individual variation, which is widespread, leading Macken and Ferguson (1987) to reject what they call a 'deterministic' acquisition models. They point to the idiosyncrasies of input, and the fact that individual learners choose from a variety of solutions for any given learning difficulty.

There is often no clear correspondence between native language patterns and interlanguage errors (Odlin 1989), so transfer is no longer seen as an all-encompassing explanation for L2 acquisition. Moreover, it is unclear whether transfer is more common the older one gets, or whether it simply predominates the beginning stages of learning. This is difficult to ascertain since the relevant mechanisms are intrinsically unobservable: transfer may be neuro-physiological, as when the learner notices, but cannot adjust to, a new articulatory pattern; or essentially cognitive, as when certain features are unnoticed or false equivalences are drawn.

In sum, theories about the intersection of L1 and L2 during the learning process raise compelling questions but provide few definitive answers. It is also remarkable that debates about underlying mechanisms still tend toward a traditional, confined view of SLA, overlooking interaction, learner agency, and context as critical forces in acquisition.

2.5 Possible advantages of early bilingualism

There is still a popular notion that, at least in the short term, early childhood exposure to more than one language delays verbal development or causes gaps in linguistic knowledge, although research increasingly points to cognitive benefits. An early testament to this relationship comes from Lambert's (1977) study, in which French–English bilingual children posted higher scores than monolingual children on intelligence tests – *intelligence* defined for this purpose as greater cognitive creativity and the ability to find multiple solutions to problems. Current thinking is that early childhood bilingualism bestows cognitive advantages, and for phonology specifically, it could hold open categorical perception and articulatory habits beyond a narrow critical period.

2.5.1 Metalinguistic and phonological awareness

It is now well attested that bilingual children have greater metalinguistic awareness, defined as "the ability to separate nonverbal conceptual meanings from corresponding words in different languages" (Gonzalez and Schallert 1999). This is presumably because, during acquisition, they naturally compare the two languages. Metalinguistic awareness has implications for phonological awareness, described as the ability to consciously recognize and reflect on segments, phonemes, and sound patterns and sequences, and to creatively manipulate them to produce rhymes, alliteration, and new words through rule-based sound substitutions (Verhoeven 2007).

To test for any unique effects of bilingualism on phonological awareness, Verhoeven (2007) tracked the proficiency of 75 bilingual Turkish kindergartners in the Netherlands over the course of their first school year (ages 5–5 and a half years at the start). According to pre- and post-tests of auditory discrimination, productive and receptive lexical tasks, sentence repetition, and story comprehension, children with the most proficiency in both languages showed the greatest phonemic and phonotactic awareness; they were able to identify and recombine separate phonemes into new words. Because reading was taught at the same time, their developing literacy likely benefited phonological awareness as well (see also Bialystok et al. 2003).

Verhoeven's investigation underscores two important points: (a) the development of phonological awareness is connected to the acquisition of other language abilities, especially literacy; (b) additive bilingualism, where both languages are well supported in early childhood, can stimulate cognitive flexibility and lead to higher proficiency in both languages (Gonzalez and Schallert 1999; cf. Bialystok et al. 2003). This is essential for understanding the possible advantages those with an early onset have over older language learners. Perhaps their greater phonological awareness accounts for a more complete acquisition of distinct sounds, while late learners have a greater tendency to conflate similar sounds, or fail to notice certain contrasts altogether due to the overriding salience of L1. We explore a few of these questions below.

2.5.2 Underlying phonological representations

Central to the theoretical debates on phonological development and attainment is the following question: Do bilinguals access distinct L1–L2 phonological representations, or just one overarching set for both languages? If we knew the answer to this question, perhaps we could figure out whether performance differences really represent differences in underlying competence.

For child bilinguals, "it is an open question how [they] structure their phonetic representations," write Burns et al. (2007). Some data suggest that L1–L2 representations overlap to an appreciable degree (Burns et al. 2007 refer to Flege's work here). Others maintain that the systems are necessarily separate if exposure to L2 takes place long after L1 acquisition. Baker and Trofimovich (2005) address this question through an analysis of vowel production among early and late bilinguals of English and Korean. Transfer was apparent for the pronunciation of vowels similar in L1 and L2, but the transfer effects were relative to AO: The older the learner, the more likely she resorted to transfer as a strategy. Late bilinguals tended to merge two or more similar vowels into a single category. This suggests bidirectional transfer since some reorganization of L1 vowels was implied. By comparison, early bilinguals appeared to establish distinct categories even for similar vowels, demonstrating fine distinctions in vowel height and frontedness in English and Korean (e.g., for /ɛ/ in each).

MacLeod and Stoehl-Gammon (2010) present an intriguing study of bilinguals in Canada, all of whom had acquired both English and French prior to age 12, and who continued to use both languages on a daily basis through adulthood. Participants were separated into two groups: (a) simultaneous bilinguals, who had acquired both languages by the age of 3 years; (b) sequential bilinguals, who had acquired the second language between the ages of 8 and 12 years (N= 10 for each group). They examined vowel height and advancement, and VOT production of stop consonants. A carrier phrase such as "*I can say mud again mud*" was used for the targeted words, and acoustic analyses on extracted phones determined that both sequential and simultaneous bilinguals distinguished between similar French and English consonants, as they did for similar vowels. There were no significant group differences overall. For VOT values on voiced bilabial stops (e.g., /b/), neither group was exactly native-like, but they were similar to one another. The data therefore suggest that despite differences in AO, these bilinguals were able to set, and maintain, contrastive acoustic values for consonants and vowels, even for those that were very similar across the two languages (ibid.: 415). In other words, both groups seemed to effectively separate underlying representations of L1–L2 sounds. Importantly, MacLeod and Stoehl-Gammon emphasize linguistic experience as a significant factor for developing phonological knowledge. They attribute the sequential bilinguals' accuracy to the high social value of both French and English within their language community, which could well have encouraged ongoing use of both languages, leading to relatively balanced competence (ibid.).

An interesting tangential debate is whether bilinguals are truly capable of equal competence in both languages. Some maintain that there is always a dominant language, determined by both frequency and depth of use. Guiora and Schonberger (1990) insist that a bilingual's pronunciation can only be truly native-like in the dominant language because pronunciation is inextricably tied to the linguistic ego. A 'double language ego' is impossible in their view. In their examination of Hebrew–English bilinguals in Haifa, Hebrew was the dominant (school) language, and according to their analysis, none of the twenty-nine participants was judged to have a native-like pronunciation in the non-dominant language (English), even for those who spoke it in the home. However, Guiora's subsequent study with colleagues on French and Dutch bilinguals in Belgium yielded incompatible results (reported in Spoelders et al. 1996), leading him to admit that a construct as loosely defined as 'linguistic ego' is not a suitable proxy for language dominance. The question is nevertheless an interesting one, since fluent bilinguals typically retain some noticeable phonological traces of each language (noted in previous section).

2.5.3 Uniqueness of bilingual language processing

A side-by-side comparison of early and late bilingual processing in L1 and L2 can yield valuable insights for a theory of age effects, plasticity, and the question of underlying representations; however, nearly all of this research is devoted to morphosyntactic or lexical processing. While the Anchoring Hypothesis predicts that processing patterns in early language acquisition are simply repeated for subsequent languages, regardless of AO (Paradis 1997), definitive evidence for phonological processing is scarce. Some neural imaging data suggest that native speakers access the primary auditory cortex to a greater extent than non-native speakers during phonemic discrimination tasks, while non-native speakers have greater activation in the inferior frontal lobe (Callan et al. 2004). Much more study is needed on a variety of phonologically related tasks.

L1 and L2 processing have been tracked for early vs. late bilinguals in order to document whether proficiency level or 'stage,' age of onset, or even task type, best predicts speed, efficiency, and the location and intensity of neural activity. Those who begin acquiring another language in very early childhood show similar activation in both languages, and in ways similar to native speaker monolinguals, even for the non-dominant language (Stowe and Sabourin 2005). However, it is unclear whether age matters more than experience, as shown by Perani et al. (1998). They first noted significant processing differences for high proficiency vs. low proficiency late bilinguals (after AO=10+ yrs.) bilinguals of Italian and English on several tasks (not phonology related), and compared these activation patterns for early bilinguals of Spanish and Catalan on the same kind of tasks. The high proficiency bilinguals processed language in overlapping ways, regardless of early vs. late onset, and significantly differently from those who had exposure – but inconsistent use – of both languages from early childhood. Simply put, if early onset is not actually critical, consistent use seems to be a prerequisite for native-like processing.

Summarizing the neural imaging data overall, Wattendorf and Festman (2008) point to some commonalities in the emerging picture of bilingual processing:

- The dominant language presents greater neural activation than the non-dominant language.
- The less dominant language requires more processing effort and is noticeably slower, presumably because it is not fully automatized (see also Weber-Fox and Neville 1996).
- For highly proficient bilinguals the same regions are activated for both languages. For less proficient bilinguals, hemispheric activation is not necessarily parallel for L1 and L2.

One obvious consideration in this context is relative L1–L2 dominance. Bilingualism is rarely balanced; there is typically a dominant language that is processed more efficiently in terms of allocated neural space and speed. Birdsong (2006) is therefore right to question the role of age as opposed to proficiency, as proficiency appears by recent accounts to be a better predictor of neural activity (for example, see Steinhauer et al. 2009). We should note, however, that neural imaging data do not illuminate any effects of real-time processing differences on actual performance in a natural setting. Put another way, neural allocation differences between early vs. late learners do not, in and of themselves, imply a lack of fluency, only that L2 users may employ other, compensatory processing pathways to perform the same task.

2.5.4 Early passive exposure to L2

A handful of studies indicate that early exposure to a language predicts success for later phonological acquisition, even if that exposure is brief or sporadic. Tees and Werker (1984) show that exposure to Hindi and English before age 2 years has a positive effect on phonemic discrimination later in life. Their late learners of Hindi who had early childhood exposure were able to discriminate Hindi phonemic contrasts that monolingual English speakers could not perceive without training. Early overhearing may hold open conceptual categories that would otherwise close within the first few years of life.

Early exposure could further advantage pronunciation accuracy according to Knightly et al.'s (2003) study of adult learners who overheard Spanish in a natural setting from 0–6 years of age. Their study measured several segmental and suprasegmental features in read-aloud and narration tasks, including VOT and voicing patterns, along with speech rate and phrasal boundaries marked by stress. Childhood overhearers were compared to late learners and native speaker participants on a 5-point accent scale. Those with childhood exposure were significantly more native-like for VOT patterns in word-initial and word-medial obstruents (/p, t, k/), but ranked only midway between the native group and adult late learners on other voicing patterns tested. And although the benefits did not extend to every task type, accent for the narrative task was significantly correlated to childhood overhearing. (Interestingly, this advantage did not extend to morphosyntax, according to grammaticality judgments and other tasks.) The authors propose that early exposure allows for the precise discrimination of voicing distinctions – a fine point to be sure, but such features could signal a non-native speaker voice to the listener's ear. Another possibility is that early exposure predicts greater authenticity in rhythm, juncture and stress as much as it does for segmental nuances, and the narrative task brings those features to light more effectively than does isolated word recitation.

2.6 Conclusion: reframing the age debate for L2 accent

We cannot yet pinpoint what drives phonological development and determines its outcome in a second language. It seems that various factors play into it, but predicting their influence at various points along the acquisition continuum is difficult. Is their relative prominence determined by age of the learner or by the particulars of their L2 experience? Some intriguing inconsistencies in the research include:

- Specific universal processes could be differentially affected by age, with deletion more common among younger age groups (10–12 years) and epenthesis favored by older learners (post-adolescence and well into adulthood) (Riney 1990, cited in Lin 2003).
- Strategic preferences could well shift as a function of task type, with formal, decontextualized tasks more subject to frequent epenthesis (Lin 2003) as a function of task-related monitoring differences.
- Bidirectional influence, seen in mergers of L1 and L2 sounds, is not well understood, and the same must be said for unattributable substitution phenomena, overgeneralizations that never regularize, etc. Are these manifestations of knowledge restructuring, or performance-based or stylistic variation?

Ultimately, all such phenomena rely not just on intangible, possibly deterministic forces at work, but on the learners' own self-awareness, monitoring, and conscious learning strategies (see Osburne 2003; Yule et al. 1987 – more in Chapter 6).

This discussion has shown that phonological development involves universal patterns and transfer that operate on both perception and production, observed across a range of discrimination and production tasks and for various L1–L2 pairs. At the same time, second language phonology is tempered by language-specific constraints and individual decision-making (Leather 1987; Macken and Ferguson 1987). These are not unrelated processes; where L1 and L2 are perceived by the learner as typologically disparate (such as English and Japanese), she will tend to avoid direct transfer (Faerch and Kasper 1987; Kellerman 1983). We also note the relevance of category salience; learners may be 'pre-programmed' by L1 to notice certain L2 features, but they can certainly adjust this, either with or without training. We have further seen that even L1 phonology is dynamic, indicating that underlying representations are not actually rigid. The in(ter)dependence of L1 and L2 is a theoretical tangle that is unlikely to be resolved soon.

By all indications, different processing mechanisms come into play at different stages, or levels of proficiency, and to the extent that these coincide with age, it is easy to assume that they are biologically determined. But if older L2 learners process the target language in ways dissimilar to native speakers, this could well be due to experience level more than to age of onset. The crucial question is therefore: Who has access to consistent, interaction-based experience and who does not? Older learners typically have less consistent and complete input, but where input is in fact sufficient, they can excel compared to younger learners (Muñoz 2006b). Perhaps their advanced cognitive development allows them to engage with the input differently, and they self-initiate interaction and seek explicit feedback that addresses their learning needs more efficiently than do children (Granena 2006).

It should go without saying – but it hasn't always – that every learner brings to bear a unique cognitive style and set of abilities, otherwise thought of as talents, preferences, and limits. These learner-specific factors operate alongside language-specific and context-specific factors. Individual variation is ubiquitous, in other words, and while it is sometimes dismissed in the cognitive paradigm, this is precisely what calls to question a hypothesis as all-encompassing as the CPH. Beyond knowing that cognition and neurobiology shift over the lifespan of the individual, there is fundamental uncertainty whether neurobiological age actually determines language acquisition outcomes. Furthermore, it is unclear whether maturation represents a truly pivotal point in language-learning-related capacities.

It has long been assumed that the special challenge of phonology is owed to some neurobiological decline or cognitive interference. Acquiring a new sound system depends on mechanisms that may become less efficient with age, and at the same time, the foundations of L1 become stronger with increasing use, thus, the more likely it is to interfere with our ability to notice fine distinctions in a new language. We know from the data on childhood bilingualism that experience – in particular *ongoing use* – can make the difference for native-like vs. non-native-like attainment. Those who enjoy early onset have far greater opportunity for consistent and meaningful interaction over time, which improves outcomes in accent. Even upholding a strictly cognitive perspective, the relevance of this relationship can hardly be overstated; experience represents opportunities for practice and feedback that affect selective attention, self-monitoring, and knowledge restructuring (see Chapter 6). Early exposure also implies a deeper psychological and social investment, another factor shown to be significant for long-term phonological attainment.

The age question will likely continue to fascinate researchers. Scovel described the CPH some twenty years ago as a compelling hypothesis, not because it deals solely with a neurological phenomenon affecting the acquisition of a specific skill, but because it asks how nature and nurture work together "through time" to "form the foundation for all human learning" (1988: 5). To appreciate its contribution to SLA, we should consider what a critical period means in social, psychological, biological, and neurological terms, for learning always takes place within a broader context. In Scovel's words, applied linguists (like most scientists) "are infatuated with dichotomies" – here: whether one *can* or *cannot* learn to speak natively after childhood. But the simplicity of such dichotomies obscures reality. The factors responsible for phonological acquisition are interwoven in the unique relationship between learner and context. With this in mind, we turn to an integrated look at intrinsic and extrinsic factors in L2 accent, focusing on the individual learner.

3 Accent and the individual

The quest for universal patterns of language development has guided linguistics research for decades, including the field of SLA, which has assumed an acquisition continuum characterized by constraints, for the most part defined in cognitive terms. At present, however, there is growing interest in individual differences as key to second language development. The framework for this new paradigm, Dynamic Systems Theory (DST), describes language acquisition as driven by various language resources "cobbled together in real time" as learners negotiate language identity as a function of who their interlocutors are and what activities they are engaged in (Larsen-Freeman 2011: 54). Language learning is viewed as chaotic, messy, and far less predictable than previously assumed. All operative psychological, cognitive, and social mechanisms are in flux, their balance continually shifting in response to the environment (Larsen-Freeman 1997, 2009; Lowie et al. 2009; van Geert 2009). This marks an important departure from the prevailing view of interlanguage as a system fraught with errors, moving along a predetermined path toward some ill-defined, "fossilized" state (Selinker 1972). In point of fact, there is plenty of variation in both process and outcome, even among those exposed to the target language at the same age. Individual differences, both intrinsic and extrinsic, account for this variation.

Keeping in mind this emphasis on complexity and fluidity, this chapter addresses individual differences as dynamic, not a priori, traits. Intrinsic predispositions naturally respond to extrinsic factors like L2 contact and use through the development of social networks. Larsen-Freeman has stated: "Differences and variation need to move to the center of language acquisition research" (2009: 585), and Sawyer and Ranta (2001) stake the explanatory adequacy of SLA as a field on the exploration of such traits. In that spirit, we thematize this chapter's discussion around the following question: *Is a native-like accent in a second language the result of an idiosyncratic mix of neurocognitive talents, access to special language-learning resources, or a specialized orientation to language learning itself?* While the following sections present individual differences in turn, this is an organizational convenience that belies their inherent interconnectedness – a theme we will touch upon throughout.

As elaborated in Chapter 2, success in the phonological realm refers to the ability to identify and/or produce L2 sounds on level with a native speaker[1], verified through perceptual or production tasks incorporating contextualized and/or decontextualized formats. Acoustic analyses of production data indicate that new tonal and phonemic categories, and especially subtle features like vowel quality, aspiration, and voice onset time, are notoriously difficult to master when L1 and L2 categories are similar, but not exactly alike (e.g., the difference in English between the phonemes /ɪ/–/i/ or between the allophones $[t^h]$ – [t]). Even listeners completely unfamiliar with the language in question can accurately hear the difference between native and non-native speakers (Major 2007). This suggests there is something unique, and salient, about a non-native accent, likely due to the kinds of subtleties mentioned, but also to a host of features that deviate in some way from the listener's expectations regarding speech rate, pause patterns, rhythm, and the like.

Unquestionably, the late L2 learner's task is daunting, given that phonological fluency implies a mastery of so many features simultaneously. Those who can fool the native ear have been called successful, if not exceptional, but there are few in-depth studies of such cases. Importantly, early onset with the target language is not necessarily a factor in their success.[2] Moyer's 2004 mixed-methods study of immigrants to Berlin offers critical insights into the profiles of two Turkish men, both of whose families had immigrated to Germany when they were just 4 years old. We might reasonably expect both to sound native-like in German given their very early exposure, but only one did. One-on-one interviews clearly reveal disparate levels of desire to assimilate. Only the one judged to sound native expressed positive attitudes toward the German language and culture; the other was decidedly negative. This had long-term repercussions for the activities he chose to engage in, and the people he developed ties with, as he consciously limited his social networks to exclude Germans. In other words, his attitudes and self-concept precluded full linguistic and cultural assimilation.

In a subsequent study of L2 users of English living in the US, Moyer (2007a) discovered a set of factors shared by two participants whose accents were rated as native-like for most production tasks:
- immigration (to the US) by age 5;
- 13 or more years' residence in-country;

---

[1] While calls for the demise of the native–non-native construct are common in the sociocultural literature (e.g., Golombek & Jordan 2005), the intent here is to understand the nature of phonological skill, thus the native speaker construct is a necessary point of comparison on phonetic, prosodic and discursive levels.

[2] 'Exceptional' and 'successful' are used somewhat interchangeably in the literature, though 'exceptional' sometimes refers to a higher threshold, i.e., nativeness as opposed to very advanced or near-native.

- an intention to stay in the US for at least 5 more years;
- consistent use of English among native speaker friends within multiple social contexts;
- a strong and consistent desire to sound native;
- a strong sense of comfort assimilating to American culture (see also Moyer 2004).

Others who reported several, but not all, of these aspects of L2 experience and positive orientation did not fare as well *despite an equally early start*. This suggests that success in the phonological realm (and by extension, 'exceptionality') is best explained by an optimal combination of *experience* and *orientation*, rather than neurobiological age alone. Attitudes, goals, and behaviors directed toward language learning develop in conjunction with meaningful language use, and this takes shape in unique ways for each learner.

3.1   Intrinsic individual differences

In *On language memoir*, Alice Kaplan (1994) describes her experiences learning French, and befriending a speech therapist named Micheline while in Paris as a young American student:

> I went into her office wanting to work on my French, and she recorded my voice on her tape recorder. I heard my foreign intonation, which she called my "song." "You'll never get rid of that song," she said, "but what does it matter?" I wanted to hire her, pay her thousands of dollars, to rid me of it. "Speech," Micheline told me, "is the highest and lowest human function, the *endroit charnière* [pivotal place] between the mechanical grunt of the vocal cords and the poetry of cognition" ... I was surprised by the strength of my desire for a new self. I had wanted to trade in my voice, even its timbre, for another one. Micheline – whose life's work was to help people with problems of voice and identity – saw this before I did and encouraged me to relax. Why didn't I want to relax with my accent and my mistakes? What was at stake? (67–70)

Alice's struggle is a manifestation of many potential, perhaps even competing, influences, only some of which she may have control over. What this chapter's discussion will show is that those who end up sounding native-like or near-native are proactive in their learning; they pursue optimal sources of input and positively shape their own attitudes and motivation. In other words, they bring to bear myriad cognitive, experiential, and socio-psychological resources on the acquisition process.

What exactly do we know about how successful learners approach the task of phonological learning? Few researchers have tested multiple factors at once to get a full picture of their L2 experience, much less an understanding of how their orientation toward the target language and culture develops over time. Suter (1976) gave an early indication that many factors are relevant, including: aptitude for oral mimicry, age of onset, length of residence, degree of concern for pronunciation, years of instruction, gender, and various types of motivation. Moyer's (2004) study of late learners of English analyzes 35 factors, among them: gender, age of onset, length of residence, intensity and consistency of motivation to acquire the target language, self-concept in that language, self-rating of pronunciation, desire to sound native, total years of formal instruction, contexts for language contact and use, and strategies for improving pronunciation. Many such factors demonstrate statistical significance for accent on the full range of controlled and extemporaneous tasks, but equally informative are: (a) the correlations linking biological, experiential and socio-psychological factors; (b) the relative strength of context-specific, interactive language use as compared to age of onset (AO) and length of residence (LOR).

Another study to investigate instructed learners comes from Elliott (1995), who found that desire to sound native was significant for repetition tasks (repeating after a native speaker), as well as read-aloud passages and spontaneous speaking. Among the factors tested, only field independence, associated with an analytical style and metalinguistic strategies, was significant. Indeed, cognitive factors may go a long way in explaining exceptional learners (discussed in 3.3.4).

Elliott's conclusions are cautious, and for good reason: Little is known about the interconnectedness of cognition and affect. The desire to sound native and an analytical learning style may contribute to self-initiated strategies involving mimicry, rehearsal, self-monitoring, etc. At the same time, the predominant context for learning is important to consider in studies of long-term attainment. Those who overwhelmingly rely on instructional contexts may prioritize cognitive strategies advantageous for the phonological loop function (involving the rehearsal of sound sequences), thereby enhancing memory. By contrast, uninstructed learners may rely on more implicit mechanisms or utilize different parts of the brain to acquire new sound patterns. These are just a few possibilities. Below, we summarize some of the more frequently cited intrinsic factors involved in L2 phonological attainment.

3.1.1 Aptitude

It is often said that some people have a 'knack' for imitating accents, but there are few concrete measures for what this means in real terms. The Modern Language Aptitude Test (Carroll and Sapon 1959) famously tests phonetic coding ability – the ability to identify distinct sounds and retain sound–symbol associations – but this is applied to language-learning aptitude in general; there is no such battery that delves deeper into phonology-related skills as a whole. The empirical work has framed phonological skill or talent in terms of the following observable behaviors:

- the ability to mimic native speaker-modeled words and phrases (Markham 1997; Purcell and Suter 1980; Reves 1978; Thompson 1991), either with or without targeted training beforehand;
- the ability to perceive new sound categories with the same precision as native speakers;
- the ability to read aloud written sentences or short passages in a way comparable to native speaker controls, either with or without targeted training beforehand.

All of these tasks are presumed to reflect *aptitude* of some kind – a somewhat mysterious, internal trait thought to be separate from, and impervious to, external influences (Jilka 2009). In general, aptitude refers to the ways that mental abilities and processes interact with learning conditions and novel information (Dörnyei 2006). This includes higher-order processes such as analysis, inference, etc., and lower-order processes like pattern recognition (ibid.). For phonological skill, the relevant mechanisms likely include hearing, perception, memory, articulatory flexibility, or some combination of processing skills. Absent detailed knowledge about how phonological skill develops over time, no comprehensive model exists to explain relevant aptitudes or talents.

Considering how little is known about what underlies phonological aptitude, Piske et al. (2001) question whether any language-related talents are truly innate, rather than something built by experience. Based on her review of the brain–language talent research, Reiterer (2009) argues for a confluence of factors, some of which are best categorized as 'nature,' others as 'nurture'. In reality, it could well be the interaction of nature and nurture that matters most, as is the case with the factors mentioned below.

3.1.2   Memory

There is wide support for the idea that aptitude in language learning, and phonetic coding ability itself, is a function of memory (see Bowden et al. 2005; Sawyer and Ranta 2001). Working memory (WM) – the temporary storage and manipulation of information used for language comprehension and production – is a major focus of aptitude research, in particular regarding specialized components such as the phonological loop function. The phonological loop refers to the recall and rehearsal of auditory stimuli such as new sound sequences. It is held to be critical to language learning, assuming that "the ability to keep an item longer in working memory considerably enhances the chance that it is being processed and stored in [long-term] memory" (Lowie et al. 2009: 132). Rysiewicz (2008) finds a correlation between associative memory (as opposed to rote) and higher test scores for reading, writing, listening, lexicon, and grammar among learners of English, yet he concedes that associative memory may not be useful for all SLA contexts. In his estimation, immersion learning does not rely on the same analytical and memorization skills that instructed formats require (cf. Sawyer and Ranta 2001; see also Safar and Kormos 2008). Robinson's 1995 study seems to suggest, however, that all learning conditions, implicit and explicit, benefit from the capacity to identify sequence and organization – an analytical aspect of aptitude – as opposed to straight, rote memorization (cited in Skehan 1998). Another theoretical quandary is whether memory continues to be significant beyond the early stages of language learning. Skehan (ibid.) argues for its ongoing influence, but Hummel's (2007) investigation does not support this claim.

Despite many unanswered theoretical questions, there is a growing consensus that phonological memory plays a prominent role in language learning and the development of literacy, but few claims are made about what that means for phonological development itself. Golestani and Zatorre (2009) assume that individual differences in WM account for the variation they observed among English speakers learning Hindi dental–retroflex contrasts and a tonal pitch contrast. However, Rota and Reiterer (2009) show mixed results for WM as a correlate of overall phonological fluency for 66 adult German learners of English. As classically measured – by digit or word-span tasks that require the recall of sequences of varying length – WM may account for little of the variance in phonological attainment, according to Munro (2008). He speculates that successful learners have some sort of 'sensory memory' that encourages attention to fine phonetic detail, which they uniquely store and use later on to perfect accent.

Because current work on memory, and even the phonological loop, is almost exclusively directed at lexical and grammatical retrieval, only tentative assumptions about memory's involvement in phonological development are possible, and this surely depends on the individual's cognitive capacities and the learning situation too, since that has implications for frequency of exposure, focus on form, and feedback opportunities (see Chapter 6, Section 3 for discussion of these constructs).

3.1.3 Hemispheric preference, musical 'talent,' and experience

Another potential explanation for the variation seen in L2 phonology relates to the prominence of the right hemisphere (RH) during language processing. The idea is that greater reliance on the RH could boost suprasegmental accuracy since tone and melody are thought to be processed there. (The left hemisphere, or LH, is associated with phonemic processing at the level of syllables and words.) While males appear to be LH dominant during various language processing tasks, females are bilateral by comparison, which could account for their observed superior performance on such tasks, as well as verbal scores on major test batteries (see Burman et al. 2008; Imaizumi et al. 2004; Lindell and Lum 2008; Rymarczyk and Grabowska 2007), and studies of long-term attainment in L2 accent (Asher and Garcia 1969; Diaz-Campos 2004; Munro and Mann 2005; Moyer 2010; Tahta et al. 1981; Thompson 1991). Gender aside, if the early stages of language learning are characterized by greater RH involvement as a rule (Obler 1993), perhaps L2 learners who end up sounding native are those individuals who, for whatever reason, continue to process language in a bilateral fashion (more in Chapter 2, Section 2.3).

Does musical talent constitute any advantage for phonological learning? This is a popular idea, but there is little evidence to support it (Piske et al. 2001; Tokuhama-Espinosa 2003), and some research casts doubt on any music–phonology interface. Gottfried (2008) recently found that musicians more accurately perceived and produced tones in Mandarin (having no previous knowledge of the language), but only for a subset of the tonal patterns tested. Interestingly, both musicians and non-musicians struggled with mid-rising and low-dipping tonal contrasts. Overall, the 'experts' did not consistently outperform non-experts (the non-musicians). Musical 'talent' may have more to do with experience than innate abilities since these musicians were able to work with some tones more accurately than others. Musicians are likely LH dominant while listening to music (Bever and Chiarello 1974) – the same pattern seen with native speakers of tonal languages – whereas novices (non-native speakers) process tone bilaterally (Sereno and Wang 2007 – more in Chapter 2, Section 2.3).

The fact that phonetic and prosodic processing respond to experience is fundamental to the idea of cue weighting, the tendency to prioritize familiar features when discriminating new perceptual categories. An important question is whether advanced L2 users weigh certain cues as native speakers do. Guion and Pederson (2007) suggest that native speakers of tonal languages attend to different prosodic cues in an unfamiliar language than do listeners from a non-tonal language background (see Iverson and Kuhl 1996). There is, however, no reason to assume that cue weighting cannot be developed, given sufficient input and practice, as learning capacities naturally evolve over one's lifespan (Dörnyei 2005; Lowie et al. 2009).

Whether aptitude relates to overall intelligence, as maintained by Oller (1983, cited in Sawyer and Ranta 2001), or to more general cognitive abilities (Skehan 1998), the current state of research offers few specifics about how aptitude might influence language learning, much less phonological learning. One possibility is that the accurate perception of new sounds and suprasegmental patterns makes native-like production possible. Nardo and Reiterer (2009) find that rhythm and pitch perception significantly correlated to production abilities in accent for 66 learners of English. There is scarce evidence thus far of this type, namely, that what L2 learners do in terms of perception extends to production (or vice versa) (see also Sereno and Wang 2007).

Taking a broader view, neurocognitive processing is not the only relevant aspect of aptitude. Some kind of cognitive–affective interface is likely central to long-term success. The Rota and Reiterer (2009) study on accent (mentioned above) compared the significance of WM with: (a) mental flexibility, based on Raven's Progressive Matrices for reasoning and abstract thinking; (b) intelligence, defined as selective attention and reaction time during task-switching; and (c) empathy, based on a questionnaire to measure sensitivity and concern over fictitious vs. real-life situations. For their advanced speakers of L2 English, there was far more consistent and widespread significance for empathy than for the other three factors. Of particular interest is the fact that empathy correlated to phonetic coding ability, suprasegmental perception, imitation ability for an unknown language (Hindi words), and self-professed enjoyment of imitating accents. This suggests a cognitive–affective interface, long touted by a few researchers (e.g., Schumann 1994), but rarely treated experimentally. Future studies should target the potential connections between selective attention, enjoyment of sound pattern mimicry, and sensitivity to suprasegmental features.

3.1.4 Learning styles and strategies

Learning styles and strategy use[3] are a logical starting point for understanding why some seem to have an edge in SLA, but the limits of this line of inquiry are obvious: The operative constructs are largely unobservable, and good data depend on the participant's self-awareness and honest disclosure. Nevertheless, typologies of strategies, as outlined by Oxford (1990), point to the varied and complex ways that learners endeavor to improve their fluency.

H. D. Brown has written: "If I were to try to enumerate all the learning styles that educators and psychologists have identified, a very long list of just about every imaginable sensory, communicative, cultural, affective, cognitive, and intellectual factor would emerge" (2007: 120). But even with decades of inquiry now, it is still unclear how learning styles affect language learning, particularly over the long term (Dai 2006; Yabukoshi and Takeuchi 2009). The relevant research has emphasized vocabulary, grammar, listening, reading, and writing skills, with scarce attention to their importance for accent, but some oft-cited categories are surely relevant, e.g.: self-monitoring, selective and directed attention, self-evaluation, repetition, risk-taking, and anxiety-lowering techniques. A few such strategies are addressed, albeit minimally, in the studies mentioned below.

---

[3] *Style* refers to general learning preferences, not tied to specific tasks or contexts, while *strategy* refers to goal-directed techniques to optimize learning within a specific task or situation (see Oxford 1990).

Thompson (1991) was among the first to assess strategy use directed at improving pronunciation, but for her 36 Russian learners of English no solid connections were found. Investigating task-directed strategies, Osburne's (2003) oral protocols from 50 adult ESL learners of various native language backgrounds revealed that most engage in several accent-directed strategies: (a) they focus on tempo, volume, and overall clarity; (b) they imitate native speakers; (c) they focus on individual words and sounds that cause difficulty. All of these are cognitive[4] in nature. Still, no ratings verify the efficacy of any of these strategies.

Metacognitive strategies to improve pronunciation relate to outreach strategies aimed at increasing social contact with native speakers, as discussed in Moyer (2004). Her statistical analyses point to an advantage for those who undertake both cognitive and metacognitive strategies (the more, the better), particularly when imitating native speakers is a regular practice. Moreover, participants who focus on their pronunciation shortfalls are more likely to seek practice and feedback from social sources (beyond the classroom) – evidence for the interconnectedness of cognition and affect in language learning. The bottom line is that those with a reflective and proactive approach are more likely to attain a more authentic, fluent accent.

Even with this supportive evidence, it is appropriate to pose a basic question here: Do learners' efforts actually target the skills most relevant to judgments of phonological fluency? A common perception is that sounding foreign is primarily a matter of segmental accuracy. In their survey of 100 adult ESL learners of various native language backgrounds, Derwing and Rossiter (2002) report that 55 percent cite pronunciation as a contributing – if not the main – cause of communicative breakdowns. In the Moyer study cited above, 40 percent of the participants refer to persistent segmental difficulties while just 13 percent report ongoing problems with intonation. Derwing and Rossiter believe the significance of segmental errors is overblown. In reality, suprasegmental fluency may be more important for judgments of accentedness (Anderson-Hsieh et al. 1992; Elliott 1997; Moyer 1999).

Learning styles and strategies are undoubtedly connected to personality, yet we intentionally leave aside this Pandora's box because personality has rarely been addressed in the empirical work on phonology (as for SLA overall), and available research paints an inconsistent picture (see Dörnyei 2006; Sawyer and Ranta 2001). Casual mention is often made of factors like risk-taking, extraversion, sociability, empathy, etc. as relevant (see Hu and Reiterer 2009), but, as with aptitude, these are typically referred to as static traits. Logic dictates

---

[4] *Cognitive* strategies include practicing, analyzing, repeating, summarizing, whereas *metacognitive* strategies refer to goal-setting, self-evaluation, reflecting on learning, seeking practice and feedback, etc. (see Oxford 1990).

that they shift with age and learning circumstances, however. As an example, adult learners are surely more reluctant to seek out practice with unfamiliar native speakers. Indeed, Victori and Tragant's (2003) study of 766 English classroom learners in Spain demonstrates that younger learners enjoy getting to know native speakers and studying with peers. They also report listening closely, imitating, and practicing sounds out loud with their native-speaking friends. Older learners expressed a preference for passive activities like listening to songs and watching films in the target language.

A holistic view of the learner acknowledges the importance of individual beliefs, self-knowledge, and even awareness of strategy effectiveness (Dörnyei 2006). Implicit in this view is a recognition of learner agency, or self-regulation. Good language learners take charge of their learning; they create opportunities for practice outside the classroom and use various strategies to recall what has been learned. Furthermore, they *invest* in the target language within its "socially constructed context" (Brown 2007: 233). A desire to sound authentic in the second language is the logical impetus behind self-initiated strategies to improve phonological accuracy. Not everyone wants, or tries, to sound native, but without that drive it is hard to overcome the features that mark one as a non-native speaker.

3.1.5 Gender differences

The question of gender differences often comes up in discussions of individual differences in language ability and language use. Two well-established lines of inquiry investigate gender from very different perspectives: (a) neurocognitive explorations of underlying gender[5] differences in language processing; (b) studies of socially conditioned language performance along gender lines. Below, we summarize current strands in the research and present questions for future work on gender and L2 phonology.

In their review of gender differences in L1, Burman et al. (2008) identify areas where females excel compared to males, including the age at which they begin to talk as infants, the speed with which they acquire vocabulary in the native language, and the creativity of their language. Kelman (2007), however, cites no obvious gender differences among 91 preschool children ages 3–6 years for phonological awareness, defined as the awareness of, or ability to manipulate, sounds and sound contrasts independently of meaning (Piske 2008: 155f.). Still, the common wisdom is that school-age girls reliably outpace boys for verbal and written language skills, and that this extends to foreign language

---

[5] *Gender* is most often used in terms of language performance, i.e., as a social construct, whereas *sex*, a prenatal characteristic, is the term common in the neuro-biological research. Here, I use *gender* in keeping with the practice of much L2 phonology research.

learning as well. One possible explanation is that males and females differ in terms of verbal memory and processing approach (Chipman and Kimura 1999), possibly owing to hormonal effects on phonological discrimination ability (see Reiterer 2009; Ullman 2005). Debates persist regarding differences in neural organization and endowment as another explanation. Schiffler (2001) maintains that Broca's area is 20 percent larger and Wernicke's area 30 percent larger for females than for males, but Wallentin (2009) discounts differences in terms of either gray matter size or the allocation of processing space.

These debates notwithstanding, there is no dispute about one essential gender difference: Males appear to be LH dominant during many language processing tasks while females are bilateral processors by comparison. Lindell and Lum (2008) showed bilateral activation among females and a male preference for LH lateralization, according to neural-imaging data. This difference was especially pronounced when the task required the discrimination of homophones with vastly different spellings (e.g., *use – ewes*). The authors suspect that the male visual field is more highly activated in such instances (see Clements et al. 2006; cf. Sommer et al. 2008). Burman et al. (2008) provide further evidence that boys ages 9–15 process words differently depending on the modality (visual vs. auditory) whereas girls seem to access a "supramodal language network" regardless of task mode. Whether bilateral processing makes females especially adept at interpreting the emotional significance of prosody is another matter for debate (see Imaizumi et al. 2004; Plante et al. 2006; Rymarczyk and Grabowska 2008).

Gender is rarely addressed directly in L2 phonology research. It is practically a footnote in some cases (e.g., Diaz-Campos 2004; Preston and Yamagata 2004), and support for its relevance is inconsistent. Asher and Garcia's 1969 study indicates a temporary female advantage for pronunciation, diminishing with increasing length of residence. By contrast, Thompson's (1991) female participants with a long residence in-country continued to show phonological superiority on read-aloud and spontaneous speaking tasks (cf. Tahta et al. 1981).

One crucial question is whether gender really exerts an independent influence on language acquisition, or whether it is confounded with attitudes, motivation, age of onset, etc. Flege et al. (1995b) blame contradictory evidence on the failure to effectively separate gender effects from age of onset, and their own attempt to do so was inconclusive. Another case in point is Munro and Mann (2005). They found a significant advantage for female Mandarin speakers learning English, but gender interacted significantly with age of onset (AO). Other studies show no significant gender differences on various task types (Flege and Fletcher 1992; Elliott 1995; Moyer 2004; Olson and Samuels 1982).

Recently, Moyer (2010) reported an independent gender effect for degree of accent among 42 learners of English in the US on a series of read-aloud and extemporaneous speaking tasks. Tasks beyond the word level, i.e., involving phrase-level suprasegmentals, indicated the greatest advantage for female participants. Correlation analyses explored whether gender's significance was attributable to affective or experiential factors, but no significant male–female differences were found for: (a) use of the target language beyond the classroom; (b) desire to sound native; (c) instructional experience; (d) attitudes toward L2 and its culture (cf. Flege et al. 1995b). Furthermore, ANOVA (analysis of variance) tests found no significant interaction between gender and LOR or AO, pointing to a possible intrinsic difference between males and females, at least for suprasegmental skills. The gender difference was strongest among learners with an AO earlier than 9 years, and learners with five or fewer years' residence in the target-language country (as in Asher and Garcia 1969).

There is a need to clearly delineate the boundaries of any possible gender effect, i.e., how gender actually affects performance, much less long-term attainment. Furthermore, if any RH benefit is tied to stage of learning, a female advantage should evaporate at the advanced level. Data are needed to tease this influence apart from the age factor as well. Perhaps most intriguing are any underlying differences in attention and memory, i.e., whether females notice, retain, and/or recall certain phonetic or prosodic features with greater efficiency, or whether they uniquely associate prosodic cues with meaning as a result of any special sensitivities to tone.

Differences in male–female speech style have long been documented, and some classic patterns obtain for L2 as they do for L1. Major's 2004 study of ESL learners reveals stylistic differences for four casual speech features (palatalization, deletion, assimilation and use of *-in'* for *-ing* present participle), with males producing significantly more casual forms than females – a likely carryover from native language behavior. Imai (2005) found something unusual, however. She analyzed both AO and gender for vowel devoicing in Japanese – a non-standard feature. In her study, younger females used this feature far more frequently than did males or older speakers, contradicting the sociolinguistic truism that women prefer standard forms (cf. Adamson and Regan 1991). Other studies highlight females' use of different pitch patterns depending on interlocutor gender and status – a clear indication of accommodation and solidarity effects (Daly and Warren 2001; Lewis 2003).

More than a few researchers suspect that females are more concerned about pronunciation accuracy than are males (e.g., Thompson 1991). Spezzini (2004) contends that her female non-native speakers are judged to be more comprehensible because of their adherence to the standard, ideal pronunciation. Her male participants oriented their speech to that of their peers and received lower accent ratings. If females are indeed better attuned to standard norms, it may lead them to use certain metacognitive strategies to improve their accent. Reflective protocols, longitudinally applied, are needed to substantiate this.

While evidence for intrinsic differences appears to be mounting, lab conditions and limited processing tasks are still narrow in scope; they exclude various external factors that interact with gender. The Polat and Mahalingappa (2010) study is an important exception. They undertook a study of 121 Kurdish children and adolescents learning Turkish. Clear advantages were found for female participants regarding the density and multiplexity of their social networks, namely, the depth of bonds among members of the *speech community* and the range of interaction types practiced within those groups (see Milroy 1987, cited in Polat and Mahalingappa 2010). These factors were found to be highly significant for accent ratings. The boys relied more on peers from their same ethnolinguistic background instead, and this behavior was correlated with a stronger foreign accent. The authors hasten to add that because gender is socially constructed, few generalizations can be made beyond this study's "immediate sociocultural realities" (ibid.: 29). Even so, an essential conclusion is that accent stands to gain as the L2 community is increasingly valued.

Some observed gender differences are likely an artifact of the instrument, at least in part. Males and females appear to respond to certain tasks or survey items in dissimilar ways (Bielska 2008). Furthermore, they may receive differential feedback from classroom teachers (Kissau 2007), or have different responses toward certain learning environments, all of which can lead to different degrees of mastery. And as mentioned, the age factor may confound results. Many citations of gender differences in foreign language learning come from studies on adolescents, who are surely susceptible to anxiety or resistant to risk-taking. Davies (2004), Henry and Apelgren (2008), Heinzmann (2009) and MacIntyre et al. (2003) all document male–female differences in adolescents' self-concept in FL, their willingness to communicate, their perceptions of FL achievement, and their attitudes about the value of learning another language in general. In short, depending on age and circumstance, males and females may orient themselves differently to language learning.

Some have suggested that immersion-style SLA triggers bilateral processing regardless of gender, thus nullifying any potential female advantage (Galloway and Scarcella 1982). A more sociocultural take is that the gender construct affects many aspects of SLA including learning resources, values placed on bilingualism, etc. It is clear that in an immigration context, gender can predict differential access to L2 resources. A scenario prevalent in the sociocultural literature goes something like this: A female immigrant stays at home, according to cultural expectations or other norms, while her husband works outside the home. This presents him with greater opportunity to develop L2 fluency via multiple and varied social networks. She has limited access to transportation, is unable to attend target-language classes, and does not engage in cultural activities beyond her immediate community. This is just one of many possibilities, but the bottom line is that social conditions relevant to gender can determine the course, and extent, of language acquisition.

3.2 Socio-psychological factors

For some late language learners, accent is the only linguistic hint of their non-native status. The presumed intractability of accent is typically described in two opposing ways: either it is essentially a social-psychological problem, or it is proof of a predetermined biological limit on acquiring sound categories and articulation patterns (see Chapter 2). In *A Time to Speak*, Scovel (1988) takes a stand on this conundrum:

> Why is it that emotional factors interfere with the learning of the phonology of a foreign language after puberty but do not ultimately impede the acquisition of any other linguistic skill? ... It simply does not seem logical to me that emotions work for good or for ill at the highest degrees of one level of language learning (phonology) but do not seem to influence the very highest reaches of any other level. (95)

For Scovel, the answer is unequivocally biological, as phonology involves lower-order, neuro-muscular skills. But if pronunciation "constitutes a higher manifestation of self-representation" (Jilka 2009: 4), it may very well be influenced by affective factors that shape the learner's approach to the task. There is ample evidence to support this position. Below, we discuss these important individual differences, beginning with the question of what is at stake when one takes on a new language identity.

3.2.1 Identity, acculturation, and the 'linguistic ego'

> [L]anguage equals home ... language is a home, as surely as a roof over one's head is a home ... [To] be without a language, or to be between languages, is as miserable in its way as to be without bread. (Kaplan 1994: 63)

No matter the specifics of the learning environment, communicating beyond one's linguistic comfort zone can be difficult, particularly for adults. Accent, as an essential aspect of our identity, can be the site of resistance when we do not wish to yield our established sense of self, or it can be the gateway to integration into another culture. The kernel for this idea gained popularity decades ago, when identity was portrayed as a sort of 'linguistic ego,' with accent at its center. Adolescents and adults, it was assumed, are especially sensitive to their own ego boundaries while children freely play with language and mimic new sounds without inhibition. This presumably explains why children end up sounding native in any language while adults rarely lose their foreign accent.

Guiora and colleagues (1972 and 1980) famously set out to prove that self-consciousness constrains the acquisition of a non-native accent. They administered varying doses of alcohol to 87 college FL learners (and in another study, valium), with the result that small doses improved accent somewhat.

Of course these controlled substances may have simply lowered anxiety; there is no proof that they actually invoked 'empathy' or redrew ego boundaries, as the authors surmised (see Schumann 1975). Block (2007) criticized this work on the grounds that it did not reveal "how individuals normally interact with others" or make choices about "how they wish to sound in a second language" (53). This, and other, legitimate critiques notwithstanding, the assumption is still intriguing: that self-concept is based in the native language(s), and that it profoundly affects phonological skill building after childhood.

Around the same time, socio-psychological models advanced the study of psychological processes relevant to language learning, as elaborated in the work of Gardner, Lambert, Clément, Giles and Byrnes, Schumann, and others. Much needed attention was thereby paid to the social context of SLA and the difficulties implied by *acculturation* – the process of adopting certain values and traits of the target-language culture while still maintaining ties to the native language group (Schumann 1978: 78).

Empirical work in this area is once again lively after languishing for some time. Nowadays, quasi-experimental and psychometric studies are typically carried out in instructed immersion environments which provide rich opportunities to examine ethnolinguistic vitality and cultural affiliation as significant for language attainment and acculturation (e.g., Gardner et al. 1999; Hogg and Rigoli 1996; Labrie and Clément 1986; Noels and Clément 1989). Another important focus of this work speaks to the ways that sociocultural experiences in the target language affect self-confidence in the second language and beliefs about language learning overall (Labrie and Clément 1986). At the same time, the sense of conflict that can accompany language learning has been underscored, to wit, Clément and Kruidenier's (1983) description of motivation as an "antagonistic interplay" between the desire to integrate into the new language community and the fear of losing ties to the mother tongue culture.

Identity is obviously linked to acculturation for those who live in the target-language country, yet this issue has received little direct attention in the L2 phonology literature. One exception is Lybeck's (2002) study of 9 American women living in Norway who felt hindered by their inability to get beyond a strongly American identity and a sense of cultural distance, especially as their attempts to speak Norwegian were so often met by their interlocutors' rapid switch to English. Those who said they now "accept this new part of themselves" despite initial difficulties had better accents, according to Lybeck (ibid.: 181). She attributed their success to the establishment of native-speaking networks of family and close friends, which allowed them to overcome feelings of distance and improve their L2 learning (ibid.: 177). Specifically, those networks were the means by which they acquired linguistically and culturally appropriate behaviors (ibid.: 184). This theme is echoed in Hansen's (1995) investigation of 20 German-born adult immigrants in the US, where

English *speech community* size and cohesiveness were statistically significant for degree of accent. On the other end of the spectrum, language shock, defined as fear of embarrassment, criticism or ridicule in speaking the target language (ibid.: 313), demonstrated negative correlations.

Schumann (1975) characterizes the initial challenges facing an adult immigrant L2 learner as follows:

> Just when inhibitions must be reduced in order to learn the second language, the anxiety caused by language [shock] and culture shock increases inhibition and reduces ego flexibility. The learner is caught in a circular trap – he must have ego flexibility to learn the second language, but contact with that language and its culture causes the ego to become rigid. At some point the circle must be broken. (226)

Otherwise, Schumann maintains, the individual will not engage with native speakers and language acquisition will suffer (ibid.: 232). An interesting counterpoint here is the finding that some, perhaps wary of this circular trap, set out to avoid other L1 speakers in order to hasten the process of social, and by extension linguistic, acculturation (Moyer 2004; Muñoz and Singleton 2007).

Sociological models of SLA have now diverged: The established paradigm still examines problems of self-concept and acculturation through psychometric methods; a newer one does so by way of ethnographic and narrative approaches grounded by an emphasis on context and learner agency. The inspiration for this paradigm shift, from the early 1990s on, comes from Vygotsky's writings on the nature of human activity as goal-driven and anchored in social interaction (e.g., Vygotsky 1987). By implication, identity is highly personalized and fluid by virtue of the fact that it is continuously (co)constructed through interaction. This newer paradigm further distinguishes between a traditional portrayal of language as a commodity – something of value to be acquired – and a view of SLA as the process by which learners gradually become members of a new (L2) community (Pavlenko and Lantolf 2000). Accordingly, Marx describes the need to understand identity as follows: "Identity is ... not to be viewed as a fixed or stable characteristic of an individual, but rather as a process of continuous change and permutation which is comprised of cultural identity, social role, and discursive voice [Kramsch's terms]. Because a person may affiliate himself with more than one culture or language, it is possible to hold multiple identities" (Pavlenko and Lantolf 2000: 266).

If identity is a practice with great symbolic value, and language is its medium, then the adult immigrant faces a special predicament. As the mother tongue fades from active use but the second language is still relatively undeveloped, a "semantic twilight zone" arises (Pavlenko and Lantolf 2000). During this phase, the learner appropriates the voices of target-language speakers to project an L2 identity – an inauthentic performance, but a temporary necessity, according to the theory. Thus ensues a kind of cognitive and affective dissonance. Pavlenko and Lantolf excerpt memoirs to illustrate this process, as in this quote from E. Hoffman's *Lost in Translation: A Life in a New Language* (1990):

All around me, the Babel of American voices, hardy Midwestern voices, sassy New York voices, quick youthful voices, voices arching under the pressure of various crosscurrents ... Since I lack a voice of my own, the voices of others invade me as if I were a silent ventriloquist. They ricochet within me, carrying on conversations, lending me their modulations, intonations, rhythms. I do not yet possess them; they possess me. But some of them satisfy a need; some of them stick to my ribs ... Eventually, the voices enter me; by assuming them, I gradually make them mine. (167)

In her own description of this tension, Marx (2002) recounts her experiences as an (L1) Canadian English speaker residing in Germany. Relying nearly exclusively on German to get by, she admits to appropriating others' voices in an effort to gain cultural acceptance – 'culture' being essentially "reflected in the melody and pronunciation of the second language," as she puts it (ibid.: 268). To avoid being labeled an American, she first experiments with a French accent in German (French was her first foreign language), and changes her outward appearance to fit her new, projected image. After one year she consciously decides to emulate a native German sound instead, hoping to sound culturally competent (in her words). During this time her use of English was very restricted. By the end of her second year, she notices gaps in her English lexicon and orthographic accuracy, and says she is surprised to hear German intonation patterns in her English. After three years, Marx moves to the US with her English pronunciation still noticeably altered. Again hoping to avoid being labeled an American, she prefers to hold on to her 'foreign' accent in English. Marx' story depicts a very conscious struggle to develop, and to manipulate, both her native and non-native accents as a way to signal identity.

Another case study illustrates the sometimes unpredictable fluctuations that mark the accent–identity connection. Major (1993) describes an American woman living in Brazil whose (L1) English phonology was influenced by Portuguese voice onset time (VOT) for /p, t, k/ in casual speech (although not according to formal read-aloud tasks). Major notes that she had long been deeply immersed in Brazilian culture and language based on 12 years in-country, and she assessed herself as 'able to pass for native' (Major's analysis of her VOT in Portuguese and impressions from other native speakers of Portuguese confirmed this). Other learners in the study with much longer residence (thirty-four to thirty-five years) were far less successful in their efforts to acquire Portuguese and reported feeling 'strongly' American. Not surprisingly, they retained a strong American accent. Attesting to the dynamic nature of identity, this advanced learner's attitudes shifted shortly before the time of data collection; she was increasingly disillusioned with Brazil and moved back to the US shortly thereafter. Whereas Major had noted a Portuguese accent in her English while in Brazil (he was initially convinced that she was a native speaker of Portuguese), he noted that she sounded fully American during their conversation one year later. She confirmed the shift, portraying it as a reflection of her new cultural affiliations. In this sense her story epitomizes what Gatbonton et al. (2005) have called the L2 learner's constant pressure to renegotiate identity vis-à-vis both the mother tongue and the target-language groups (492).

Such introspective work highlights identity as "multiple and shifting" (Norton Pierce 1995), while reminding us of the significance of agency. The conscious control and manipulation of accent is striking, and this is seldom (if ever) considered in discussions of age-related constraints on accent. Moyer (2004) discovered that some advanced L2 learners enjoy playing with language identity; they pretend to be native speakers while traveling outside the target-language country (112). One behavioral correlation worth noting here is that those who say they enjoy passing cite significantly more L2 contact sources, i.e., they use the target language in more domains than do those with an identifiably foreign accent (Moyer 2004). This could be a circular relationship of course; the more authentic contact one engages in, the more native-like one's accent becomes, and the more one enjoys experimenting with a new (L2) identity.

A meta-awareness of identity as relevant for accent was first noted by Zuengler (1988), and Piller (2002) has recently shown how flexible some advanced language learners can be in this regard, mimicking regional and social accents for effect. Along the same lines, Rindal (2010) describes Norwegian learners of English who conscientiously shift between American vs. British pronunciation as a stylistic practice, in response to perceived contextual appropriateness, e.g., through realization of /r/ in various environments, and intervocalic /t/. Yet while some may delight in their ability to pass, Piller says they also face a dilemma:

[T]hey just don't want to be perceived as members of a particular national group right away. Indeed ... they prefer not to be reduced to their original national identity. At the same time, they do not necessarily want to be perceived as native speakers either [at all times], because that would negate their achievement in learning an L2 to a very high level and being interesting as a person from somewhere else. (2002: 194)

In other words, by sounding native, they give up a piece of their own history as well as their accomplishments, and this can be a painful trade-off (see also Grazia Busa 2010).

If some L2 users (just like native speakers) manipulate their accent to project certain cultural and linguistic affiliations, others are less able, or consciously choose not to do so. Berkowitz (1989) has asserted that those who "already feel secure, socially accepted, and approved of" no longer feel the need to accommodate their interlocutors linguistically (102f.), preferring to maintain their own vernacular style with the accent they are most comfortable with. This is understandable, given what is at stake. Gardner notes that the language student acquires not just new words, structures and pronunciation patterns, but the symbolic social meanings contained therein (1979: 193). This is a concern even for classroom learners, who intentionally mispronounce words to preserve their affiliation with peers (Lefkowitz and Hedgcock 2006). Let us therefore be mindful that *not* being a native speaker constitutes an identity in itself (Marx 2002). Some individuals endeavor to hold on to their foreign accent as an essential link to their self-concept and linguistic heritage (Moyer 1999, 2004).

Concretizing the identity–accent connection has proven difficult. Quantitative analyses confirm a link between phonological attainment and self-concept, sense of confidence in L2, the intention to reside in-country, and other identity-related constructs (Moyer 2004). Looking at behavioral manifestations of identity, Noels (2005) confirms that individuals with a strong sense of self in the target language tend to use it actively, and Moyer's (2004) study of immigrant L2 users verifies a link between their sense of linguistic confidence and a growing feeling of cultural and social belonging. Introspective, longitudinal approaches are needed to understand how identity influences the development of social networks and other opportunities to use the target language.

Finally, identity is treated here within a discussion of intrinsic constructs, but it holds obvious external significance as well. As per Bucholtz and Hall (2005), identity is built and maintained on social ground (587), meaning that it is neither *a priori* nor strictly internal – an aspect of the learner's mind. Any given speaker is heard through the filter of his listener's expectations. To this point, Gatbonton et al. (2005) confirm that listeners associate the degree of a speaker's accent with the depth of their ethnic affiliation. Post-structural notions of identity emphasize how the L2 user's ethnic or national background can affect whether the host community expects full linguistic and cultural assimilation (Gardner 1979). These expectations, in turn, condition her opportunities to engage with native speakers. While the consequences are not always negative – after all, some groups and their accents are highly valued – discrimination and limited access to resources for undervalued groups are prevailing themes in the literature. (Chapter 4 treats this topic in detail.)

3.2.2   Motivation

How can researchers adequately formulate a model for SLA given that social conditions are infinitely varied? Recent scholarship takes the individual learner as its starting point and poses a basic question: What drives the language learner in what is ultimately a very effortful task? Borrowing from psychology and

education to flesh out a new working definition of motivation, scholars generally agree on these principles:
- Motivation is a kind of super construct that incorporates attitudes, intentions, efforts, self-concept, desires, goal-setting, planning, self-reflection, the expectation of rewards, and a desire for new challenges. These many factors operate on at least two levels: the first, a more intrinsic, self-determined orientation and the other a more outward, extrinsic one (Noels 2005).
- Motivation is dynamic; it evolves as efforts, goals, and plans are reconstructed in response to new conditions and achievements. This means that its essential qualities, including orientation and intensity, shift as well.

A practical approach is now needed to test motivation's relevance. An early attempt to do so distinguished between *instrumental* and *integrative* motivation. *Instrumental* motivation refers to the drive to satisfy specific goals such as passing a language class, learning to read in another language for the purpose of translation, etc. The desire to affiliate with the target-language culture is usually referred to as *integrative* motivation. This dichotomy has predisposed researchers to take an either/or approach, and no definitive evidence has quieted debates about the efficacy of one over the other. Some argue that the dichotomy itself does not hold water. Clément and Kruidenier (1983) ask: Is the desire to "know more about the target language art, literature and culture" an integrative or an instrumental desire? This depends on the intent and understanding of the learner (274). The *instrumental*, or intrinsic, aspect has been sidelined of late, in favor of exploring the parameters of *integrativeness*.

Phonology research has long measured motivation in conjunction with other affective factors, but its treatment has been fairly simplistic. Purcell and Suter (1980) confirmed the significance of integrative motivation for the pronunciation accuracy of 61 learners of English, and there is well-cited support for the significance of instrumental motivation for very advanced learners of other languages. Bongaerts and colleagues (Bongaerts et al. 1995 and 1997) examined the pronunciation skills of highly motivated L2 learners who were employed as teachers of the target language. In one of their noteworthy studies, they selected 10 Dutch speakers to complete a sentence read aloud based on their apparently exceptional pronunciation (1997). All cited a keen interest in sounding native given their chosen profession, and about half were judged to be indistinguishable from the native speaker (NS) controls. A 1995 Bongaerts et al. study offers parallel results, with a similarly motivated group landing consistently within the native range for a range of tasks.

Among 24 highly motivated graduate students who also taught German, Moyer (1999) found 14 who overlapped with the NS controls on one or more tasks, but just one was judged to sound native across the board. For him and the others, an instrumental orientation was statistically significant. In a subsequent study of L2 users living in Berlin, however, Moyer (2004) found that an integrative motivation was most significant for accent, as was the *consistency* of that motivation over time (motivational *intensity*, as a scalar measure, was not). Perhaps the setting for each study affected the results: In the first, most of the participants intended to pursue German as an academic profession while remaining in the US; those in the second study were immersed already and surely felt immediate pressure to find a linguistic comfort zone as a result. A subsequent study of 42 non-native speakers of English residing in the US attested to the significance of a *combined* personal and professional motivation (Moyer 2007a; see Flege et al. 1999 for similar results). One could thus reason that motivation type matters little, as shown in Muñoz and Singleton's (2007) examination of two exceptional learners of English. One had a decidedly integrative motivation, the other instrumental. Remarkably, both sought greater fluency and described their efforts to that end despite already sounding native-like.

An important question is whether *instrumental* motivation encourages any unique learning strategies, as compared to *integrative* (or vice versa). In the end, the consistency of one's motivation over time probably matters more than anything else. The bidirectional, or even circular, nature of motivation is an issue as well if fluency feeds motivation, and not just the other way around.

Finally, motivation should be examined in relation to meta-awareness and a metacognitive orientation. Specifically, we need to know how successful learners set goals, plan, act, evaluate outcomes, and reassess their approach. Two relevant constructs in this context are self-determination and self-efficacy, defined as the perceived likelihood of success and a sense of autonomy when setting specific goals (Brown 2007; Noels 2005). Smit (2002) found only weak correlations between learners' perceived ability to improve pronunciation and the grades they earned in a pronunciation course. On the other hand, Moyer (2007a) asked L2 English users whether they thought they could improve their pronunciation, and those that did received significantly more native-like accent ratings on several tasks.

Motivation essentially bridges personality and cognitive style, but we are still puzzling out how it affects language acquisition. Looking forward, it is noteworthy that Gardner and Lambert emphasized accent in their original definition of integrative motivation forty years ago. As they wrote, an "integrative and friendly outlook toward the other group ... can differentially sensitize the learner to the audio-lingual features of the language, making him more perceptive to forms of pronunciation and accent" (1972: 134). There appears to be a special connection between accent and motivation. Learners likely adjust expectations and efforts toward phonological skill-building as they encounter new challenges, redefine goals, accomplish new milestones, or realize that their needs have changed. It is this dynamism that presents the biggest empirical challenge.

3.2.3   Attitudes and learner investment

Closely related to motivation are attitudes – toward language learning, toward the target language itself, and toward its culture and community of speakers. Only a few attitudes have been consistently tested for their connection to accent, most notably:
- concern for pronunciation accuracy;
- desire to sound native;
- self-rating of, and/or satisfaction with, accent and overall L2 attainment;
- attitudes toward the target language and culture.

Several studies report a positive correlation between accent and a concern for pronunciation accuracy or desire to sound native (Elliott 1995; Flege et al. 1995b; Moyer 2007a; Purcell and Suter 1980; Thompson 1991), but others do not (Moyer 2004; Oyama 1976). Self-rating is sometimes used as a stand-in for external evaluations by native speaker listeners or a test battery of some kind, but also as a way to measure self-determination (e.g., Moyer 2004; Noels 2005).

The target-language attitudes construct is obviously the most difficult to measure, and it has been the least consistent in statistical analyses. For example, Oyama's 1976 study found no solid connections between a positive orientation toward the target-language culture and accent. Thompson (1991) similarly found no significance for accent based on any preference for American culture, pro-American orientation, or impressions of American people for her 36 Russian learners of English residing in the US. Moyer has variously measured related attitudes, such as perceived ease of establishing contact with native speakers, comfort with linguistic and cultural assimilation in the target language, and intention to reside long term (more than 5 years) in the target-language country (2004, 2007a), with the last two factors significantly correlating with accent.

There is little doubt that attitudes play some role in phonological attainment, however, the directness of that relationship is uncertain. Considering the (typically) decontextualized measures of these constructs, we do not yet understand the degree to which they are interrelated, nor how they shape the learner's efforts vis-à-vis accent. For example, *self-rating* correlates to perceived self-efficacy and attitudes toward the target-language culture (Moyer 1999, 2004, 2007a), and may signify a metalinguistic orientation as well. *Concern for accuracy* and *desire to sound native* may also relate to cognitive strategies like imitating native speakers, practicing aloud, asking for feedback, reflecting on problem sounds, etc. More direct instruments are needed to verify the relevance of these interrelationships, especially across different learning conditions.

Perhaps attitudinal factors are significant insofar as they reflect an underlying integrativeness, defined by Masgoret and Gardner as an "openness to identify with another language community" (2003: 126). Integrativeness is relevant for the classroom learner too, whose connection to the target language is based on at least two things, according to Dörnyei: (a) the cultural and intellectual values he associates with the language; (b) his own ideal self-concept, reinforced by achievement and success in his endeavors (2003a: 6). In simple terms this means that, as with motivation, it is not so much a question of *this* attitude vs. *that* one, but the overall depth of investment in the language that directs how one utilizes L2 input.

Taking a conservative line, Piske et al. (2001) downplay any direct link between accent and attitudes, but up to now, attitudes have been treated in a relatively isolated way. It has not been clear how they work in relation to L2 experience. This is key, because, as Dörnyei (2005) puts it, L2 learners are "self-regulators" who proactively integrate internal and external forces:

> It makes a great difference ... if someone consciously plays down any negative influences and focuses instead on forward-pointing and controllable aspects, thereby putting things in a positive light, or if the same person dwells in negative experiences without making an effort to move on. (90–1)

This observation is personified by one late learner of German whose accent is rated as native or near-native on a variety of speaking tasks in Moyer (2004). "Dora" is a Polish-born immigrant with little informal exposure to German before moving to Berlin, and despite having a very limited social network there, she is intensely motivated to acquire the language. By her own account, fluency in German is integral to her self-image, and any attrition – even occasional difficulty retrieving a word – is felt as a loss to her core identity. Perhaps most fascinating about Dora is her approach to limitations. Where her social connections are few, she devises strategies to gain greater exposure to the language. Where she encounters cultural conflict, she reconstructs these experiences to put a more positive spin on them. Dora's orientation exemplifies a fascinating coupling of less-than-optimal circumstances with optimal psychological orientation; she redoubles her efforts in response to setbacks. (It is also worth noting that she can cite exact phonetic contrasts that still cause her difficulty – a testament to her metalinguistic awareness.) Her proactive approach recalls Taylor's (1977) assertion that behaviors can reinforce attitudes, just as attitudes encourage (or discourage) certain behaviors.

Contrast Dora with Drew, an American in the same study, who is an unsuccessful learner as far as accent goes. Drew is defiant about his desire to maintain cultural distance from Germans, citing no desire to integrate into his surrounding community. Drew was rated at the bottom of the scale for accent, so his attainment squares well with his attitudes (in fact, Drew says he prefers to sound American). Although he describes German as increasingly important for his future career, Drew actively rejects any feedback on his accent or grammar. In Dörnyei's terms, Drew has failed to 'move on' – to integrate internal drives with external circumstances and experiences. This uncomfortable juxtaposition highlights the difference between intention and investment as Norton Pierce (1995) defines it – the reality of having multiple desires within a complex social history. Drew has managed to do what he feels he must in terms of linguistic fluency, thus exhibiting intention, but with limited risk on a personal level. Drew purposefully holds back on accent – the aspect of the language that symbolizes integration for him.

All L2 users, regardless of learning environment, must develop a sense of self in the target language. This process is best explored through qualitative, longitudinal means so that shifts in attitude and affiliation, and their accompanying advances or retreats in linguistic skill, can be documented.

3.3 Experience and input

There is an emerging consensus that language learners owe their phonological fluency, in large part, to the quality of their cumulative L2 experience (Jia and Aaronson 2003; Flege et al. 2006; Moyer 2004, 2009). Two points should be borne in mind, however: (a) fluency cannot develop without sufficient input; (b) individual orientation guides the strategic use of that input. This means that learners make choices about how to utilize the language available to them in accordance with their own goals and learning styles. If the 'successful learner' is our reference point, we need to investigate how she makes best use of a linguistic environment that is nearly always limited in terms of both quantity and quality.

Input is the basis for acquisition; it is literally the language that we see and hear (Krashen 1982). As we make sense of that language via form-meaning connections, input is converted to 'intake' – that "subset of the input ... from which grammatical information can be made available to the developing system" (VanPatten and Cadierno 1993: 227). At the phonological level, speaking allows us to develop intelligibility, which is crucial to communicative skill, and in turn, helps us to form social bonds. Flege concretizes this point with his example of a child learning to produce Spanish as opposed to English: He must learn to produce an unaspirated /t/ "whereas the L1-English child learns to produce an aspirated [tʰ]. As a result of this kind of phonetic learning, children are soon identified as belonging to a specific *speech community*" (2009: 176). This is surely tougher for adults, considering the inevitable social–psychological challenges and likely interference from the first language. Some may demonstrate initial advantages in both perception and production, but within a relatively short span of time, younger learners tend to surpass them (Aoyama et al. 2008).

New (L2) categories are likely heard through the filter of L1 "even when the constituent L2 phonemes do not exist in the L1 or are produced in a phonetically different way" (ibid.). This applies to prosody as well (see Bent et al. 2006;

discussion in Chapter 2, Section 2.4.2). Flege (2009) further argues that L2 learners are influenced by the foreign accents of those around them, but Trofimovich et al. (2001) demonstrate that with greater exposure (here: length of residence), they adopt more sophisticated analyses of L2 phonemic and allophonic relationships. For example, those learning English eventually realize that different word-initial and word-final realizations of /r/ are not actually separate phonemes, but that /i/ and /ɪ/ are, allowing them to distinguish meaning, such as between *beat* vs. *bit*. Time on task is essential, but not sufficient, for such realizations.

There are many ways to understand *experience*. At the most basic level, it is time on task, measured as weeks, months, or years of instruction and/or immersion. Although such measures are ubiquitous, they can lead to false assumptions, e.g., that X amount of L2 exposure will lead to Y outcome. A quick look at the age factor demonstrates the fallacy of this assumption. Children residing in-country will, as a rule, attend schools in the target language, become friends with native speakers, and increasingly rely on their new language across varied contexts. Their experience is far deeper and more varied, while adult learners often come to the task with unique resources and constraints (psychological, cognitive, social, etc.), making it hard to compare their experience in terms of *quality* even if years spent in-country are equivalent.

3.3.1   Length of residence

One construct that does not clearly differentiate exposure from meaningful experience is *length of residence* (LOR). On its own, LOR is a one-dimensional measure, and as a result its significance for accent is rather unreliable across studies (Asher and Garcia 1969; Flege et al. 1995b, 1997, 1999; Moyer 1999, 2004, 2011; Oyama 1976; Thompson 1991 – see Piske et al. 2001 for discussion). The issue is not whether adult language learners accrue a specific amount of time on task, but whether they have sufficient opportunity, and inclination, to acquire native-level mastery. LOR, as a simplistic measure, guarantees neither. Where LOR does show main effects, it is arguably the *quality* of that residence that matters. Time spent in-country must represent the kind of language use that signifies "a variety of speech acts over a wide range of situations and topics," and consistent participation "in social settings effectively dominated by the L2" (Muñoz 2008: 585).

LOR is commonly tested as an influence on production and perception at the segmental level (Flege et al. 1995a, 1997b; Flege and Liu 2001; Jia et al. 2006; Trofimovich and Baker 2006; Trofimovich et al. 2001), but rarely for its potential contribution to suprasegmental skills. One exception is Trofimovich and Baker's 2006 study on 'melody', defined as stress timing (rhythm)[6] and tonal peak alignment, vs. 'fluency,' defined in terms of pauses and overall speech rate. Using a low-pass filter to preserve frequencies relevant only to prosody, the authors compared acoustic analyses to listener ratings for thirty Korean learners of English. Main effects for LOR were substantiated for suprasegmental ratings overall, but the acoustic analyses found an LOR effect for stress timing only. The most experienced group, averaging 10 years' residence, closely approximated the NS controls for melody, but not for fluency; their speech was still noticeably slower. The authors' conclusion is that melody can improve with in-country experience, but fluency is a function of processing constraints and therefore subject to a sensitive period.

Comparing different populations, Flege and Liu's (2001) study of sixty Chinese immigrants to the US speaks to the quality of in-country residence for students, in particular. On tests of phonemic recognition, listening comprehension, and grammaticality judgment, LOR revealed significant, main effects for student participants, as opposed to non-students. The authors surmised that the input received by these two populations differs, namely that the students benefit substantially from targeted practice and feedback. This is another indication that the significance of LOR relies on real experience, and so much the better when that occurs in varied communicative contexts. Optimally, a longer LOR significantly correlates to greater interaction among NS friends, greater use of L2 overall, and less use of L1 (Moyer 2011) – each of which predicts a closer-to-native accent.

An analysis of quantitative and qualitative data in Moyer (2004) underlines additional reasons why LOR deserves closer scrutiny:

- LOR is highly correlated to several psychological variables, including a sense of satisfaction with phonological attainment, a personal motivation to acquire the target language, self-ratings of fluency, and the intention to reside permanently in-country.
- LOR is relevant for the social realm, correlating to frequency of interactions with native speakers – a factor whose significance for accent overall is on par with AO and LOR.
- LOR is significant cognitively insofar as it correlates to years of target-language instruction, the opportunity for communicatively based language instruction (as opposed to grammar–translation), the amount of formal feedback received on pronunciation, and types of targeted phonological training received.
- LOR relates to learners' desire for formal vs. informal L2 experience: As more time is spent in-country, personal contacts become the greatest resource in their pursuit of greater fluency. At the same time, the desire for

---

[6] Stress timing indicates variation in syllable duration according to patterns of phrasal stress (English is a stress-timed language, Korean is not).

instruction decreases. Those personal contacts are seen as critical to social integration, according to participants' reports.

Most factors listed here are also significant for the accent ratings themselves, suggesting that extended in-country residence confers real advantages for phonological attainment if it signifies rich target-language experience.

3.3.2 L2 use

Time on task seems far less consequential for phonological attainment than consistent, interactive language practice, but are certain contexts especially beneficial? Below, we consider language as daily or weekly hours, and according to specific contexts, before turning to the connection between L2 use, language dominance, and attrition in the mother tongue.

Almost without exception, positive evidence for L2 use refers to segmental precision, i.e. the perception and/or production of individual sounds, whether measured as days per week, hours per day, or as rough approximations of frequency, as in 'never' to 'frequent' (Diaz-Campos 2004; Derwing et al. 2007; Flege et al. 1995a, 1999, 2002; Flege and Fletcher 1992; Flege and Liu, 2001; Jia et al. 2006; MacKay et al. 2006; Moyer 2011; Thompson 1991). As an example, Diaz-Campos (2004) used a paragraph read-aloud task to test the effects of language use beyond the classroom during a study abroad program for twenty-six English-speaking learners of Spanish. When language use beyond the classroom reached four hours per week or more, or occurred at least four days per week, it correlated significantly to better accent ratings. Muñoz (2011) also found that hours of target-language contact beyond the classroom was significant for a phonetic discrimination task among learners of English in Spain.

Looking at L2 use in a more detailed way, Jia et al. (2006) examined the perception and production of 131 Mandarin speakers learning English in the US for challenging vowels distinctions such as: /i/–/ɪ/, /æ/–/ɛ/ and /ɑ/–/ʌ/. Those with the highest percentage of English use across varied contexts were rated best. In fact, this was the only significant experience factor for recent arrivals (those with an average of one to three years' stay). A few additional studies describe use according to mode, e.g., TV viewing, speaking, reading, and writing (Flege et al. 1999; Moyer 2011). Not surprisingly, the oral–aural mode correlates most significantly to accent. Furthermore, Moyer (2011) shows that the total number of modes cited as consistent sources of practice is also significant for accent, confirming that even passive activities can be beneficial.

Not all interactive contexts hold equal value, to be sure; some naturally denote greater social and emotional significance than others. For example, speaking to a close friend at the local tavern surely requires more of a personal investment in the language than it takes to conduct minor business at the post office or grocery. An examination of contextualized L2 use shows that extended interactions occurring at home or in other leisure domains are significant for phonological fluency, whereas formal encounters at work or school are not (Moyer 2011; see also Derwing et al. 2007). This recalls Thompson's (1991) study of Russian immigrants to the US whose pronunciation benefitted from at-home L2 use as opposed to workplace communication (see also Purcell and Suter 1980). Going a step further, interaction with native speaker friends was tested separately from non-native friends in Moyer 2011, and regression analyses confirm its independent predictive power for accent.[7]

A summary of the language use research confirms the following relationships:
- An early arrival and a longer residence in-country predict greater L2 use, which in turn predicts greater gains in both segmental and suprasegmental skills.
- When it comes to L2 use, more is better, but *informal* L2 use – beyond the classroom or workplace – is especially advantageous for pronunciation accuracy, and especially when native speakers are the primary phonological model.
- In terms of processing modes, the aural/oral mode seems to have special significance for phonological acquisition, but consistently using L2 across various modes is also beneficial.
- Simple tallies of language contact hours are not necessarily informative unless they account for L2 use *relative to L1 use*. Those who strongly favor their mother tongue(s) are far more likely to sound foreign in the second language (more below).

Optimal language use provides the means to develop contextualized fluency. Where such opportunities are consistent, the target language is likely to take on deep functional and symbolic value in the learner's life. The implications this transition has for identity and related factors are obvious. More effort must therefore be made to directly address how language use affects cultural affiliation and sense of self in the language.

3.3.3 Language dominance

At some point, the individual living in-country may find herself relying more on the target language than the mother tongue. Bilinguals whose use of L1 outweighs that of L2 tend to produce longer utterances in L1 than in L2 (Flege et al. 2002). They also sound noticeably different from those who use the second

---

[7] See also Moyer 2005 and 2006 for findings on syntactic acquisition and listening comprehension, respectively.

Experience and input 77

language as much, or more, than the first (Flege et al. 1997a; Moyer 2011; Piske et al. 2001).

As characterized by Flege et al. (2002), the issue of L1–L2 balance revolves around a few key points:
- *language use*: the frequency with which the two languages are used, and with whom;
- *language history*: the contexts and ages at which the two languages are acquired;
- *language function*: the purposes for which the L1 and L2 are used (570).

Thinking about individual differences, we might ask: Is the balance of language use determined by external conditions or by internal drives? Would restricting L2 to instrumental, as opposed to social and emotional, functions somehow stifle the acquisition of accent? How can we explain child immigrants who may become L2 dominant but still have a foreign accent?

Language dominance is a deeply personal phenomenon, best understood at the level of the individual learner, but a few generalizations can be made nonetheless. Looking at its influence on accent, Flege et al. (1999) detail language use among 240 native speakers of Korean living in the US. Not surprisingly, amount of L2 (English) use correlates positively to accent ratings on a read-aloud task, and maintains its independent significance according to a regression analysis, even after controlling for AO. A critical observation is that those who arrived as children received significantly more education in the US, used more English in daily life, and reported less use of Korean overall. Those who arrived aged 12 years or older reported a more balanced use of English and Korean, and were less likely to become English dominant. This was later confirmed in the Flege et al. (2002) study of Italian bilinguals in Canada, confirming a fundamental link between accent, AO, language use, and language shift.

Up to this point, no common standard has been established to assess language dominance. Some researchers adhere to an 'automaticity' quotient to show which language is stronger; they literally count excessive pauses and false starts (Derwing et al. 2007); others measure the length, speed, or duration of L2 utterances (Flege et al. 2002); or test reading abilities (see Flege et al. 2002 for discussion); still others simply ask participants which language they would eliminate if forced to do so (Cutler et al. 1989, cited in Flege et al. 2002). Although these assessments capture some of the linguistic impact of language shift, they do not show us what the process looks like up-close, and over the course of time.

Jia et al. (2003) present a longitudinal view of how this takes root, tracking Chinese immigrants to the US over a period of three years. Their data show how younger children make the transition to English in the home environment more quickly and easily than their older siblings, even when exposure amounts are comparable. The authors hypothesize that language dominance actually comes in response to a shift in language *preference*, which they carefully tracked over the course of the study. Immigrants who arrived after age 8 reported that they preferred Chinese over English, and wanted to retain strong ties to their heritage culture, even after three years' residence in the US.

Language dominance is an important consideration for phonological attainment precisely because it signifies the role of target language in the learner's life: Where L2 effectively replaces L1, it performs not just instrumental, but emotional and social functions essential to a sense of self. Those considered exceptional, phonologically, tend to be L2 dominant in the home, which surely intensifies their desire – and efforts – to sound native (see conclusions, Section 3.5).

3.3.4 L1 attrition

Thompson (1991) has speculated that giving up or losing the mother tongue leads one to acquire a second language accent indistinguishable from natives. But would such a shift actually affect accent in the mother tongue? Recall Major's account of an advanced L2 speaker of Portuguese (referenced in Section 3.2.1): Not only did her L2 accent gain and lose ground in accordance with her changing cultural affiliations, her (L1) English accent similarly shifted as she, by turns, embraced or disavowed a Brazilian identity. Similarly, Marx' account of her own shifting L1 and L2 accents begs the question: Would her English pronunciation ever return to its original, pre-immersion state if, say, she returned to Canada?

Major describes L1 parameters, rules, underlying representations and other categories as "neither fixed nor stable" (1992: 203), and Cook (2003) asserts that for anyone who learns another language, the L1 system is "fundamentally and irrevocably changed," regardless of age of onset (cited in Schmid and Köpke 2007). Language attrition and the bidirectionality of language influence are gaining attention, given that bilingualism is rarely stable or balanced; like the process of SLA, its nature is dynamic.

Where the mother tongue loses ground to the second language, attrition can range from a complete loss of proficiency to slight modifications in production that would strike a native's ear as somehow off-target (Major 1992: 203). For perception, the ability to detect a native accent in one's own mother tongue does not seem to diminish, even after some attrition (Major 2010). At the level of production, attrition-related modifications can be very slight indeed. Major (1992) examined VOT values for voiceless stops (/p, t, k/) for five adult native English speakers living in Brazil who had acquired Portuguese to varying levels. In keeping with his first hypothesis, the three residing in Brazil with the strongest foreign accent in Portuguese retained English VOT values most like those of his American native speaker controls, though they were not exactly parallel. The surprise was that for two participants, neither their Portuguese nor their English VOT values were native-like. Either way, the English pronunciation of all five participants had shifted as a result of their experience learning, and living with, Portuguese. Because all used English throughout their daily lives in Brazil as EFL teachers or administrators, Major reasoned that a lack of L1 use could not be the cause of this attrition. Why, then, would their English undergo change? Was it a matter of the predominance of L2 in certain domains? If they used Portuguese in the private realm among other native speakers this would imply a function central to personal expression. Further details on the patterns of their language use could substantiate this development.

A detailed analysis of L1 attrition and L2 use comes from DeLeeuw et al. (2010), who studied changes in L1 (German) accent on a larger scale. Participant groups were comprised of 34 native German speakers living in Anglophone Canada, 23 living in the Netherlands, and 5 controls living in Germany. The expatriates' age was 61 years on average, with an average LOR of 37 years. Altogether, 14 of these native German speakers were judged to be *non*-native based on a short film-retelling task. Interestingly, the quality and quantity of their ongoing contact with native German speakers was more significant for accent ratings (in German) than was either age of arrival in the Netherlands or LOR.

Paradis' Activation Threshold Hypothesis (2007) predicts that language disuse gradually leads to language attrition, but it is unclear which aspects of phonology are most susceptible to loss in such a process. Presumably, basic phonetic categories are maintained, but fine voicing distinctions and subtle features such as final stop consonant release, vowel height, and even muscle tension, could all be subject to shift (see Sanchez 1995).

Schmid and Köpke (2007) discount the notion that attrition is a strictly one-directional and destructive process, e.g., that L2 'takes over' L1, or that it is an unusual occurrence; all bilinguals experience changes in their L1 system depending on the extent of their exposure to, and active use of, the second language (3) (see Hyltenstam et al. 2009). Prescher (2007) introduces a psychological perspective, asking how aware long-term migrants are of their own L1 attrition. In her interviews with Germans living at least ten years in the Netherlands – all of whom migrated as adults – she discovered that some willingly and quickly adapted to their new L2 selves, but experienced a level of rejection later on by family and friends in Germany who said they had a Dutch accent. Some were actually 'scolded' for being foreign even though they could not themselves perceive the relevant changes in their speech. An especially interesting finding is that those who had been away from Germany longest expressed the greatest desire to "return to their original identity and language" (ibid.: 201) – a reminder that language shift is not necessarily irreversible.

We began this discussion of experience by acknowledging that success in SLA relies on sufficient input. That implies ongoing opportunities to use, not simply be exposed to, the target language. *The aspect of language experience most significant for accent is apparently the degree to which one engages meaningfully and authentically with native speakers of the target language.* Thus, contexts for language use must reach across formal boundaries into the personal realm, and interactions must extend beyond perfunctory exchanges. Expressive, social, and affective functions are a necessary foundation for such language practice, and perhaps a flexible language ego or a special propensity for empathy comes in handy as well. Younger immigrants usually enjoy advantageous circumstances regarding input and practice, while adults must strive to structure language use opportunities in optimal ways. For classroom learners, the relative lack of authentic practice (especially with native speakers) can be an insurmountable obstacle. In the next section, we consider how some L2 users who are deemed to be especially successful make this happen.

3.4   Exceptional language learners

Much has been made of exceptional cases in L2 phonological attainment. Selinker (1972) famously estimated that 5 percent of learners are capable of reaching a native level in a second language despite having a late start (past childhood). Over the years, a handful of studies have sought to discover the underlying nature of such exceptionality, and here we look at several such cases to discover what they have in common.

In one oft-cited study, Ioup et al. (1994) present data from an adult, immersion learner of Egyptian Arabic they call "Julie." At the time of the study, Julie had lived in Egypt for twenty-six years and had long since adopted Arabic as her home language, speaking it with her children as well as her Egyptian-born husband. Julie describes herself as someone with a talent for accent mimicry and she reported no problems with Arabic pharyngeals and uvulars. In the early stages of her untutored immersion, she frequently imitated native speakers, and eight out of thirteen native listeners agreed that she sounded native. The authors attribute Julie's success to a conscious attention to form and her concern for pronunciation accuracy. Another non-native speaker, "Laura," reached a similar level of success, but via a different route: She studied formally for many years, ultimately earning her Ph.D. in Arabic. She also married an Egyptian and took a job teaching Arabic. There is no remarkable difference between them in terms of accent despite the different paths they took to get there. (Another finding of interest is that both Julie and Laura were able to also discriminate regional dialects of Arabic on a listening task, with perfect accuracy – better than some of the native controls.)

In a recent study, Muñoz and Singleton (2007) detail two exceptional profiles from among twelve advanced learners of English living in Spain. One learner, Elena, is best described as having an integrative motivation: she is living in Ireland, married to an Irishman, and all of her friends are English-speaking Irish. Elena, from the beginning of her time in Ireland, has made a conscious effort to avoid Spanish speakers, only using it to visit with family members. Marga was also rated as native, but she is less oriented toward cultural affiliation. Instead, she has an overwhelming desire to master all linguistic aspects of English because, as she puts it, she loves the language. Both describe their conscious approach to acquiring English – they monitor their own progress and fluency constantly, *still*, and seek out ways to improve, especially through interactive contact.

Moyer (1999) also documents an exceptional learner judged to be more consistently native-sounding than any of the actual NS controls, on every task. At the time of data collection, he had studied German just five years, and was largely self-taught. By his own account, he spent hours listening to German exchange students to absorb the sounds before going abroad himself. As someone with a self-described fascination with the language and culture, he successfully assimilated linguistically and culturally in his two years there.

At this point, it is tempting to categorize these learners as simply 'having a good ear'. Indeed, this was Ioup et al.'s suggestion. But a closer look shows that all felt a deep connection to the target language, and all took a conscious, reflective approach to the learning process, regardless of their differing amounts of formal instruction (some had very little, or none at all). In short, all directed their attention to the sounds of the language in order to emulate native speakers. This cognitive orientation is also evident in Nikolov (2000), who describes several late learners of Hungarian and/or English rated as native-like for accent. Nearly all are married to native speakers, and they are quite conscious and proud of their language attainment. They actively seek ways to improve their fluency through both interactive and receptive means, socializing with native speakers and frequently reading and listening to the target language through TV and film viewing. Molnár's (2010) description of an exceptional learner of German is a similar testament to the importance of extensive – indeed, primary – use of the target language, along with great pride in attainment, and a commitment to sounding native.

So, is a metalinguistic orientation key to these learners' success, or is an integrative orientation essential? This brief comparison, along with a few profiles cited earlier, point to some specific ways that exceptional learners approach accent:
- through metacognitive strategies – planning; goal-setting; the adoption of strategies aimed to improve authenticity; continuous self-monitoring of progress;

82 Accent and the individual

- through cognitive strategies – practicing; analyzing; explicit attention to challenging segmental and suprasegmental features; asking for feedback; imitating native speakers;
- through ongoing concern for pronunciation accuracy and/or desire to sound native;
- through strong identification with L2 – maintaining a positive orientation toward both language and culture;
- through consistent use of the target language – relying on L2 to accomplish various speech acts across multiple domains, especially the home environment with family and/or friends; using L2 across multiple modes (reading, speaking, listening).

What is striking here is that these learners mobilize all means necessary and available – cognitive, affective, and social. And, as for investment, all had integrated the target language into their lives in deeply meaningful ways, relying on it for most expressive functions.

Long ago, Schneiderman and Desmarais (1988) speculated that exceptional learning is directly tied to greater neurocognitive flexibility, allowing for faster language acquisition and less interference from L1. McLaughlin (1990) similarly argued that such learners have greater "plasticity in restructuring their internal representations of the rules," employing meta-analysis and reflecting on the efficacy of their learning strategies (170f.). Schneiderman and Desmarais advocated for the importance of a strong associative memory, bilateral processing, and an ear for phonetic detail, but also a strong motivation and plentiful access to L2 input. Obler straightforwardly described exceptional learning as ideally combining neurological talent and risk-taking tolerance (1989, 1993). These are all interesting points, yet it seems that exceptional outcomes in accent do not require extraordinary talent or predisposition; they do, however, rely on an *adaptive* combination of cognitive, social, and psychological factors supported by meaningful experience, i.e., consistent interaction across a range of contexts.

3.5 Conclusion: gaps in theory and method

Scholars have expended tremendous research energy trying to figure out the secrets of successful L2 learners (Bialystok and Hakuta 1994: 157). Step one, as per Stern (1975), is to clarify how they internalize the rules and procedures of the target language, understanding that good learners are active initiators who take personal responsibility for their progress. (Poor learners, by contrast, are passive or even resistant to learning a new language.) Step two would be to establish a list of good practices, taking into account individual and contextual differences. "If someone is learning a language informally on the streets of a new country, then the advantage probably falls to the more gregarious learners,"

Bialystok and Hakuta note (1994:158). In more structured environments, gregariousness could be less advantageous, or even penalized. It is this appreciation for the interactions between context and personal orientation that SLA scholars are now attuned to, and for no other skill is this interaction more relevant than for phonology.

This chapter has presented a number of intrinsic factors as possible explanations for outcomes in L2 phonology, including: aptitude, memory, bilateral processing, learning strategies, and gender – all of which could somehow direct attention to phonetic or prosodic nuances or account for some unusual ability to perceive new sounds, if not produce them with greater flexibility. Also addressed were a host of socio-psychological and experiential factors that speak to individual orientation, as well as input and practice opportunities. These, too, could attune the learner's ear and encourage her to conscientiously practice new, challenging sounds and sound patterns. With all of this in mind, we reconsider the question posed at the outset:

Are those who manage to acquire a native-like accent simply anecdotal cases of phonological genius? Alternatively, do they enjoy extraordinary resources that support language learning more effectively, or do they have a unique orientation to the task of language learning?

Table 3.1 summarizes the significant intrinsic and extrinsic factors, based on available quantitative and qualitative evidence, that work in complementary fashion to achieve this end.

- The neurocognitive evidence draws our attention to several important areas for future investigation: (a) possible differences in perceptual acuity based on processing preferences, which could facilitate the discrimination of new sounds and sound patterns (how this connects to production is still unclear); (b) an analytical approach that involves selective attention, repetition, imitation, and practice which presumably help to restructure knowledge and improve fluency. We also stressed the learnability of skills relevant to

Table 3.1 *Intrinsic and extrinsic factors relevant to L2 accent*

Neurocognitive realm		Social-psychological realm		Experiential realm	
Cognitive strategies	Metacognitive strategies	Desire to sound native/concern for pronunciation accuracy	Comfort with L2 culture	L2 use across contexts, esp. informal environment	Long-term residence in-country
Memory	Bilateral processing	Social strategies to increase L2 use and contact with NS	Consistent motivation	L2 use across modes	L2/L1 balance in favor of L2

accent, and noted that experience actually changes the way that language is processed. This suggests that the need for special talents has been exaggerated, but more empirical clarity is needed on the aptitude issue overall, and especially for phonological acquisition.
- The socio-psychological evidence underscores the importance of *investment* and *self-regulation*. Successful learners are proactive; they continuously monitor their progress, regardless of their stage of learning. Furthermore, their beliefs about the value of the target-language influence how they structure L2 input and use. As for constructs like motivation, consistency is key but so is flexibility; the successful learner appears to reorient himself in response to the conditions at hand, i.e., in the face of social and linguistic limitations. Implicit in this realm is the willingness to undertake cognitive and/or social strategies that benefit phonological acquisition.
- Finally, experience is an exciting new frontier in L2 phonology research. It essentially connects language use and *investment*, and allows us to better understand phenomena such as language shift. To unravel its explanatory potential, quantity and quality must be clearly delineated, as well as the relative balance of L1–L2 use.

In this discussion we have conceptualized success in phonological attainment in terms of individual differences, not to discount the role of age but to underline its inherent relationship with significant, covarying influences. Individual differences in L2 phonology have yet to be addressed in a comprehensive way, however. In the quantitative paradigm, they are typically treated in a disconnected manner, losing sight of their integral relationship with the learning context. A qualitative, introspective approach allows us to explore the dynamic development of accent and sense of self in the target language, yet this kind of work is still rare. For example, we do not know how localized, context-driven episodes of 'passing' eventually develop into routine aspects of linguistic performance.

Future work will direct greater attention to the ways that accent is shaped by social interaction, and delve more deeply into the long-term significance of the learner's intention to assimilate linguistically and culturally. Our task is to study predictive factors not as stand-alone influences, but as pieces in the larger picture of the L2 learner's needs, desires, and opportunities to develop native-like fluency. And more scholars will hopefully address why it is that, even if learners realize that a standard-sounding accent has greater currency, some choose to sound *not-quite-* or even *not-at-all* native. The next two chapters are devoted to this question of reception, and the broader consequences of sounding foreign.

4 Accent and society

> Your accent carries the story of who you are – who first held you and talked to you when you were a child, where you have lived, your age, the schools you attended, the languages you know, your ethnicity, whom you admire, your loyalties, your profession, your class position: traces of your life and identity are woven into your pronunciation, your phrasing, your choice of words. Your self is inseparable from your accent. Someone who tells you they don't like the way you speak is quite likely telling you that they don't like you.
>
> Matsuda 1991: 1329

Davies (2000) believes that listeners detect a speaker's foreignness based on a range of discursive behaviors, and this makes sense; lexicon is an obvious clue, and any gaps in cultural knowledge or any interactive missteps would also send an immediate signal. But these aspects of fluency notwithstanding, accent is particularly salient; it spans motor skill, audition, and cognition, which support a veritable orchestra of intonation, pitch, rhythm, stress, pause, tempo, syllable duration, and elision, not to mention phonetic precision, all of which provide an immediate picture of the speaker's identity. No wonder then that, based on speech samples of just a few seconds or less, we can ascertain non-nativeness with great reliability – there are many layers of acoustic information to go on. But too often, sounding identifiably non-native has negative consequences insofar as it triggers assumptions in the listener's mind about other traits. In a 1997 article, Walter Olson recounts a story that could occur anywhere:

Consider the controversy that engulfed the town of Westfield, Massachusetts a couple of years ago [in 1992]. The town's school system had assigned instructor Ramon Vega to an experimental program where he'd teach language skills to first and second graders. Some parents had trouble understanding Vega's conversation themselves, and worried that their kids might have the same problem. Four hundred of them proceeded to sign a petition asking that instructors in early grades be proficient in "the accepted and standard use of pronunciation." When word reached Boston, all hell broke loose. The state education commissioner charged the parents with "bigotry." The National Education Association rushed through a resolution at its annual meeting decrying disparate treatment on the basis of "pronunciation" – quite a switch from the old days when teachers used to be demons for correctness on that topic ...

Westfield, a rather gritty mill town, [is] heavily populated by first and second-generation ethnics. In fact it should come as no surprise that immigrants are often strong supporters of setting high standards for English proficiency: Not only do they see fluency as critical to their children's success, but they keep running into that arch frustration: dealings among novice English speakers whose original languages are not the same. Westfield Mayor George Varelas, himself a Greek immigrant with a marked accent, backed the parents. "Persons like myself... should not be" in charge of 5- and 6-years olds' first language skills. "I would only impart my confusion and give them my defects in terms of language." (1997)

The idea that foreign-accented teachers are unfit models for young students runs counter to the evidence that a child's grammar and phonology are largely set by the time he goes to school (Milroy 1998), and that his peers – not his teachers – are the greatest influence on his lexicon and discursive style (Battistella 2005). The Westfield controversy underscores a more basic assumption, however; that those with a non-standard or foreign accent lack overall linguistic competence. Olson seems to support this view, and even the mayor apologizes for his apparently *fluent* English. We can only assume that his apology is unfounded; without solid linguistic skills, he surely would not have been elected to represent his city.

Olson's further descriptions of the 'daily hassles' of interacting with foreign-born service personnel (who, in his view, should take accent reduction courses) serve as a reminder that negative attitudes toward non-standard accents are often the public face of deeper forms of discrimination. Like many sociolinguists, Lippi-Green rightfully disdains the idea that those who speak in non-standard ways are uneducated or lazy, and that they could simply change their accent if they chose to do so. Any such links to personal character are purely social, according to Milroy (1998); they rarely stem from communicative problems.

In any language – native or not – *everyone* has an accent, yet the idea of a neutral accent standard persists in our collective consciousness. Where did this idea come from, and why does it hold such sway? First and foremost, a standard provides a reference point for correctness. Its corollary purpose is no less important; it "ultimately forms part of our view of social structure, and of our own place within it," Crystal reasons (1987: 3). In essence, we locate ourselves and others through our ways of speaking.

In this chapter we explore the idea that accent operates on an immediate level, as a communicative construct, and on a broader social level through its associations with prestige and status as well as stigma. The following questions guide the discussion:

- Where do we get our ideas about an accent standard given that language variation is ubiquitous?
- What are the communicative consequences of a foreign accent, and are these in response to social or linguistic criteria?

- Do stereotypes hinder our ability to 'hear' non-native speakers and to interact with them successfully?
- In what ways can a foreign accent hinder cultural integration over the long term?

As much of the relevant research focuses on English as a second language, ESL/EFL will serve as the chapter's primary reference. We begin with the question: Has there ever been a single standard for pronunciation in English?

4.1 Historical perspectives on a standard accent in English

Let your articulation be clear and distinct ... Let each syllable and the letters which compose it be pronounced with a clear voice, without whining, drawling, lisping, flammering, mumbling in the throat, or speaking through the nose. Avoid equally a dull, drawling habit, and too much rapidity of pronunciation; for each of these faults destroys a distinct articulation. (Noah Webster 1789)

Standardization – the codification of pronunciation, grammar, lexicon, or spelling for a given language variety – is often set in motion by political paradigm shifts such as declarations of independence, regime change, etc., or the publication of literature that leads to a canon, as with Luther's translation of the Bible into German and Wycliffe's translation of it into English (Wardhaugh 2010: 31f.). To the extent that this standard becomes necessary for professional and social mobility, it soon symbolizes the heritage and identity of a society (ibid.). Through its association with print media, literature, the courts, and the educational system, the authority and prestige of a language standard is unquestioned, even by those who speak in non-standard ways.

The eighteenth century is the period most strongly associated with language standardization in Britain, Europe, and the newly founded colonies in America. Dictionaries and grammar books proliferated, and their forewords promoted correct usage as a social necessity. The prevailing attitude was prescriptivism, "the view that one variety of language has an inherently higher value than others, and that this ought to be imposed on the whole speech community" (Crystal 1987: 2; see also J. Milroy 1999). The most esteemed variety for English was that spoken by the elite of London, and authoritative sources of the time advocated proper pronunciation as an important marker of status.

Samuel Johnson's *Dictionary of Pronunciation* (1755) and John Walker's *General Idea of a Pronouncing Dictionary* (1774), *Dictionary of the English Language Answering at Once the Purposes of Rhyming, Speaking and Pronouncing* (1775), and *Critical Pronouncing Dictionary* (1791) are popular titles from among hundreds of volumes and essays which decried working-class speech and regional dialects. Linguist and educator James Buchanan made the case for correct pronunciation as follows: "How unbecoming are discordant and jarring sounds in the mouth of an otherwise polite gentleman or lady" (cited in Mugglestone 2003). Such titles as *Vulgarisms and Other Errors of Speech*, *Mind Your H's and Take Care of Your R's*,[1] and *Common Blunders in Speech and How to Avoid Them* captured the widespread derision of 'sloppy' and 'barbarous' speech as socially unacceptable. "It was clear that the ... spoken language you used (accent, tone, style and vocabulary) was laden with social significance," writes Crowley. "To make a mistake was not simply [an] ... error but a social faux-pas" (2003: 108).

This preoccupation was evident in the New World as well, as linguists, teachers, and philosophers debated the merits of establishing an American standard even while acknowledging the inevitability of linguistic change (see Finegan 1980, 2004; Kahane 1992). Early on, it was understood that American English would diverge from its British roots given its contact with indigenous and immigrant languages. Noah Webster was a vocal supporter of the American 'brand,' and famously predicted in his *Compendious Dictionary of the English Language* (1806) that American English would overtake all other languages within fifty years. To this end, he urged uniformity and stability in American English in order that the "population of this vast country ... throw off their leading strings and walk in their own strength" (*American Dictionary of the English Language*, 1828, cited in Baron 1982) – a reminder of the tension between a British-centric sense of social prestige and hierarchy vs. an emerging American patriotism (Aviel Roshwald 2011, p.c.).

Debates over linguistic correctness became increasingly dogmatic in nineteenth-century Britain (Crystal 2003). Crowley (2003) describes the desire for standardization in England as nothing short of a move to preserve rationality, civility and allegiance to country. The establishment of a public education system in the mid-nineteenth century promoted a unified pronunciation standard for children of all backgrounds but prescriptive spelling norms did little to reduce regional and social accent variation as intended (Mugglestone 2003). At the same time, regional standards were emerging in Scotland (e.g., in Glasgow and Edinburgh) and in Newcastle, distinct from those in London (see Milroy and Milroy 1985b).

The nineteenth-century trend toward social equality in the US was accompanied by the fear that linguistic variation threatened a nascent national identity (Battistella 2005). Jacob Cummings, in his 1819 *Pronouncing Spelling Book*, warns: "If we consider the great importance of preserving uniformity in our

---

[1] *H*-dropping – a 'low prestige' variant – occurs at the onset of words such as *who* (which sounds like /u^w/ in Cockney dialect, e.g.) and on words like *which* and *whether*, distinctly aspirated as /w^h/ in earlier times. This is an ongoing shift in American English according to Labov (2006). Milroy and Milroy (1985a: 93) suggest that *h*-dropping came to be regarded as "sloppy, lazy, and ugly." Similarly, the *r*-lessness of some American dialects was considered prestigious as recently as the early twentieth century, they add, before being associated with lower social classes (as in New York or other northeastern cities) around the time of World War II.

country, and of avoiding what already begins to be called northern and southern pronunciation, no attempt to preserve harmony ... will be regarded as too minute" (quoted in Baron 1982: 35). Unlike in England, however, there was no obvious locus for a standard, and the founding fathers had decided against a national language academy, as proposed by John Adams. At the time, a sizeable portion of the population in the Northeast spoke German. Some feared it would overtake English (Benjamin Franklin most famous among them), but no official law was passed to prevent this. In hindsight, this is often lauded as a sign of tolerance, but it was also pragmatic – few doubted that English would quickly supplant all other foreign and indigenous tongues.

The turn of the twentieth century saw the stigmatization of languages other than English in the US and bilingual education was eradicated as immigration peaked and a monolingual ideology emerged. Educators and politicians championed the importance of assimilation, and linguistic unity and correctness were central to that creed. One educator urged America to wage war on "her poor, indistinct and inelegant speech" – often found in the mouths of American teachers, in her view – thus holding back "the development of her national good breeding, refinement and culture" (McLean 1927: 79). Founded in 1911, the National Council of Teachers of English dictated grammar and spelling standards, yet acknowledged in a 1945 publication that "all language usage is relative" and that good English is "that form of speech which is appropriate to the purpose of the speaker" and "comfortable to speaker and listener" (cited in Finegan 1980: 105). This conciliatory tone was probably unusual; debates about linguistic standards as a tool for maintaining social order intensified against the backdrop of the world wars and continue to the present day.

The birth of mass media in the twentieth century drew further attention to 'correct' pronunciation as a supraregional ideal. In the interest of enhancing intelligibility while projecting a certain degree of authority, the British Broadcasting Company (BBC), founded in 1922, famously promoted a speaking style and accent called received pronunciation (RP).[2] Considered a supraregional accent, RP represents the educated upper and upper-middle classes (Trudgill 1999) and as such it quickly gained prestige and became the standard for international ESL/EFL classes around the world. As the norm for the Church of England, and among the Royal Family, its status can hardly be overstated, but James Milroy (1999) connects it to class discrimination throughout the twentieth century; those who did not use RP were routinely denied professional opportunities (19). But because high-status accents can also be stigmatized, the younger generation is moving away from it now (ibid.: 38), and the British

---

[2] Daniel Jones coined the term in 1918 (Crystal 2003).

media increasingly allow accent variation in order to avoid appearing overly conservative or arrogant (Mugglestone 2003).

US broadcast media similarly promoted their own accent standard. As compiled by James Bender, the National Broadcasting Company's (NBC) *Handbook of Pronunciation* encouraged (1943) each local broadcaster to "use the pronunciation that is spoken by the educated people of the area served by the station" to avoid "being difficult to comprehend or alienating." At a national level, the stated goal was 'General American,' a generic, Midwestern pronunciation typical of male voices, according to the handbook. Lippi-Green notes that the rigor of the BBC effort has never been matched by the Americans (1997: 137). This is understandable, since democratic ideals, along with historical migration patterns, prevented any localized group from garnering special authority in this regard. In other words, 'network American' has never been marked for class (L. Milroy 1999).

The current English-only movement in the US claims that today's immigrants should follow in the footsteps of early immigrants and quickly transition to English. Yet bilingualism was the historical norm in America, and churches, schools, and newspapers promoted languages other than English through the late nineteenth into the twentieth century (see Bailey 2004; Wilkerson and Salmons 2008). Nonetheless, the connection between national unity and a national language standard is not lost on Americans, says Battistella:

Assimilation treats the speech of certain mainstream groups as setting the standard for language, and by extension, other cultural and social values as well. Assimilationism also assumes that a single Standard English is socially good – fostering mobility, political unity, and common values. (2005: 148)

In other words, a standard unifies members of a larger social and political community, even if only an imagined one (as Benedict Anderson, 1983, has described it).

Milroy and Milroy (1985a) suggest that standardization is born of the desire to limit or control language change, especially toward external influences perceived to threaten a sort of cultural invasion. France officially controls the influx of English lexicon through its Académie française, Quebec restricts public use of English in order to promote and protect French, and Germany's linguists and laypersons have long debated how to deal with the rapid adoption of English terms into German. Such promotion of a 'standard language ideology' typically means that any language variety other than the standard is socially degraded (Chand 2009; Joseph 1987).

To be sure, some dialects and accents – native and non-native – are valued while others are stigmatized. Furthermore, cognitive dissonance can result when a priori ideas about the prestige of a given accent are challenged. Imagine a radio interview with an astronomer or cardiac surgeon discussing the latest scientific discovery in her field. A German or British accent would hardly surprise the listener, but because of cultural stereotypes, the same could not be said for an Appalachian or Mexican-American accent.

Context can also affect how tolerant we are of foreign accent. Minerva Perez, a fifth-generation Texan from the Rio Grande Valley, held a television news anchor position in Los Angeles from 1986 to 1992, where she read the news in standard 'broadcast' English but pronounced her own name with an authentically Spanish accent. Some listeners complained, others reportedly sent hate mail, and her supervisor allegedly decried the practice as "jarring to the ear." Perez eventually moved to another anchor position in Houston and remarks on the transformation in Los Angeles since: "The culture itself is changing the vernacular ... More Latino journalists coming on board are saying their name correctly" (Canto 2006).

At this moment in history, we once again find an increased interest in accent coinciding with rapid population shifts. Historically, such shifts have called into question basic assumptions about citizenship and national identity. Thus, the accent standard is once again a timely issue – one that will evolve in tandem with the politics of immigration and minority representation.

Beyond the UK, US, Canada, Australia, and New Zealand, aka the "Inner Circle" (Kachru and Nelson 1996), RP has been historically lauded and taught as the most prestigious English accent even though just 3–5 percent of the population of England actually uses it (Trudgill and Hannah 2008). In the 'Outer Circle,' English is a second language used in official contexts such as government, law, business, and education. Indeed, it is frequently the language of personal communication as well, depending on the educational level of the speaker (e.g., in India, Pakistan, Singapore, etc.). In those countries where a unique regional variety has evolved, RP is still a useful reference point. Jenkins (2002) illustrates this function in her analyses of ESL communication breakdowns. Where speakers are aware of the potentially unintelligible features of their own pronunciation, they endeavor to adjust in order to approximate the (usually British or American) standard (ibid.: 95). But should each such context teach its own English accent, rather than upholding a more traditional model? As numbers of ESL speakers in the Outer Circle increase, and as 'Expanding Circle' countries such as Japan, China, and Indonesia increasingly adopt English for specific purposes, the call for a unitary, global pronunciation standard will be increasingly challenged.[3]

In this context, the whole notion of *nativeness* has become murky, if not downright controversial. Many scholars disdain the native speaker construct as

---

[3] For pronunciation differences in international Englishes, see Trudgill and Hannah 2008. For historical background and current usage patterns of World Englishes, see Melchers and Shaw 2003. Moag (1992) outlines the process of indigenization in World Englishes.

passé at best. To be sure, some varieties of English around the globe are nativized by now and there is a desire to move beyond the hegemonic, colonial implications of the native–non-native distinction. Sharma concedes that these indigenized varieties represent an unusual sociolinguistic challenge: "They can neither be straightforwardly subsumed under models of individual second language learning nor under models of native variation" (2005: 194). They are effectively hybrids, based on colonial varieties of native English, which have taken on local features (ibid.). Even 'Indian English' refers to multiple varieties within India that represent local ethnicities and linguistic backgrounds (Chand 2009).

So does the native speaker concept still serve any purpose? ESL teachers surely need a standard for pedagogical consistency, and many ESL learners express the desire to sound native, i.e., aligned with an Inner Circle model, even if their intended use for English is limited (Scales et al. 2006). Moreover, intelligibility beyond the local level is anchored by a supraregional (often Inner Circle) standard. For now, American and British English top the list in this regard. Whether Inner Circle standards will continue to be idealized will depend on future shifts in economic, social, and political power, and the concomitant shift in ideology that could bring.

Phonology exhibits great diversity across world Englishes, and the trend toward globalization suggests the need for some measure of comprehensibility between them, but orchestrating the use of a specific variety of English for global communication purposes is another matter, writes Nihalani (2010: 26). Wardhaugh reasons that given its social and geographical distribution "English is unlikely ever to be spoken uniformly, nor should we wish it might be so" (1999: 59f.). Seidlhofer (2004) similarly cites a 'conceptual gap' between the need for linguistic norms and the recognition that one standard cannot reasonably apply to all English speakers. That being the case, it is important to ask whether a foreign accent is really detrimental to communication. We turn to this question next.

4.2 Communicative effects of a non-native accent

The debate over whether the native speaker model is still relevant for L2 phonology has coalesced around the notion of *intelligibility*. Even if many learners of English prefer the Inner Circle model, sociocultural and pedagogical branches of applied linguistics suggest that a foreign accent is unimportant as long as the intended message is clear. There is little agreement of what this means in real terms, however; intelligibility seems to mean different things to different people (Jenkins 2000: 69). On an empirical level, segmental and suprasegmental features that affect intelligibility must first be teased apart. Second, we must consider word choice, rate of speaking, and morphosyntactic accuracy and complexity. Finally, exogenous factors invariably play a role, including listener attitudes, familiarity with the topic, situational factors, shared cultural knowledge, and so forth. In light of these complex interrelationships, the discussion below illustrates how difficult it is to substantiate the communicative effects of accent in specific terms, even when several such factors are taken into account.

4.2.1 Comprehensibility, intelligibility, and accentedness

Accent as a communicative phenomenon has been measured in terms of *comprehensibility*, or the perceived ease of global-level understanding for an entire utterance or passage, and *intelligibility*, the extent to which a word or utterance is recognized at the level of finer acoustic–phonetic detail, although some scholars have used intelligibility to emphasize interpretability or apprehension of the speaker's intended message in a general way (see Derwing and Munro 1997; Field 2005; Jenkins 2000; Munro and Derwing 1999; Pickering 2006).[4]

Both constructs lend themselves to scalar measure, and intelligibility is often verified through a transcription task as well. Here, the listener fills in blanks on a written transcript (a *cloze* test) based on what she hears, thus confirming recognition of the words themselves. The potential for listeners to compensate for phonetic/phonemic mistakes by writing what *should* have been said is especially likely in longer, non-ambiguous passages, thus affecting the reliability of this technique. Some researchers therefore force the listener to choose between predetermined forms. Despite these fairly straightforward instruments the evidence is fraught with ambiguities, and we see right away that *intelligibility* and *comprehensibility* are highly subjective judgments that bring to bear many factors; some intrinsic to the listener, some to the speaker, and some entirely situational or external in nature. As will be seen, distinguishing one from another continues to pose a challenge.

In an early study, Smith and Rafiqzad (1979) found significant correspondence between native and non-native listeners' comprehensibility ratings, intelligibility transcriptions, and accent ratings of ESL speech samples representing mostly Asian and South Asian L1s. Speakers with the same mother tongue background as their listeners were generally deemed more comprehensible (see also Bent and Bradlow 2003; Derwing and Munro 2005; Kennedy and Trofimovich 2008) but passage difficulty was also statistically significant. In this case, the native controls generated longer and more complex utterances and were found less comprehensible by non-native listeners. By contrast, Hayes-Harb et al. (2008), Major et al. (2005), Munro et al. (2006), and Van

---

[4] In this section, we will use the terms consistent with the individual study under discussion.

Wijngaarden et al. (2002) indicated no intelligibility advantage for speakers with the same linguistic background as their listeners. For example, Chinese listeners in the Major et al. (2005) study found Chinese-accented speakers of English less comprehensible than Spanish- and Japanese-accented ones (see also Ortmeyer and Boyle, 1985). Of relevance here is the finding that listeners can acquire 'talker independent' comprehension for a given accent with repeat exposure (Bradlow and Bent 2008). These seemingly contradictory findings indicate that comprehensibility works bidirectionally; the speaker and the listener each play a role, so broad generalizations are still premature. (We address the social implications of this in the following sections.)

Gupta (2005) draws attention to another curious phenomenon: Some listeners are better than others at comprehending *unfamiliar* accents. Of relevance here is the Smith and Bisazza (1982) study in which American listeners understood Asian- and South Asian-accented English better than did the Asian and South Asian ESL/EFL listeners. Perhaps native speakers more readily adjust for phonological variation, and when it comes to comprehending foreign-accented speech, language expertise trumps accent familiarity (see Kennedy and Trofimovich 2008). Whether this is a function of attention to specific linguistic cues is a matter for future investigation.

To complicate matters, it appears that intelligibility/comprehensibility ratings and actual comprehension do not necessarily match; it depends on who is talking. Schmid and Yeni-Komshian (1999) observed that both native and non-native listeners judged L2 pronunciation errors more leniently than native speaker errors, and this leniency increased with degree of accent (see also Garrett 1992). In terms of actual comprehension, however, errors occurring within heavily accented passages were less likely to be identified than those in mildly accented passages. This is a good indication that greater processing effort is required to get at a speaker's meaning when her speech is heavily accented.

Digging deeper into the issue of comprehensibility vs. intelligibility, the statistical overlap between them is readily apparent. Derwing and Munro, working in the context of ESL in Canada, have endeavored to disambiguate them, but in so doing raise even more questions about their real nature. For example, before listening, their participants often cite segmental errors as key for judging *accentedness*, yet grammar, prosody, and speech rate apparently all come into play. Intelligibility and comprehensibility are similarly multivalent, it seems. Derwing and Munro nonetheless argue for 'partial' independence of all three for the following reasons:

(1) a strong accent does not necessarily imply poor intelligibility (Derwing and Munro 1997; Munro et al. 2006);
(2) accent ratings tend to be 'harsher' than comprehensibility ratings, which are, in turn, harsher than intelligibility ratings (Derwing and Munro 1997; Munro and Derwing 1999);

(3) the correlation between grammar and accentedness is slightly more significant than the correlation between grammar and either comprehensibility or intelligibility (Derwing and Munro 1997; Munro and Derwing 1999).

Though interesting, these distinctions do little to clarify either the essence of these constructs or the boundaries between them. Even degree of accent – a seemingly straightforward measure – involves more than just phonological performance.

One empirical priority is to pinpoint those features most relevant for intelligibility. Voice onset time (VOT) for word and syllable-initial consonants appears significant (Cesar-Lee 2000 for L2 French; Gonzalez-Bueno 1997 for L2 Spanish; Riney and Takagi 1999 for Japanese learners of English), as is syllable duration (Cesar-Lee 2000 and Setter 2006 for L2 English), and vowel quality (Setter 2006). Schairer (1992) proposes a hierarchy of sorts, with vowel quality most significant.[5] Accurate production of consonants comes next (cf. Riney et al. 2005), followed by syllable-level phenomena such as elision, which can affect vowel quality, especially under conditions of assimilation or neutralization. Linguistic environment is key according to van Els and deBot (1987), who caution that "acoustic aspects of the speech signal are not necessarily directly linked with its perceptual ones" (149). As an example, segmental errors occurring in word-initial position seem to affect comprehensibility disproportionately (Bent et al. 2007), likely because categorical perception[6] relies on fine VOT distinctions in word-initial position (Riney and Takagi 1999). Although the evidence is sparse, this is an intriguing issue for future study.

Intelligibility, according to many, is a function of suprasegmental accuracy above all. For it is prosodic information that "provides the framework for utterances and directs the listener's attention to information the speaker regards as important" (Anderson-Hsieh et al. 1992: 531). Holm (2006) confirms the significance of intonation and segment duration for intelligibility and judgments of accentedness, and Low (2006) offers similar evidence. In a micro-level comparison of vowel quality and word-level stress for intelligibility, Field (2005) manipulates both, presenting *second* as *seCOND*, both with and without changes to vowel length in the second syllable. Stress shift is the most significant predictor of intelligibility, according to seventy-six listeners from various L1 backgrounds (native listener controls made similar judgments). Rightward stress shifts are even more problematic than leftward ones (e.g., *FORget* or *CONtain* as opposed to *seCOND*). In a stress-timed language such as English, correct stress on the first syllable of a word is critical because listeners construct

---

[5] This fits nicely with Nihalani's (2010) emphasis on vowels as a fundamental point of difference, and sometimes confusion, in world Englishes as well as regional varieties within the Inner Circle.
[6] As in the distinction between /p/ and /b/, and thus between *pat* vs. *bat*.

word boundaries around expectations of stress.[7] A mispronunciation such as *foLLOWED* could lead listeners to interpret subsequent utterances around notions of *load* or *flowed* (ibid.), resulting in possible miscommunication.

The importance of phrasal stress for intelligibility gets close attention in several additional studies. In Jenkins (2002) data, the error '*I smoke more than you DO*' in response to the question, '*How much do YOU smoke?*' led to communication breakdown between two non-native interlocutors despite three attempts to clarify. Along similar lines, Kang's (2010) native listeners judged accent more harshly when non-native speakers' pitch range was reduced, and word stress was erroneously placed on function words like *the*. Hahn (2004) provides another critical piece of support for the significance of stress: Here, listeners had trouble recalling the content of the speech sample when stress was misplaced – a sure sign that suprasegmental accuracy is critical to interpreting meaning.

Other recent investigations suggest that intonation, pitch range, and pitch movement are all crucial reference points for global and detailed comprehension in native/non-native interactions (e.g., Kang 2010; Pickering 2009). As Pickering puts it, "intonational cues are particularly vulnerable to misinterpretation" and can lead to negative attitudes when they are understood to be rude, uncooperative or unfriendly (2009: 237) (see next section). Of relevance here is Wennerstrom's (1994) study of Spanish, Japanese, and Thai ESL speakers who completed both a reading and a free speaking task in English. None consistently used pitch contrasts to signal meaning as native speaker controls did. In a subsequent study, Wennerstrom's (1998) Mandarin Chinese ESL speakers did not increase pitch levels at rhetorical junctures that corresponded to topic shifts. This correlated to their global language score in English, lending support to Wennerstrom's assertion that intonation is not simply a matter of style, but constitutes a meaning-bearing grammatical system in its own right, as the means by which we interpret the semantic relationship between proximate utterances.

In addition to these phonological criteria, many other linguistic and paralinguistic factors contribute to intelligibility. Comparing phonological accuracy to other levels of language, Gynan (1985) concludes that morphosyntax is more salient for native Spanish speakers' judgments of beginning Spanish learners' intelligibility, but for intermediate learners, neither grammar nor phonology are significant. Ensz (1982) also finds significance for grammatical accuracy when it comes to intelligibility ratings of L2 French speakers, but Janicki's (1990) study of L2 Polish shows phonological features to be more significant than grammatical ones. Advocating a different focus altogether, Albrechtsen et al. (1980) contend that linguistic accuracy is just one consideration; in their view, overall error frequency matters most (cf. Eisenstein 1983). It seems that both

---

[7] Approximately 90 percent of content words in English place stress on the first syllable, according to Cutler and Carter (1987), cited in Field (2005).

the speaker's general proficiency level and the distinctive features most salient in the target language contribute to a hierarchy of intelligibility criteria.

A wide range of discursive and non-linguistic features contribute to intelligibility as well, including: familiarity with the topic (Gass and Varonis 1984); semantic content (Kennedy and Trofimovich 2008); background noise (Rogers et al. 2004; van Wijngaarden et al. 2002); perceived speaker personality (Albrechtsen et al. 1980); discourse strategies (Albrechtsen et al. 1980); task type (Derwing et al. 2004); and speech rate (Anderson-Hsieh and Koehler 1988; Derwing and Munro 1997; Kang 2010; Munro and Derwing 1998, 2001; Trofimovich and Baker 2006). Even head movement and facial motions that correspond to pitch and loudness have demonstrated an independent effect on speech intelligibility (Mumhall et al. 2004).

Considering these complexities, intelligibility is obviously difficult to nail down empirically. It is intrinsically connected to several levels of language, to the language-specific salience of certain phonological and grammatical features, and to situational factors, including the nature of the interaction and the relationship between interlocutors. Shared cultural knowledge is also a factor to consider, as this could smooth over any communicative misstep. In other words, intelligibility at the word level may not be the biggest stumbling block to native–non-native interactions. And where it does interfere with communication, it is all but impossible to predict how interlocutors will negotiate their way past it.

Discourse-level studies that involve longer passages and more complex situations remind us that listeners must be able to notice contextual cues and make adjustments for phonological errors in real time. Some L2 users simply do not have the skills or intuitions to do so, as shown in Jenkins (2002), where communication failed upon a phoneme substitution of /l/ for /r/ in the phrase *red car* (i.e., *let car*) despite the fact that the speaker was pointing to a picture of a red car. Jenkins writes that for some critical errors, "context and co-text do not provide much help in clarifying meaning" (ibid.: 91). Setting the case of /l/–/r/ confusion aside, Jenkins asserts that some quintessentially English phonemes can be substituted with no cost to comprehension, e.g., voiced and voiceless *th* (/θ/–/ð/). For example, French speakers of English may use /z/ or /s/ to replace *th*, while South Asians use a /d/ or /t/ (Melchers and Shaw 2003). More complicated are varieties such as Singapore English, which uses a reduced set of final consonants and consonant clusters so that words end with glottal stops or nasals ([bæŋ] for *bank* and [i:ʔ] for *eat* (ibid.). Here, substitutions amount to deletions that could critically hamper comprehension. Interlocutors can use collaborative discourse strategies such as pause, repetition, back-channel cues, and so on, to negotiate past such points (Pickering 2006); however, some L2 users have less facility with such strategies. Other substitutions are more subtle, e.g., involving vowel intensity, height, and duration in unstressed syllables in English (as shown in Lee et al. 2006), and such cases may be more difficult to negotiate past if they are not readily recognized.

Jenkins asserts that pronunciation is "by far the most frequent and the most difficult to resolve" cause of communication breakdown (2002: 87) and this is surely the impetus behind her quest to establish a non-negotiable 'core' of phonological features for English as an international lingua franca. Yet this core is limited to the segmental level; she dismisses many suprasegmental features as inconsequential, citing pitch movement as unteachable, for example. Jenkins' proposed Lingua Franca Core of intelligibility features for English has drawn criticism in part because it belies the natural development of regional phonologies (see Dewey and Jenkins 2010; Seidlhofer et al. 2006; Trudgill and Hannah 2008). It is these local variations that help learners "acquire their national flavor," and thus they may hesitate to forego them in favor of any imported standard (Nihalani 2010: 33; see also Pickering 2006). Finally, L2 users' reasons for acquiring English, and thus their goals relative to attaining a specific sound, are idiosyncratic as well (Scales et al. 2006: 717).

As a final point, perceptions of accentedness, intelligibility, and comprehensibility show high inter-rater reliability within studies, suggesting a minor role for individual factors such as language familiarity (Munro et al. 2006), yet to claim that any such construct is unitary would be premature; we have no evidence that listeners of different backgrounds actually *process* accent in the same ways. Riney et al. (2005) discovered that Americans listening to Japanese-accented English rely more on segmental cues when assigning accent ratings, while their Japanese counterparts rely on intonation, speech rate, and overall sentence duration. In the end, however, the two groups' ratings closely agreed. Kennedy and Trofimovich (2008) also confirm that listeners both familiar and unfamiliar with specific accents arrive at similar ratings despite actual differences in comprehension. And, as noted, the relative salience of specific cues in each listener's own L1 surely influences the phonological features they attend to most when processing a foreign accent. Evidence from a recent ERP, or event-related potential, study by Conrey et al. (2005) support this assertion, since neural processing differences were observed between those whose dialects contain a specific distinctive feature and those whose dialect does not. It is thus too early to take these constructs at face value; we must know more about the underlying mechanisms they represent.

Thus far we have emphasized the fact that closely controlled tasks do not capture the dynamic qualities of intelligibility and comprehensibility. Also noted here is the complex interplay of linguistic, individual, and situational factors involved in any determination of intelligibility. Still to be addressed is how the perception of foreign accent affects the actual course of interaction. Specifically, we are interested in the kinds of adjustments listeners make when a speaker is difficult to understand, and whether such adjustments correspond to communicative problems alone, as opposed to pre-existing attitudes toward the accent in question. The following sections explore phonological accommodation and the extent to which interactive behaviors are governed by a priori attitudes.

4.2.2   Phonological accommodation

It is well known that interlocutors shift their speech features in response to one another. Linguistic accommodation is a dynamic, communicative behavior said to take two directions – either *convergence* or *divergence*, depending on whether interlocutors hope to minimize or increase social distance (Beebe and Giles 1984; Thakerer et al. 1982). On an affective level, the direction and extent of accommodation reflects a desire for approval, an interest in maintaining or asserting a positive social identity, or an expectation of social reward or acceptance (Giles et al. 1991). Accommodation directed at improving communicative efficiency (i.e., comprehensibility), such as adjusting utterance length, speech rate, gesture, facial expressions, and even lexical or morphosyntactic complexity, is said to be cognitively motivated (ibid.). Where non-native interlocutors are significantly less proficient than their native interlocutors, 'foreigner talk' may serve as an accommodation of sorts (see Ferguson 1971). This morpho-syntactically reduced register is marked by slower, more deliberately pronounced words, using frequent repetition. It is debatable whether foreigner talk is truly facilitative, namely, whether it helps the non-native listener's comprehensibility or acquisition in general. Context is key to understanding accommodation, as gender, age, familiarity, and topic are prominent influences on how we modulate speech behaviors (Giles and Coupland 1991; Jones et al. 1994).

In specific terms, vowel and consonant quality are subject to adjustment, and suprasegmentals such as vocal intensity, speaking rate, pause length, and pause frequency can indicate accommodation as well (Natale 1975, cited in Pardo 2006). Evidence comes from Coupland's (1984) documentation of exchanges in a UK travel office. In the business of customer service, the office assistant, Sue, is presumably motivated to accommodate her many clients for both affective and cognitive reasons. Sue's use of /h/, intervocalic /t/ and certain consonant clusters all shift in response to each client's dialect, effectively charting a spectrum of standardness in her accent. Garrett (2010) describes the delicate balance that Sue must strike between projecting a competent, trustworthy image and social desirability at the same time. In short, accommodation merges multiple objectives and must be negotiated carefully to achieve the desired effect.

Accommodation does not always follow the principle of prestige or favor. Even in the high-stakes situation of a job interview, Willemyns et al. (1997) noticed that job applicants converged less often toward interviewers with the more prestigious accent, and more often toward the interviewers with the *less* prestigious one (here: 'cultivated' vs. 'broad' Australian accent).[8] What could explain this? Thakerer et al. (1982) note that we seek to differentiate ourselves from others to the extent that: (a) we recognize them as belonging to a different group; (b) the perceived costs for our accommodation behavior are "proportionally lower than the anticipated rewards" (214). In other words, we sometimes calculate that cost–reward balance in favor of preserving our own positively valued identity (ibid.: 218). Willemyns et al. interpret their male subjects' behavior in this way since many had expressed strong preference for the lower status accent on a pre-task questionnaire. Post-interview data raise an interesting problem, however: Job applicants tended to describe their male interviewers as having the 'broad' accent even though the authors had carefully balanced both accent types (and genders) in that role. Presumably then, the male interviewees did not *intend* to diverge from their interlocutors in each case. Because they had misidentified them, they must have thought they were *converging*. This confusion underscores the need to ask direct questions about linguistic behavior and attitudes in conjunction with such tasks.

In the accommodation literature there are references to situational behaviors leading to long-term shifts but very few studies examine this directly. Pardo (2006) gave native English speakers from different regional backgrounds a paired information exchange task, and observed convergence for some aspects of vowel and consonant quality. Not only did the convergence intensify over the course of the interaction, it continued into a follow-up, non-interactive speaking task. In a longer-term, informal study, Shockey (1984) observed four Americans living in England whose phonology increasingly took on certain British features over a period of several years, most notably the use of /t/ instead of /d/ for intervocalic /t/, such as the word in *latter* (the American pronunciation would sound like *ladder*). Shockey assumes affective as well as cognitive motives for this shift, since the intermedial flap of the American /t/ can affect comprehensibility (where there is a need to clearly distinguish *ladder* and *latter*, for example). To support her argument, she compares this feature to postvocalic /r/. Here, she maintains, the Americans feel no need to accommodate British *r*-less-ness because even if their retroflex /r/ makes them sound distinctly American, it does not cause any confusion. The general consensus is that accommodation patterns need a specific impetus, present over a longer period, to become permanent features of a speaker's idiolect.

Thus far, the evidence cited pertains only to native speakers who adjust to other *native* regional and social dialect features. Studies of second language

---

[8] The distinction is based largely on vowel quality, as the authors describe it, e.g., for /ai/ in *library*, which is [laɪbɹɪi] in the cultivated variety, and [lɔɪbɹɪ] in the broad accent.

accommodation are quite rare by comparison, and tend to focus on *disaccommodation*, where the L2 speaker diverges in a presumed effort to preserve his language identity (see Bourhis et al. 1975). In Bourhis et al. (1979), trilingual Flemish students "muttered and whispered disapproval" of an interlocutor whose pronunciation maintained a distinct ethnic Francophone quality during a conversation they carried out in English (cited in Giles et al. 1991). Such behaviors typically spike in response to threatening topics or tones. Zuengler's (1982) pilot study of 13 ESL speakers examined several pronunciation features in the language elicited by 3 different prompts, one of which was 'threatening': the informant's mother tongue (Greek or Spanish) was described as unimportant in the US context and the claim was made that those who wished to use it should return to their native country. Zuengler noted a decrease in accommodation under the threatening condition (see also Bourhis and Giles 1977, cited in Zuengler 1982).

The research has overwhelmingly focused on accommodation as a socially motivated behavior, and some have investigated specific constructs as relevant in this vein. Looking at empathy, Berkowitz (1989) assigned 26 of 52 adult Dominican ESL learners to a treatment group where the teacher related a story of immigration to the students' own lives, asking about their personal experiences and expressing a desire to understand the issue from their point of view. Non-verbal signals such as eye contact and smiling complemented her approach. The other 26 in a control group discussed only basic comprehension and grammar points with no (intentional) verbal or non-verbal signals of empathy. Speech samples were collected from interviews that directly followed the class discussions. Students who gave the teacher the highest empathy ratings were significantly *less* likely to use standard pronunciation of consonant clusters, prevocalic /r/, and some neutral vowels. The author interpreted this as a sign that those students felt no pressure to converge toward the teacher's standard pronunciation. In other words, empathy improved self-acceptance of a foreign accent rather than provoking accommodation. Several methodological concerns preclude any generalizations here, but it remains an important question how psychological constructs like empathy and solidarity affect phonological accommodation.

It is imperative to show that for a given interaction, relevant phonological features are repeated sufficiently to signal a real behavioral shift, and are not just random variation characteristic of an interlanguage phase (Coupland 1984). Indications are that intermediate and advanced non-native speakers can adjust their pronunciation in response to their native interlocutors, but there is much to learn about their communicative vs. affective motivations for doing so. Far fewer scholars have concerned themselves with how native speakers accommodate non-natives even though they presumably have more resources to call upon during interaction than do their L2 interlocutors

(Derwing et al. 2002: 247). Coupland calls for more investigation in this area since "phonological behavior is known to be socially meaningful ... in a regular and specific way, unlike utterance length" (1984: 66). With this in mind, we now consider how accent is imbued with social significance in the listener's mind.

4.3 Reactions to non-native speech

According to Garrett, an attitude is a learned, not innate, "evaluative orientation to a social object" (2010: 20). Decades of language attitudes research affirm that accents are widely associated with social values like correctness, desirability, prestige, and power. Giles and Coupland (1991) describe how very minute variations in our speech can set a negative evaluation in motion:

> [E]ven a single vowel or consonant sound, contrasting with ... our expectations, can have evaluative repercussions for its utterer ... [S]light and inherently trivial details of pronunciation can clearly take on crucial social significance when they index differences in 'standard' vs. 'non-standard' language use, with their echoes of prestige, class and competence. (32)

This is to say that having an accent not only affects whether others understand us, but how they judge us as social beings as well.

When it comes to attitudes toward *native* accents, the standard/non-standard dichotomy is most salient (e.g., Cargile and Giles 1998; Milroy, L. 1999), as native speakers are aware which social and regional accents are held in high esteem and which are ridiculed. When faced with L2 speakers, the distinction *native–non-native* is front and center in our minds, with various social and contextual factors coloring our reactions to any discernible accent. Below, we explore the nature of such attitudes as we juxtapose individual preferences with broader notions of prestige, and demographic factors like race, class, and gender.

4.3.1 Prestige, prejudice, and familiarity

Accent is in the ear of the beholder as much as it is in the mouth of the speaker. In the UK, RP is favorably associated with education, competence, self-confidence, and intelligence (Brown et al. 1985). A British accent is highly regarded in the US too, but Cargile and Giles (1998) emphasize the difference between *attractiveness* and *status* in this context. RP's association with a conservative, reserved image means that it can be unattractive for some situations in the US. Even research from the UK shows favor for regional accents rather than RP when situations call for humor, friendliness, and generosity (ibid.). Coupland and Bishop (2007) recently undertook a large-scale online study supported by the BBC as part of a wider project called "Voices." With data from 5,010 respondents across the UK who evaluated 34 different English accents, it is clear that social attractiveness and status are sometimes in conflict, evident in respondents' ratings of Australian vs. Northern Irish English and many regional dialects – high marks for attractiveness can accompany low ones for status.

Attitudes toward accent have traditionally been tested indirectly through a technique called the *matched guise*, pioneered by Lambert et al. (1960). Here, a single speaker reads a text in several different accents while other linguistic factors are held constant to the extent possible; the passage itself is the same, and the speech rate, pitch patterns, and voice quality are presumably consistent (Giles and Coupland 1991). The goal is to clearly isolate accent as the trigger for perceptions of personal traits like intelligence, confidence, ambition, sincerity, trustworthiness, friendliness, etc. This technique has inspired decades of language attitudes research.

In an early test of the matched guise, Lambert et al. (1976) asked listeners in Caribou, Maine to react to a range of accent types, including European French, supraregional Canadian French, Canadian English, and local dialects of both languages. Listeners rated perceived friendliness, trustworthiness, intelligence, physical fitness, and even physical attractiveness and height along a scale, e.g., with 'very friendly' on one end of the scale and 'not friendly' on the other. Speakers whose accents were associated with the working class were generally rated less intelligent, less active, less good-looking, shorter in stature, and less truthful. The European and supraregional Canadian French-accented speakers were deemed more trustworthy, more active, taller, and so on – clear affirmation that accent conjures up attitudes of a personal, and socially relevant, nature.

Hu and Lindemann (2009) employed the same premise in their investigation of 38 Chinese ESL learners who heard a native Cantonese woman read words and sentence-length items in English. For some items, they were told the speaker was native Cantonese, for others they were told she was American. Their task was to identify pronunciation features in each sample, with the sentence-level task producing an interesting result: When told the speaker was American, listeners reported hearing fully released final consonant stops (*dog* as /dɔgʰ/, as opposed to unreleased /dɔg̚/ – a stereotypical Chinese English feature). This occurred regardless of whether these final stops were actually released in the speech sample. When the speaker was said to be Cantonese, listeners accurately heard the release feature as it (alternately) occurred. Hu and Lindemann explain this as follows: Learners idealize a native target-language accent, and this interferes with the accuracy of their listening. In contrast to native listeners, non-natives may not reliably distinguish native from non-native speakers for colloquial or non-standard varieties (Scales et al. 2006; cf. Alford and Strother 1990; see Niedzielski 1999 for similar findings among native speakers).

The field of folk linguistics, or perceptual dialectology, confirms that accent desirability is also a matter of local preference and covert prestige (Niedzielski and Preston 2003; Preston 1999). When presented with speech samples representing various regional accents, US native speakers consistently favor those who sound most like their own regional dialect, while accents revealing great geographical distance are often deemed unfriendly, inauthentic, or untrustworthy, even if more 'correct.' This demonstrates a clear in-group effect that trumps overt prestige. Indeed, an accent deemed too correct or too standard can be disparaged as condescending and arrogant (Lindemann 2003).

To observe everyday accent attitudes, Preston famously employs a task in which native speakers locate regional accents by labeling a map of the US. The results often illustrate how simplistic (and off-base) our assumptions about accent can be, even for our mother tongue. Extending this kind of work to an international L2 focus, Lindemann (2005) asked American undergraduates to locate and describe the English spoken in various regions while looking at a world map without country names. In a complementary task, students rated the English spoken in each of 58 countries listed according to correctness, friendliness, and pleasantness on a 10-point scale. They also rated their familiarity with each variety. By incorporating open-ended data with scalar response types, Lindemann provides critical insights on the interplay between familiarity and cultural stereotypes:

- In Western Europe (France, Germany, Italy, etc.) comments such as 'speaks English well' and 'comprehensible' were the norm. The label 'broken English' was often used to describe other L2 Englishes.
- Familiarity does not necessarily indicate preference. Here, Mexican-accented English, which was very familiar, received low scores and garnered the most negative comments overall.
- Positive attributes were significantly interrelated, but a few distinctions were apparent (e.g., German and Russian English were both described as correct, but not pleasant).

One possible interpretation is that when faced with familiar accents, listeners make more nuanced (here: hierarchical) judgments, whereas when they hear – or in this case, merely imagine or recall – unfamiliar ones, cruder generalizations come to the fore.

Confirming just how arbitrary such attitudes can be, Kang and Rubin (2009) alternately displayed a false guise photo of two similarly dressed men – one Anglo-American and one Asian – as listeners heard speech samples from a male native speaker of English. The authors' assumption was that seeing the photo before hearing the speech would pre-empt expectations about language ability based on ethnic and social criteria – a phenomenon they call "reverse linguistic stereotyping." They set out to prove that such preconceived ideas actually affect comprehension. The statistical analysis bore this out.

Listeners who had reported negative associations with Asian speakers before the listening task performed significantly worse on a cloze-format comprehension test thereafter, as compared to those who did not express such attitudes. There is evidence that L2 speakers also draw conclusions about job status, friendliness, and appearance based on the standard–non-standard dichotomy in the target language – also correlating to comprehensibility (see Eisenstein and Verdi 1985, cited in Major et al. 2005). As Major et al. put it, positive attitudes aid comprehension while negative attitudes interfere with comprehension (ibid.: 44).

All indications are that listener attitudes affect comprehensibility and influence perceptions of speaker believability as well. Vornik et al. (2003) compared the tendency of New Zealand listeners to be misled by someone with a 'powerful' and/or a 'socially attractive' accent; both factors significantly correlated to the listeners' propensity to accept misinformation. In a similar study, Lev-Ari and Keysar (2010) were able to tease apart prejudice from comprehensibility. They asked 35 listeners to rate the truth value of statements such as "*Ants don't sleep*" as recited by English speakers with Turkish, Polish, Korean, Italian, or Austrian accents. Native speaker controls were also included. Listeners heard an advance disclaimer that the actual statements were provided by the researchers, yet they still assigned less trust to the foreign-accented speakers and this effect increased with degree of accent.

4.3.2   Linguistic and contextual factors

While decades of empirical work confirm that a priori notions of attractiveness and prestige mediate our responses to accent, linguistic criteria also come into play. A study by Ryan et al. (1977) found that the stronger a speaker's foreign accent, the less likely she is to be found pleasant, fluent in English, or 'a possible friend' (see also Cargile and Giles 1998). As for speech rate, Brown et al. (1985) found associations between faster speech and perceptions of intelligence and ambition, while slow speech was linked to kindness, dependability, and politeness. Contrasting native and non-native listener perceptions, Scales et al.'s (2006) L2 English listeners strongly preferred a slower General American accent while native listeners preferred faster British and Mexican-American-accented speech, even though they found the American accent easiest to understand. This suggests that speech rate and accent operate somewhat independently on attitudes.

Beyond linguistic features, contextual factors such as formality and interlocutor roles are also attitude correlates. Cukor-Avila's (1988) 49 American college undergraduates rated accent less negatively for conversational as opposed to formal speech, regardless of the specific accent (here: Spanish,

German, Arabic, Chinese, and French speakers of ESL). Similarly, Callan et al. (1983) found that Greek-Australian listeners were harsher critics of Greek-accented English when the passages represented a formal context, and Bresnahan et al.'s (2002) 311 American undergraduates attributed greater attractiveness, status, and pleasantness to foreign accents when asked to imagine that the speaker was a friend as opposed to a teaching assistant.

Familiarity seems to affect accent tolerance as well. Dailey et al. (2005) explore how *linguistic landscapes* – the use of a given language in advertising, signage, media, and other public texts – can impact attitudes: In locations with a predominantly Spanish linguistic landscape, listeners of both Hispanic and non-Hispanic background judged Spanish-accented English more favorably than Anglo-accented English (the reverse was also true). Along somewhat similar lines, Dalton-Puffer et al. (1997) confirmed that immersion experience positively influences listeners toward that environment's accent.

One of the most widely cited studies in this vein comes from Carranza and Ryan (1975), who had 32 Mexican-American listeners and 32 Anglo-American listeners – all high-school students – rate standard vs. Mexican-American-accented speech. All Anglo listeners had studied Spanish in school. Two read-aloud passages were used: one representing a mother preparing breakfast in the kitchen for her children, the other representing a teacher giving a history lesson to her class. Listeners heard both passages in standard English and standard Mexican Spanish. The 2 groups' ratings largely overlapped, with the English passages receiving higher marks for status variables such as education, wealth, success, and intelligence. Clear preference was noted for English in the school domain, but both groups preferred Spanish for the home domain. The authors had predicted a split between Anglos and Mexicans in terms of attitudes, namely that Anglo students would prefer English for both contexts. They attribute these unexpected findings to their familiarity with, and appreciation for, Spanish: "The manipulation of context demonstrates that there is another facet involved in the evaluative reaction process other than ... biased impressions which members of one group hold towards themselves or others" (ibid.: 99). As such, attitudes research should do more to account for the relative balance of contextual factors and individual preferences.

4.3.3 Demographic factors

Accent attitudes undoubtedly connect to race, class, and gender, but, thus far, speculation has outpaced hard evidence of these relationships. In the UK, L. Milroy (1999) maintains that a speaker's perceived social class is a far more powerful predictor of accent attitudes than race or ethnicity, while in the US, the opposite holds true. Yet Giles' 1970 study indicates that regional and social accents in the UK enjoy more favor than foreign ones, and within the realm of 'foreign' there are clear preferences (e.g., the French accent is preferred over Italian or German) (cited in Hamers and Blanc 2000). Cukor-Avila (1988) also finds a preference hierarchy for German and French over Spanish, Chinese, and Arabic accents in English. A preference hierarchy is also evident in Gallois and Callan (1981) for European, British, and Vietnamese accents as heard by Australians; however, gender and ethnicity of the speakers come into play (e.g., Italian females were rated more positively than Italian males). As for differences among listeners, Mulac et al. 1974 (cited in Eisenstein 1983) and Cukor-Avila (1988) find that females tend to judge accent less harshly than do males (see Coupland and Bishop 2007).

An important caveat to all this empirical data is that reactions to accent cannot necessarily be taken at face value. Lindemann's (2003) Anglo-American college students judged native Korean speakers as belonging to all sorts of ethnic groups, from Latino, Chinese, and Indian, to Japanese, unspecified 'Asian,' and 'other'. (Lindemann wonders whether US listeners are inherently more aware of ethnicity if it involves a black–white distinction, echoing L. Milroy's assertion.) Lindemann concludes that the native–non-native distinction is salient above all, but stigma is also apparent. Otherwise, she says, why would these different ethnic groups be similarly described as people who are "lazy" and/or "speak poorly"? She recommends that future studies compare many non-native accents, some stigmatized and others not, while also targeting listener beliefs about the represented groups. This would move the research past simplistic assumptions such as 'foreign = faulty'.

4.3.4 Communicative consequences

It has been said that native speakers rarely come halfway towards non-native and non-standard speakers in situations of communicative difficulty (Lippi-Green 1997). This underscores Baker's (1992) definition of attitude as comprising not just beliefs, but an 'action' component as well. When we are "especially positive about the configuration of social characteristics we see in the person, or if the purposes of communication are especially important to us, we will accept a disproportionate amount of the [communicative] burden," Lippi-Green reasons, but in the face of negative social evaluations, we reject our responsibility vis-à-vis our interlocutor (1997: 71f.). Even when all parties have reason to work toward mutual comprehension, accent can be an impediment insofar as it indexes a negative social evaluation (often about race or ethnicity). A relevant study suggests that the motivations behind communicative behaviors are more nuanced, however.

Lindemann (2002) set up a negotiation task between native English speakers and Korean ESL speakers in the US. The study included native–native interactions as well, as a basis for comparison. Among some native speakers who had expressed negative attitudes toward Korean speakers prior to the interaction, Lindemann observed two specific behaviors: (a) they failed to provide crucial feedback through either questions or statements when the information given was obviously erroneous; (b) they emitted frustrated sighs or moved to subsequent questions without signaling that they had understood their partner's contribution. These participants typically described their interactions as unsuccessful afterwards, even though most had successfully completed the information gap task. Lindemann points out that things other than accent could have impeded the ease of communication, among them the non-natives' differences in interactional style, either as a result of language abilities or cultural norms (ibid.: 425). Some of the native speakers could have also been motivated by politeness, in her view; they allowed the Korean speakers to save face by not drawing attention to every faulty or ambiguous utterance.

In this experimental setting, task success relied on persistent and clear cooperative signals, but Lindemann stresses that in everyday life we frequently ignore communicative difficulties. This does not necessarily imply rudeness or an uncooperative stance. Importantly, her work underscores the need for reflective data to better understand whether it is really accent-related attitudes, or a lack of salient social cues, that is at the core of apparently negative interactive behaviors.

4.3.5 Critical summary

This discussion has endeavored to show that there is considerable social consensus about accent attitudes, but caution is warranted on methodological grounds, as outlined below:

(1) Matched guise, the predominant technique for this research, relies on a single speaker to produce various accents, so it is hardly authentic. Furthermore, assigning social and personal traits on the basis of an audio sample is an indirect indication, at best, of the accent–attitude connection. When respondents are asked to actually label accents with their own descriptors, or are asked to rank certain accents in terms of attractiveness, results may differ from those obtained from a matched guise of audio samples (see Garrett 2010).

(2) Studies risk bias through the instrument itself. The researcher's choice of adjectives – individually and on balance – can position the listener to arbitrarily connect personality and physical traits to accent. The wording of the questions can similarly lead responses and thereby skew results. Garrett cites MacKinnon's (1987) study on attitudes in Scotland that included this question: "Do you disagree with our *well-considered* view that Welsh children should be *perfectly entitled* to learn Welsh?"

(my emphasis) – hardly a neutral choice of words. Open-ended items with neutral prompts (as in Lindemann's work) ensure free associations.

(3) Of further threat to internal validity is the potential *mis*identification of speakers' backgrounds. Because ratings connect cultural stereotypes to specific accents, when listeners misidentify the accent (or are purposely misled), their assignment of personal traits may be misinterpreted as a result. (NB: Lindemann's 2003 listeners correctly identified her native Korean speakers just 8 percent of the time.) To clarify the criteria that contribute to ratings – be they linguistic or non-linguistic – introspective instruments are needed.

(4) We should remember that listener reports can be misleading, as shown in Lambert (1965) where participants' attitudes toward ethnic groups did not synch up with their ratings (discussed in Garrett 2010). Dörnyei (2003b) attributes the occasional gap between what respondents report to believe and what they really believe to a desirability bias, the tendency to provide the answer perceived to be most desirable. Other possibilities include self-deception and the tendency toward acquiescence – agreeing with sentences despite being unsure or ambivalent (ibid.: 12f.).

More direct measurement of the connections between accent and attitudes is necessary to avoid misinterpreting isolated listening tasks. To wit: One study sheds light on the term *broken English*, which seems unambiguously negative at first glance. When asked to elaborate on this response, Lindemann's (2005) participants described 'broken' as a reflection of specific features – pause frequency, deletion of the verb *to be*, etc. – none of which implies incomprehensibility (210–11), much less prejudice.

In short, artifacts of the instrument can misdirect conclusions about attitudes expressed on either close- or open-ended response types. Moreover, we know little about how interlocutors actually behave when faced with an accent that is either difficult to understand, or evokes an unwillingness to share the communication burden for other reasons. These are critical questions for future work.

4.4 Strongholds of accent stereotypes

Of special interest is the extent to which individual attitudes and any accompanying behaviors are shaped by broader social stereotypes, those shared beliefs that exaggerate similarities among group members and differences between groups (Garrett 2010: 32). Insofar as stereotypes categorize people in an oversimplified way, they are a cognitive shortcut (Bakanic 2009: 74). Typically, esteemed characteristics are attributed to the dominant group while less-valued qualities are attributed to minority groups (ibid.: 89). Speech criteria are common reference points for stereotypes, e.g.: voice quality, intonation, lexicon, and speech style (de Klerk and Bosch 1995: 18). Media (sometimes unwittingly) promote these stereotypes through both informational and entertainment venues, and they are reinforced anecdotally as well.

Sociolinguistic research has long been interested in stereotypes, bolstered by Social Identity Theory in the 1970s, which proposed that humans identify and categorize one another on the basis of (perceived) group membership (Tajfel and Turner 1979). Stereotypes are a part of this tendency; they allow us to size up a person with minimal effort, according to Merskin (2011), and once these 'scripts' develop, we are more likely to see familiar associations as truths. Still, there is much debate about exactly how stereotypes lead to specific discriminatory behaviors (Enteman 2003:16), and how highly differentiated emotions and/or conscious effort can override them (see Devine and Sharp 2009; Fiske et al. 2009; Mackie and Devos 2000). Both neurocognitive and sociocultural paradigms struggle to establish a causal link between the psychological foundations of stereotypes and their social consequences because they presumably operate both implicitly and explicitly (see Bakanic 2009), and self-disclosure of bias and discriminatory behavior has obvious potential shortcomings (e.g., the *desirability* problem mentioned above).

One recent study presents a fascinating glimpse into the human propensity for social categorization based on accent, solely as an auditory criterion, as compared to race, which is visually salient. In a series of experiments, Kinzler (2008) was able to show that:

- infants had a basic preference for a native vs. a foreign accent as evidenced by length of gaze;
- 10-month-olds reached selectively for toys offered by native speakers, as opposed to non-native speakers, but the 'same-race' vs. 'other-race' factor did not make a difference as long as the speaker had a native accent;
- 5-year-olds who looked at photographs and heard speech samples of other children indicated a preference to befriend those with a native, rather than a foreign, accent, including native speakers of another race (intelligibility was not a factor).

Kinzler concludes that accent is a primary criterion for social categorization from infancy throughout childhood, more so than is race. Looking at older children, Nesdale and Rooney (1996) verify the salience of ethnic stereotypes associated with accent as early as 10 years of age.

With these important theoretical questions as a backdrop, this section spotlights a few practical contexts – broadcast media, the classroom, and customer service – to show how accent stereotypes in the public sphere often exaggerate cultural, educational, and social differences between foreign speaker and native listener (or consumer, as the case may be).

4.4.1 Media portrayals of non-native speakers

What children learn from the entertainment industry is to be comfortable with same and to be wary about other, and that language is a prime and ready diagnostic for this division between what is approachable and what is best left alone. (Lippi-Green 1997: 103)

Broadcast media institutions are powerful in part because they are pervasive. The Nielsen Company estimated that as of 2009, the average American spent about 5 hours a day watching television and about an hour a day on the internet (Nielsen Company 2009).[9] They also provide a vicarious experience, shaping our perceptions of people and events we would not otherwise encounter firsthand (Elliott 2003: 12). "[I]t is a given that media of all types sell more than the literal product of information, persuasion, or entertainment. From the choice of who or what counts as newsworthy to deciding which body images promote sales," media managers are largely responsible for what is presented as important and valuable (ibid.). In media studies this is termed *priming*, calling attention to particular issues while ignoring others, and *framing*, the persuasive power of media that causes its audience to adopt its stance by virtue of how it portrays an issue (Lim and Kim 2007: 317).

News outlets, the film and television industries, and internet outlets are all sources of information, misinformation, entertainment, and powerful pictorial imagery. As such, they have the power to suggest and reinforce consistent associations through sound and imagery. Imagine an evening news story that plays images of African-American youths on a street corner in baggy clothing while reading a story on crime rates, for example. Even if unintentional, the combination of factual information and superimposed imagery effectively lends credibility to a stereotype without referring to race per se (Abraham 2003). Assuming that such images and information are packaged in similar ways over time to the same audience, the cumulative effect may strengthen stereotypes (see DeFleur and Dennis (1998), cited in Merskin 2011; Gerbner (1969), cited in Lim and Kim 2007).

The entertainment industry is rife with stereotypical depictions of non-native speakers, exaggerated for dramatic or comic effect. A 1998 *New York Times* article, "Hollywood Now Plays Cowboys and Arabs," describes how Arab-American actors can suddenly find work in Hollywood if they have a dark beard, speak with an accent, and don't mind playing a terrorist, hijacker, or the like (Goldstein 1998). Of course, these stereotypes can themselves be parodied, such as in *The Simpsons* or *South Park*. Such (mis)representations of foreigners are a staple of comic and dramatic television shows, movies, and stand-up

---

[9] This average does not reflect the considerable – and quickly changing – age, regional, and gender differences in TV viewing and internet use.

routines, going back to Charlie Chan, a fictional Chinese-American detective in the 1920s, and continuing on through Sid Caesar, Peter Sellers, Eddie Murphy, George Lopez, and Dave Chapelle, among others. Today, the punch lines of stand-up comedian Dat Phan, a young Vietnamese-American, center on reenacted arguments with his Vietnamese mother whom he imitates with a strong and shrill accent, reduced English grammar, and a hard-headed insistence on the 'old ways'. Similarly stereotypical portrayals can be found by Eddie Murphy as an African prince in the movie *Coming to America*, and Sacha Baron Cohen in *Borat* and *Brüno*, where he plays a fictional Kazakh journalist and a gay Austrian fashionista, respectively. These films depict foreigners as nitwits whose accents and cultural naïveté lead them from one comic stumble to another.

Without exception, accent plays a crucial role in the overall effect of such ethnicized portrayals. One current critique speaks directly to this point: Chand's (2009) exegesis of Apu, the excessively polite and overqualified convenience store owner on the animated American satire, *The Simpsons*. Apu is voiced by Hank Azaria, who says he developed the Indian-sounding accent by mimicking a generic '7-eleven worker in Los Angeles' (Azaria 2004). Apu's accent merges /v/ and /w/ (e.g., *what* becomes *vhat*) and he misuses American idioms to the point of disfluency: "yes, yes, hot dog, hot dog, yes sir, no sir, maybe, OK," all of which reinforce the stereotype of an unintelligible Indian buffoon, according to Chand: *Simpsons* viewers are encouraged, through the repeated use of "particular linguistic and social practices, to forge a link" between language idiosyncrasies and peculiar cultural traits (2009: 398f.).

A well-known indictment of this phenomenon comes from Lippi-Green (1997), who roundly criticizes Disney films for imbuing foreign-accented characters with negative traits: too often they are poor, uneducated, criminal, drunken, oversexed, of low social station (e.g., butlers and housekeepers), or so "good-natured and dumb" that they cannot be taken seriously, such as the warthog Pumbaa in the film *The Lion King*. In Lippi-Green's view, the fact that these films are marketed to children makes their gendered and ethnicized stereotypes particularly insidious. "[E]ven when stereotyping is not overtly negative, it is confining and misleading" she writes. For example, male characters who speak American or British standard English have "the widest variety of life choices and possibilities available to them" while females and non-standard speakers occupy worlds that are "demonstrably smaller" by comparison (ibid.: 101).

Indeed, children may be more susceptible to certain stereotyped images (Oppliger 2007), yet Nabi (2007) insists we do not yet understand the psychological processes involved, and thus should not assume that audiences actually reorient their cognitive and emotional responses as a result of media stereotypes (ibid.: 137ff.). Social class, education, income level, gender, and age likely mediate how we react to such images. Individual personality is another relevant factor, since there is evidence that bias correlates to tendencies toward authoritarianism, right-wing political ideology, religious fundamentalism, and a 'social dominance orientation' (Hing and Zanna 2010).

Bakanic (2009) notes that as members of society, we are inundated with stereotyped representations; it is ultimately up to us to decide whether to act on them. Moreover, viewers likely choose programming that aligns with their established views, minimizing concern over a causal relationship (ibid.). On a positive note, Schiappa suggests that exposure to images from different sources actually complexifies our sense of foreigners, leading us beyond simplistic prejudices (2008: 3; see also Lee et al. (2004), cited in Mutz and Goldman 2010).

These ambiguities notwithstanding, one point deserves mention: To the extent that we accept stereotypes, they could well 'preset' our expectations of foreign-accented speakers' personal qualities. Chand (2009) gathered reaction data from 127 college students in California on traits such as friendliness, sincerity, and politeness as they listened to native Hindi speakers pronounce words with stereotypical phonetic–phonemic contrasts such as the *v–w* merger. Students did describe the *v–w* merger as a 'problematic' sign of disfluency and foreignness. Whether this constitutes prejudice is not overtly discussed, but some written comments were: "The first speaker was very cheerless ... and doesn't like the English language," and "Some words were said unclearly by the first speaker [Indian English] because of her accent, which in the modern world, can be seen as a signal of unreliability – if you can't understand the person, they're hard to work with" (ibid.: 403). In other words, this listener assumed a connection between accent and the speaker's reliability at work and *willingness* to be intelligible – an indication of bias, surely.

As the discussion throughout this chapter has demonstrated, those with a foreign accent considered of low prestige may face obstacles, either for reasons of comprehensibility or simply because communicative difficulty is anticipated. Sometimes a shift in the typical power balance is implied, leading to further potential for frustration, such as when a customer seeks assistance from non-native service personnel, or when a university student struggles to understand her foreign-born teacher. These two scenarios have been the center of some controversy and public outcry recently, and in the following sections we outline how businesses and academic institutions have responded to such complaints.

4.4.2 Call centers

Much has been made of the outsourcing of product orders and technical expertise for customers who place a call for English-language assistance and are (unknowingly) connected to a remote part of the world, often India or

Pakistan. A major American network, NBC (National Broadcasting Company) recently launched a new sitcom, *Outsourced* (adapted from a film by the same name), wherein an American manager must continually explain US culture, customs, and linguistic idioms to his call center staff in Mumbai. The humor plays off of the cultural ignorance of the boss and the naïveté of his employees with respect to American-style pragmatics.

In the real world, outsourced call centers offer an inexpensive way to provide 24/7 service across time zones, helping customers to solve software issues, "plan their vacations, track package deliveries, and sort out ATM card problems" (McKay 2004). But customers complain that agents are hard to understand, work from scripts, and use artificial-sounding American names. It is impossible to know whether this aggravation is a reaction to non-target-like phonological features, cross-cultural gaps, or resentment that service jobs are shipped overseas at a cost to local economies.

Companies that contract call center workers typically require workers to undergo accent reduction training and classes on culture – usually American. One such firm, Tucker International, promises the following to their business clients:

> By using a "surgical" approach to correcting the unique Indian difficulties in English pronunciation, speed, tone and style, graduates of Tucker's program sound quite different than when they started. Also, they are better able to relate to their American callers because Tucker's program teaches Indian Call Center Agents how to build rapport "American Style".[10]

Using videos, games, and interactive speaking practice in a 2-week, 80-hour program, Tucker focuses on (a) "accent neutralization and grammar improvement"; (b) listening skills to help agents recognize and respond to typical telephone routines; (c) American culture and norms for customer service. Another online company, American Accent Training, goes even further: "Trainees learn how Americans think, what is important to them, and how best to get them to respond in the desired way."[11] Before-and-after recordings of trainees are posted as proof of the program's efficacy. One accompanying description reads: "Nadia initially sounds nasal, and her speech is clipped and high pitched. She mispronounces, for example saying *woice* instead of *voice* and *wrtz* instead of *wrdz*. In her second recording she has a nice voice quality, and a good lilt to her intonation. Her pronunciation is very clear."

Several curricular elements are common in these accent training programs. Cowie (2007) gives an insider's glimpse into such a program in Bangalore called Excellence, where she spent six months working part-time alongside

---

[10] www.tuckerintl.com/callcntr_prog/indian_callcntr_detail.html
[11] www.americanaccent.com/callcenter.html

managers and trainers. Cowie describes the certification process and the curriculum, which consists of five modules: "customer care, culture, attitude, English, and phonetics" (ibid.: 319), with an emphasis on the first and last of these. Phonetics instruction targets British or American pronunciation to align with their largest customer bases, so that, for example, /t/ or intermedial flap /d/ is clear for words like *better*, and aspiration is heard on initial /p, t, k/. (Other important contrasts include retroflex /r/ in coda position[12] and velar /l/ for American pronunciation.) According to McKay's (2004) report on *24/7 Customer*, a call center training company in Bangalore, trainees are also taught pragmatic differences, such as the frequent use of *Sir* and *Ma'am* for British customers, and answering questions directly, including saying *no* to Americans, instead of hedging to be more polite. Workers even celebrate Halloween and Thanksgiving in the office to reinforce American culture. A Microsoft call center encourages workers to listen to National Public Radio, in addition to action movies and sitcoms (Dudley 2004).

By Cowie's account, clients most often described their needs as 'accent neutralization,' defined as an international, region-less, sound. But several controversial issues arise in this regard. One is the extent to which Inner Circle standards are imposed on local standards in ways that degrade or devalue them (Chand 2009); another is the degree to which a trainee is expected to take on a new identity in the course of their work, thus reinforcing an 'ideology of nativeness' that views non-native speakers as unintelligible (Chand 2009; Rahman 2009).

So, is the point of call centers to fool the customer into thinking that they have reached an American? McKay says that workers at 24/7 Customer are never encouraged to fake an accent, such as a Southern US dialect. But Cowie notes that some managers ask trainees to speak in their new accents even outside the classroom, and Rahman (2009) describes hallway posters in a call center training company in Pakistan urging its employees to stop speaking Urdu if they really want to improve their English.

Cameron (2001) disparages call centers for encouraging false biographies to go with trainees' Americanized names – a successful deception, she says, because customers cannot see their interlocutors: "[T]he voice is the only clue the customer has to the identity and location of the person she is speaking to. If customers could actually see C. J. Suman, they would have much more difficulty believing her claim to be the all-American Susan Sanders" (ibid.: 83). In Cameron's view, we believe that voices "are the willed and authentic expression of an individual's 'true' identity" (ibid.), whereas this kind of passing is a temporary performance, limited to a specific context.

---

[12] See Sharma (2005) and Rahman (2009) for more details on various phonetic, phonemic, and allophonic variations between American, British, Indian, and Pakistani English.

The motivation for the call center employee is great since managers tend to remove workers whose customers complain about their 'inadequate language skills' (Rahman 2009: 246). Cameron thus characterizes the push for accent neutralization as corporate subordination that privileges 'the brand' above all else (2000: 324).

The main impetus behind such practices is presumably not to deceive customers so much as make them comfortable by approximating what they expect to hear, and avoiding any miscommunication due to poor comprehensibility. The client companies cannot know how much experience a given customer has with any accent, much less what kinds of a priori attitudes might come into play, but they do have a vested interest in mitigating potential problems. From their perspective, a 'neutral accent' policy is the most economical (if ill-defined) approach. Insofar as it does imply a negative evaluation, this is not strictly directed at foreigners; non-standard regional and social accents in the UK and US would be seen as similarly bad for business. Nevertheless, those in power still define (if not embody) the models for 'correctness' and worth. Language thus takes center stage in a commodification process (Heller 2003: 476, cited in Rahman 2009), which only seems to be increasing with globalization (see Cameron 2000). An interesting twist on this phenomenon is the problem of international managers who interact with American subordinates. Here, the roles of power are reversed, but the cultural and linguistic divides must still be bridged (see Rubin et al. 1991).

4.4.3 The international teaching assistant controversy

The instructor does have a problem with English. His accents are on the wrong syllables. This is a distraction ...
I believe that he is capable of teaching economics but that his speech is poor.
I believe that the instructor's unfamiliarity with the English language prohibits him from expressing clear examples and analogies which are a very good learning aid. I also find myself having to concentrate on each word instead of the entire concept he is trying to communicate.
When I first realized my economics teacher was foreign, I was upset. After the first day, I was seriously deciding on getting out but now I wouldn't. I was hesitant about the ability of a foreigner to teach American economics, but I think [Abe] has done a good job. He isn't that hard to understand. I stuck on and I'm glad.
I enjoy foreign instructors very much. I find that having to listen to them more carefully helps me quite a bit ... The language gives others a chance to learn accents and it is interesting, I think. I feel students can and will get adjusted to the accent. (excerpted comments from students at the University of Texas at Austin, in Orth 1982)

The Institute of International Education reports that in 2009–10, about 3.5 percent of the 19.5 million students at US institutions of higher learning were international students,[13] with nearly half of those studying at graduate level. California ranks first in the list of US states to host them and engage them as teaching staff (King 1998), and in California, as elsewhere, the English-language proficiency and comprehensibility of international students employed as teaching assistants (ITAs) has received national attention – much of it negative.

During the 1980s and 1990s, some states across the US enacted statutes either mandating or encouraging greater control over the language proficiency of college and university instructors (King 1998: 204). At most institutions of higher learning in the US, international students must pass the Test of English as a Foreign Language (TOEFL)[14] to gain admission, and speaking is one of the assessment areas. Nevertheless, students often complain about ITAs, citing accent as the source of the problem. A *New York Times* article, "Unclear on American Campus: What the Foreign Teacher Said" (June 24, 2005) reported that complaints are particularly acute in subjects such as math, engineering, and the physical sciences where faculty shortages abound (King 1998). As the article describes, it is difficult to separate legitimate complaints from a possible issue with intolerance, not to mention anxiety about the subject matter itself.

As with intelligibility more generally, individual differences like familiarity with a given accent and the topic itself matter, but in this context, the ITA is often responsible for the student's mastery of the material and overall course grade. This undoubtedly sets the student up for greater anxiety. Parents and administrators sometimes get involved, and academic institutions feel pressure to develop policies and programs to prevent such controversies.

Spurred on by legislation in 22 states, many large universities are now offering preparatory courses for those who will become ITAs. Accent is one focus of such courses, as is awareness training on cultural differences, educational practices, and interactional style. Meanwhile, scholars have tried to tease apart comprehensibility from student expectations and stereotypes, which "can materially interfere with information uptake and exert a deleterious effect on learning" (Kang 2008: 187). But as the student comments above show, reactions to ITAs are not just about language proficiency and accent; they reveal preconceived attitudes about the value of exposure to foreigners and their potential to be effective teachers.

---

[13] The top three home countries of international students are China, India, and South Korea at 19 percent, 15 percent and 10 percent, respectively.

[14] The Test of Spoken English, originally designed to test the proficiency of international students who would hold teaching assistantships (Orth 1982), was eventually expanded to many institutional uses, but was discontinued as of March 31, 2010. The TOEFL has largely taken its place. The IELTS, or International English Language Testing System by Cambridge is another internationally recognized test for academic contexts.

Gill (1994) suggests a link between TA–lecturer accent and information recall in the classroom, but this could be due to attitudes that predispose the student's measure of attention. Rubin and Smith (1990) examined lecturer ethnicity and lecture topic as influential for attitudes toward ITAs and for comprehensibility ratings. Ninety-two undergraduate students in the US listened to a 4-minute text on either a scientific or a humanities-oriented topic while a photograph of a female 'lecturer' – either Anglo or Asian – was projected in front of them. Participants also completed a cloze test for comprehension, filled out a survey on their experiences with non-native speakers, and ranked their perceived similarity to the speaker regarding attitudes, appearance, and values. In addition, the researchers manipulated moderate vs. strong degrees of accent (produced by two native Chinese speakers fluent in English) to see whether this difference affected either attitudes or comprehensibility. Highly accented speech was perceived as 'more Asian' in both subject matters, and degree of accent correlated negatively to perceptions of teaching competence, but comprehensibility was not significantly affected. Importantly, comprehension and attitudes did correlate with the number of courses previously taken with an ITA. Also of interest is the finding that 42 percent of the participants had dropped a class at some point because the lecturer was foreign, and 57 percent felt that their grades had suffered because of the poor comprehensibility of an ITA (see also Kang 2008). In a comparable 1992 study, Rubin showed that even when listening to a standard American-English accent, listeners reported hearing a foreign accent if they were simultaneously shown a picture of an Asian woman, and this association correlated significantly to perceptions of teaching competence.

Reflecting on these results, Rubin and Smith recommend that universities train students on how to be better listeners rather than expecting ITAs to remediate their accents. To verify whether such awareness training might ameliorate "deeply held prejudices," Rubin (1992) asked 25 undergrads to observe two classes taught by ITAs, and afterwards provide them with informal feedback in the presence of a facilitator. Attitudes were measured before and after the experiment, but no changes were apparent.

In a more fully developed study addressing this same principle, Kang (2008) asked 63 undergraduates to rate ITA speech excerpted from a class lecture by Japanese, Korean, Russian, Arabic, Chinese, Nepali, and Sri Lankan ITAs. Comparing these samples to those of native speakers via acoustic analyses, Kang found significant differences in speech rate, length of utterance, and patterns of phrasal stress, pause, and intonation. These differences correlated significantly to listener ratings of accentedness, comprehensibility, instructional competence, and overall language proficiency. Motivated by the idea that working toward a common goal can benefit attitudes, Kang then asked half of the participants to complete an hour-long, informal interaction with an ITA, and afterwards rate speech samples again. This 'awareness training' phase did correlate to improved comprehensibility and accent ratings, but it did not affect perceptions of instructional competence. (A multiple regression test to compare the relative strength of attitudes, exposure to non-native speakers, and phonological criteria would have been a valuable addition to Kang's conclusions.) It seems that students can learn to be better listeners, but may not adjust their attitudes as a result of greater exposure to ITAs.

Kang's study is an important reminder that phonological features are important for understanding ITA speech. Holding exposure to non-native speech and familiarity with the topic constant, Hahn (2004) substantiated the significance of syllable and phrasal stress for ITAs' comprehensibility. And Pickering's work provides additional support for the importance of intonation and pause structure (2001 and 2004). Comparing fundamental frequencies and intonation curves for native and non-native TAs who covered equivalent science material, her statistical analyses and observational data suggest the following:

- American TAs' tonal patterns have both referential and affective value: Their use of tonal shift signals topic boundaries, marks meaning contrasts, and establishes rapport with students. Specifically, native speakers begin a new topic with relatively high pitch, use mid-pitch to continue a topic, and lower pitch when concluding or making side comments. ITAs exhibit a limited pitch range by comparison and do not consistently use pitch to mark discourse boundaries. Their comparatively flat tone and lack of pitch movement hinders the delivery of information, obscuring meaning in some cases. Moreover, it leaves students with the impression that the ITA is unsympathetic.
- Pause structure – another feature that draws attention to semantic and pragmatic boundaries (e.g. signaling topic vs. comment, shifts in topic, etc.) – is similarly off-target for the ITAs, who often do not allow time for students to respond or ask questions, as native speakers do to confirm comprehension.

In short, when tone does not effectively mark syntactic and semantic boundaries, listeners must "continually adjust their representation of the text" in an attempt to predict what will follow (2001: 249), and this inevitably reduces comprehension.

Pickering speculates that ITAs are unaware of their tonal patterns and their overall 'monologic' discourse style. In the US, students expect a more dialogic style, and the strategic use of rising and falling tone signals cooperation and negotiation between teacher and students. Pickering therefore advocates overt training on the discursive and pedagogical effects of tone so that ITAs can develop a style in line with US educational practice, given that the cultural divide in teaching style exacerbates the comprehensibility issue. ITAs must negotiate a new identity through interaction with their students, sometimes addressing the comprehensibility issue head-on, and finding other ways of assessing their own performance (Williams 2011; see also Golombek and Jordan 2005). This is more effective, Williams asserts, when they encourage questions, use frequent comprehension checks, and openly discuss their linguistic and cultural background with students. Such a proactive approach positions both parties to take responsibility for the quality of classroom communication.

At present, there is no universal standard for screening ITAs at English-speaking institutions, and pronunciation is not analyzed in any systematic, in-depth way (Isaacs 2008). The University of Iowa takes a multi-pronged approach to this issue: Prospective ITAs must first pass a language proficiency test and then complete a mock classroom instruction test, which involves explaining a concept in their field to a roomful of students and instructors. The ITA must also "show awareness of teacher–student relationships in the United States (which frequently are very different from those in the student's country), and show interest in the subject and in students as learners. Only when the student passes that test is he or she certified to teach" (University of Iowa 2000). The university's Center for Teaching works with all teaching staff on strategies to ameliorate communication problems, such as making good use of visual aids, slowing down while speaking, and avoiding facing the chalkboard while talking.

Comprehensibility is a two-way street, Isaacs (2008) reminds us, and students need to be willing listeners who can work around a foreign accent by seeking assistance outside of class, providing feedback as appropriate, and so on. The University of Iowa is one institution that explicitly makes these suggestions in its student handbook. Beyond the university, after all, students are bound to encounter many unfamiliar accents.

Two interesting studies offer an important counterpoint to the negative perspectives cited thus far. The first comes from Chuang (2010), who asked 66 undergraduate students, half native speakers and half non-native, to describe their attitudes toward ITAs and their foreign accents. Both groups expressed mostly positive attitudes, and those who described themselves as 'interculturally aware' were significantly more likely to do so. The second study, by Derwing et al. (2002), set out to prove that regular exposure to recorded speech, along with explicit instruction on the features of a specific accent (here: Vietnamese-accented English) and cross-cultural communication lessons, would improve comprehension of foreign-accented speakers and improve student attitudes toward accented speech in general. One experimental group received cross-cultural training only and the other received both cross-cultural training and accent instruction (a control group was included, and all three groups were subject to a pre-test and post-test). No significant group differences were apparent for comprehension on either sentence-length or paragraph-length listening tasks after the 8-week experiment, as all groups actually improved. However, both experimental groups indicated greater levels of empathy for immigrants, and those who were trained on the specific features of Vietnamese-accented English expressed greater confidence in their ability to interact successfully with ESL speakers. Of those in the accent instruction group, 85 percent cited a direct benefit in terms of their interactions with non-native speakers, saying they better understood how to listen carefully and appreciate the difficulties that speakers of other languages have mastering English phonology. This suggests that awareness-raising can be beneficial for native–non-native interactions, even for more formal settings like the classroom.

4.5 Conclusion: accent and assimilation

There is an essential question that underlies the research on L2 phonology and preoccupies pedagogical and sociocultural discussions today: Does having a foreign accent in a second language really matter? There are some cases where sounding native does make a difference, either for the learner's personal goals or for more institutional purposes such as high-level diplomatic work. For many other contexts the native speaker ideal is outdated and impractical, particularly in regions that have adopted a second language deeply and broadly enough that it becomes intrinsic to the local (or even national) culture. But let us also acknowledge the need for a baseline of sorts to ensure comprehensibility between native speakers and L2 users, and between L2 users across locales. Let us also remember that teachers are in a bind to establish some commonality in second language instruction and assessment across learning environments (more in Chapter 6), and many learners express a desire to sound native, whether or not that is seen as reasonable or laudable.

If intelligibility is a more realistic target for L2 phonological acquisition, coming up with a unitary definition of it has never been more of a challenge. Levis cautions that "the intuitive appeal of intelligibility ... masks a number of difficulties," not the least of which is that "judgments of understanding are particularly subject to contamination, especially from social attitudes" (2006: 253). Throughout this chapter, we have seen that attitudes toward accent typically have to do with social dimensions like ethnicity and class, education, gender, and religious background. These criteria inform our expectations for a speaker's language fluency and even a host of personal traits, ranging from kindness and trustworthiness to intelligence and competence. This phenomenon will not likely fade away as society becomes more multilingual and multicultural. It seems that differentiating ourselves from others along group membership lines is part of our cognitive and social make-up, and discomfort, or even prejudice, is sometimes associated with this tendency.

From the standpoint of theory, many questions remain concerning the construct of intelligibility, beginning with the relative importance of linguistic factors vs. non-linguistic factors intrinsic to its definition. We have noted that intonation, stress, segmental and syllable duration, consonant and vowel quality, pitch range, and even speech rate and pause structures are relevant criteria, as is grammar. L1 also plays a part in what we attend to as listeners. Those features that are salient in our own mother tongue may cause the greatest difficulty for comprehension when they are inaccurately produced in non-native speech (e.g., syllable stress in English). We have also cited an array of non-linguistic factors that play a role, including context, topic familiarity, accent familiarity, and, last but not least, an interlocutor's willingness to share the communicative burden through accommodation. The non-native speaker may have limited facility with style-shifting, not to mention less awareness of cultural and pragmatic norms that convey meaning and move the conversation along smoothly. In that vein, we have cited evidence to suggest that it is possible to increase tolerance and comprehension of any foreign accent with conscious effort. There is much to learn about how, and why, some interlocutors put forth that effort while others do not.

In this age of societal multilingualism, who sounds foreign is ultimately defined locally and negotiated between individual interlocutors, one context at a time. Having an 'ideal' accent is thus about acceptability and currency, as much as it is about intelligibility (Davies 2000: 93). On this basis, many decry the emphasis on nativeness as an ideology designed to preserve the status quo for centers of economic and political power. The long-standing focus on nativeness surely engenders insecurity among those who may not feel like legitimate speakers of the target language (Golombek and Jordan 2005).

In her essay "No Language to Die In," Greta Hofmann Nemiroff (2000) reflects on how she continues to negotiate a multilingual identity in Quebec even though she has lived there for several decades, arriving as a child from Germany. Nemiroff says she learned French and Quebec culture "through inclination, not through legislation" (ibid.: 19), but she is always asked *"What are your origins?"* when she speaks French, and feels slightly at odds as an English speaker as well:

If German inhabits my body, English clothes me in a well-tailored and somewhat elegant costume. Often I dream in English; I speak it with my children, at work, and with many of my friends.... It works for me in numerous contexts, but I dare not get too attached to it since I have been constructed as an 'other' both within and because of it. (ibid.)

This tangible unease is most prominent for first-generation immigrants, but is typically unknown to the third generation due to the process sociolinguists call 'three-generation language death'. Where the first generation may or may not acquire fluency in the language of the host country, the second generation learns it in school and tends to use it with friends as well as siblings. Typically, use of the mother tongue is limited to the home, and while some in the second generation remain functionally bilingual, many others become L2 dominant as they assimilate socially and economically (see Tse 2001). By the third generation, the mother tongue may serve as a touchstone for cultural identity only. At that point, connections to the homeland have typically faded, and there is little question of language dominance; the assimilation process is complete.

In this three-generation scenario, L2 use and literacy are the foundations upon which assimilation builds, but those who arrive as adults are ensured of neither, and they usually retain a recognizable accent.[15] Some work to change their accents even as they struggle to identify the features that mark them as non-native (see Derwing 2003). Many are motivated by a sense of shame and frustration over not being understood after living many years in-country (House 1999). This common feeling was brought to light years ago by Schumann (1978) in his account of *language shock*, the inability to express oneself in the second language with the same facility as the mother tongue. At the workplace, shame and frustration can have serious consequences, according to Sondra Thiederman:

When educated, intelligent, and accomplished people who rely on their ability to demonstrate those virtues verbally are unable to make themselves understood, they appear to others to be slow, unimaginative, and uneducated. Thousands of foreign-born professionals who are entering the United States today are experiencing this difficulty. Having been successful back home, they come here only to appear inarticulate and inexperienced – perceptions which often generate feelings of inadequacy and low self-esteem. (1991: 37)

This negative appraisal is not just internal, as this discussion has made clear. Hyman's (2002) study verifies that degree of accent, not just the accent itself, plays into perceptions of employability. Of the 51 managers polled, 76 percent said they would be unlikely to recommend hiring an applicant for a management level position if they did not favor his or her speech style. To the extent that accent affects whether we are taken seriously, receive deserving praise and promotions in the workplace, and establish close contacts in the

---

[15] Comparing language use 'other than English' in the home from 1980 up to 2007 in the US, there is a dramatic change apparent – a gain of 140 percent over that 27-year period, from just over 23 million people in 1980, to 47 million in 2000, to well over 55 million in 2007. The 2000 Census asked respondents to estimate how well each non-native English speaker in the home speaks English. Fifty-five percent responded 'very well,' but the number of those who reported 'less than very well' grew considerably, from 4.8 percent in 1980 to 8.1 percent in 2000, and they are distributed unevenly across geographical regions and across native languages (Spanish and Chinese top the list, with other languages far fewer in number).

broader community, its psychological and social significance can hardly be overstated.

Today's US immigrants are more ethnically diverse, and more educated, than at any previous time (Sengstock 2009). One-third of the US naturalized citizens and non-citizen immigrants over the age of 25 have college degrees according to US Census Bureau statistics (2008 and 2009), and the economic differences between first and second generation immigrants is substantial: 32 percent of the first generation earn $50,000 or more yearly, but that figure rises to 47 percent in the second generation. These immigrants will predictably assimilate to American society, linguistically and culturally, in incremental fashion (Sengstock 2009). Language use and language dominance are good indicators for how quickly that process takes hold. Along the way, many will encounter stereotypes and false assumptions, positive or negative, based on their accent. Some native speakers will be resistant to speaking with them as a result; others will simply let it pass when comprehensibility suffers (House 1999), not necessarily out of malice or a sense of superiority, but in some cases to allow the non-native speaker to save face, or preserve dignity. The research shows that native speakers tend toward greater leniency when an accent is strong, and feel greater empathy when they are aware of the difficulties of acquiring a new accent. Informal settings, where the stakes are psychologically low, are most likely to engender tolerance.

The field of SLA today is gradually redefining its theoretical mission, and in so doing, supports a more inclusive vision of what it means to learn another language, both socially and psychologically. While a specific agenda has yet to be delineated, there is a far greater appreciation for the connections between oral fluency and identity, and phonology is essential to both. With that in mind, this chapter has sought to demonstrate that the power of accent lies in its multiple spheres of relevance; it operates on a psycholinguistic level, it is essential to communication, and it has great symbolic value socially. If we orient ourselves primarily by in-group/out-group distinctions (Mackie et al. 2000), it is easy to see why accent triggers such differentiated responses; it offers an immediate basis for us to locate ourselves relative to others. In the words of Parrino, "We define ourselves by what we say, but more notably by how we say it. ... Our pronunciation allies or isolates us from a community of speakers. Even when we whisper, it screams out at our audience. It precedes our intentions and completes our utterances" (1998: 171). This is of great consequence in formal spheres, as is the case in less formal ones. We therefore turn our attention in the next chapter to the workplace and the courts to examine the legal implications of speaking with an accent.

5 Accent and the law

> For most people, accent is a dustbin category; it includes all the technical meanings, and a more general and subjective one: Accent is how the other speaks.
>
> Lippi-Green 1994: 165

> Everyone has an accent, but when an employer refuses to hire a person "with an accent" they are referring to a hidden norm of non-accent – a linguistic impossibility, but a socially constructed reality.
>
> Matsuda 1991: 1361

To the layperson, Lippi-Green (1994) writes, accent refers not just to phonology, but to language fluency, language style, and, ultimately, to identity. Thus, when we claim not to understand someone because of her accent, the actual issue may be *who she is*, i.e., what she represents socially. From Chapter 4 we have seen that comprehension declines if a listener believes she is hearing the voice of a non-native speaker, whether or not this is true – a powerful illustration of how bias can act as a filter on how we hear others. We noted also that in professional contexts, a neutral or 'standard' accent is often favored when the speaker's role has symbolic significance. (Recall the anecdote of the Massachusetts town where parents, the local school board, and the immigrant mayor all mobilized to keep a foreign-accented teacher out of the classroom.)

This chapter hopes to show that our tendency to favor or disfavor certain accents takes on real significance in formal, public contexts where it is associated with educational background, competence, intelligence, and authority. Equally important are common perceptions of accent as an indicator of likeability, trustworthiness, and credibility. Marketing and sales make their living off such associations, manipulating accent for everything from a car manufacturer's pitch on safety features (best in Standard American or British pronunciation, no doubt) to a cowboy's folksy endorsement for salsa made 'anywhere but' New York City. It is therefore important to think of accent in more consequential, collective terms, beyond isolated interactions, and even

beyond the individual L2 user's sense of self. To that end, this chapter is guided by the following questions:
- What are some practical consequences of sounding foreign?
- Is accent a proxy for various forms of discrimination, and if so, are some groups more susceptible than others?
- Does the non-native speaker have any protection under the law against accent-based discrimination?
- How do legal understandings of accent differ from linguistic ones, and what are the consequences of this disparity?

As a touchstone for negative attitudes toward foreigners, accent is front and center in some forms of discrimination, passed off as concerns about comprehensibility and language ability more generally. Beginning with the domains of housing and employment, we show how this manifests itself, before exploring the details of accent discrimination as a sometimes-defensible action under the law. Finally, we examine how ambiguous definitions of accent and attitudes about what is 'standard' have played a hand in case history.

5.1   Linguistic profiling

Research shows that job applicants are judged as differentially desirable, based on auditory stimuli alone; no actual in-person interviews need be conducted for some prospective employers to ascertain who is a desirable applicant and who is not. Beyond the lab setting, these kinds of judgments take shape according to this typical (actual) scenario:

Mehdi Najari, an Iranian living in Canada, applied by phone for a traffic controller job advertised in a Victoria newspaper (as recounted in Munro 2003). Najari was told that the available positions were all filled even though he called just a few minutes after phone lines for applicants opened. This response seemed suspicious to Najari, who asked a standard-accented neighbor to call in about the same position. She did so an hour and a half later and was told there were still openings, but then stated she was calling on behalf of a friend from another country. The response was then reversed, and the neighbor was told to call back in a few months. The local courts awarded Najari $2,000 for humiliation. (ibid.: 46)

Verifying this phenomenon in an experimental setting, Henry and Ginzberg (1985, cited in Cargile 2000) asked Anglos and individuals with various ethnic accents to make phone inquiries about jobs advertised in a newspaper, then compared responses received. In some cases, the Anglo callers were invited for interviews while others were told that the job had been filled.

Where such treatment is established practice, it is referred to as *linguistic profiling* – the use of speech characteristics to identify a speaker's race or ethnicity, religion, or social class, typically resulting in the denial of a specific opportunity or service. The term has long been used in clinical practice to describe the diagnosis of speech disorders, but it was John Baugh, a sociolinguist and Stanford University professor, who applied it to the practice of denying jobs and housing based on racially salient speech patterns (see Baugh 2003).[1] Though illegal, this is not uncommon. As socialized beings, we have tremendous sensitivity to acoustic features that distinguish speakers' background characteristics, and it may therefore be all but impossible for us to 'turn off' our propensity to categorize others accordingly.

Roger Shuy has verified that non-linguists can accurately and reliably 'hear race' based on a speech sample of about 20 seconds (2008), and Purnell et al. (1999) confirm that listeners can do so upon hearing just the word *hello*. Shuy has shown, however, that this ability has much to do with the speaker's social class: those at the upper-middle and upper-class ends of the spectrum sound more alike than not, regardless of race, thus the ability to hear race disappears in the absence of class-related dialect features.[2] Such fine acoustic attunement to class/race features would not apply to foreign accents unless the listener had sufficient awareness of dialectal differences that represent those social categories. Most likely, we recognize 'foreign' vs. 'native' first, and from there, determine broad categories like 'Spanish-sounding,' 'Asian-sounding,' etc., although misattributions certainly occur (see Chapter 4; also Sato 1998, cited in Munro 2003).

To some extent, our ability to categorize others on the basis of a few phonological features, absent any visual information, is remarkable. But it is arguably a fine line between that skill and the proclivity to judge another's status or worth. Baugh insists that few witnesses in linguistic profiling cases admit to using accent as a means to identify the ethnicity of others (2003: 160). This recalls Cukor-Avila's finding that some listeners are reluctant to assign personality traits on the basis of accent (1988). Conscious reluctance notwithstanding, drawing social distinctions based on speech patterns seems to be an inevitable by-product of socialization.

Most vexing for researchers – and for jurisprudence – is the accent–ethnicity connection in practice. Are they inextricably intertwined in our minds as we ascertain a stranger's employability, competence, desirability, and so on? One case that highlights this connection is *Sirajullah* v. *Illinois State Medical Inter-Insurance Exchange* (1989).[3] Sirajullah was a Bangladeshi-born orthopedic surgeon denied medical malpractice insurance on the grounds that his accent would impede communication with patients and make him more susceptible to malpractice claims. Here, the court sided with the insurance company, saying

---

[1] The Fair Housing Act (Title VIII of the Civil Rights Act of 1968) protects against discrimination in housing based on race, color, sex, religion, and national origin (familial status and physical disability were added in the Fair Housing Amendments Act of 1988, 42, USC 3601, et seq.). http://portal.hud.gov/hudportal/HUD?src=/program_offices/fair_housing_equal_opp/FHLaws/yourrights
[2] See also the early work of Trudgill and Labov.   [3] No. 86C 8688, 1989 US Dist. LEXIS 9113.

this was a reasonable basis for denying insurance, and as such, it did not constitute racial or national origin discrimination (see Section 5.3). Remarkably, the presiding judge noted that the defendants had "rejected 19 other applicants of varying races and nationalities in part because they had foreign accents that prevented them from communicating effectively." In other words, the insurance exchange made a policy of discriminating against foreign-accented individuals, so Sirajullah could not claim disparate treatment if other similar applicants were treated in the same manner. The judge's comment actually denied *any* connection between accent and race, and made several references to Sirajullah's accent as a "language disability," adding, "courts will not interfere with a bona fide business decision even if it is misguided or socially repugnant."

The denial of services is thus one manifestation of accent-based discrimination. Largely out of the public eye, applicants for jobs may also be screened according to how they speak, since suitability is commonly judged on that basis (Yuracko 2006). We turn now to how this can affect an applicant's likelihood of landing, and keeping, a job.

5.2 Accent, employability, and earnings

The US Immigration Reform and Control Act of 1986 (IRCA) prohibited employers from knowingly hiring 'unauthorized' workers. It required them to verify employment eligibility for all job applicants with some kind of official documentation (US passport, social security card, birth certificate, etc.). Upon passage, the US Congress feared that to avoid possible sanctions employers would unfairly deny job opportunities to eligible applicants who looked or sounded foreign. In March 1990 the General Accounting Office (GAO) submitted to Congress the final of three reports on whether IRCA had led to an increase in discriminatory hiring practices.[4] Data were gathered from an anonymous survey (N = 9,491) and an audit (N = 360) of employers across different regions. The GAO surreptitiously sent in pairs of applicants closely matched for qualifications, one a 'foreign-appearing, foreign-sounding' Hispanic and the other an Anglo with a neutral accent. In addition, the GAO interviewed 300 foreign and non-foreign job seekers across the US to compare the treatment they received during job searches. Data analyses confirmed that 10 percent of all employers discriminate on the basis of national origin. The GAO report noted that some employers admitted to regularly disregarding anyone with a "foreign appearance or accent," or only asking those applicants for

---

[4] *Immigration Reform. Employer Sanctions and the Question of Discrimination* (1990). General Accounting Office, Report to the Congress. The report concluded that discrimination had increased as a result of the law, and recommended streamlined verification and employer education on how to comply with anti-discrimination laws.

documentation – a profiling strategy, in other words. Indeed, the majority of complaints following the passage of IRCA came from documented workers, 83 percent of whom were Hispanic. Fifty-eight percent of all complaints concerned the refusal of employers to accept valid documents. This occurred across industry types and regions, indicating disproportionately negative treatment for Hispanic job applicants (ibid.: 43f.).

This disparity begs the question of whether accent-related discrimination is actually racial at its core, or results indirectly from external forces like IRCA or similar laws and policies. (These are just two of many possibilities.) Either way, this would mean that such decisions are not about comprehensibility, but something else entirely. We might also wonder whether such discrimination occurs more commonly at the hiring stage than subsequently, and whether it has any impact on actual earnings for those already hired.

Chapter 4's conclusion cited evidence of managers who downgraded the employability and management potential of accented speakers according to both degree of accent and type (to wit: Asian-accented applicants were seen as having greater management potential than those with a Russian accent). In reality, Asian workers in the US earn more on average than whites, Latinos and blacks, according to the Bureau of Labor Statistics, and this holds for positions at both ends of the skills spectrum, i.e., professional and non-professional positions.[5] Thus, there are documented disparities in earnings across ethnic groups. It is unclear whether accent plays any direct role, or whether legitimate criteria like educational background and professional qualifications are at the root of it. Cultural stereotypes could also be a factor.

Focusing on the impact of accent for Latinos, Dávila et al. (1993) contend that Latinos in the US suffer a significant wage gap compared to their non-Hispanic, white, and other non-native counterparts (e.g., Italians and Germans were the comparison groups in their study). They maintain that employers negatively associate Spanish accents with legal status as follows: the stronger the accent, the more likely a worker is to be undocumented, thus indicating a higher risk for labor turnover. Lower wages for such workers probably reflect this calculation, they say, and the employer's anticipation that communication barriers will eventually arise between coworkers, thereby decreasing productivity. Based on earnings data alone, these are not verifiable connections, but they highlight additional ways that accent may play into hiring and wages.

Pursuing the idea that different ethnic groups are judged according to different standards, Cargile (2000) presented 71 US college undergraduates with job descriptions and asked them to judge employability for each job type while listening to English-speaking Chinese vs. Anglo (mock) applicants, but overall,

---

[5] *Labor Force Characteristics by Race and Ethnicity* (2009, No. 1026). US Department of Labor and US Bureau of Labor Statistics. Retrieved from http://searchworks.stanford.edu/view/6742390

no significant differences were apparent. A broader comparison comes from Kalin and Rayko's (1978) study in which 203 university students evaluated the suitability of 10 job applicants based on recorded (fictional) biographies outlining their backgrounds and qualifications. Five of the (mock) applicants were of English-Canadian background, and they were rated significantly more suitable for the higher-status jobs of foreman and industrial mechanic. The other five were Italian, Greek, Portuguese, West African, and Slovak speakers of English – all judged more fitting for assembly line and custodial jobs. Significant correlations were also found between ethnicity and perceived honesty, reliability and 'promise of future progress'. The authors had closely matched lexical and grammatical fluency for the applicants by providing them with read-aloud scripts to point toward a racial, as opposed to linguistic, basis for these disparities. Similar findings come from Rey (1977), where white, black, and Cuban employers judged the employability and social and educational status of job applicants from the same three backgrounds. White applicants were rated highest overall, followed by Cuban, then African-American applicants.

Cultural and/or ethnic stereotypes undoubtedly influence employability perceptions, but *degree* of accent should also be taken into account, as this could be associated with poor language fluency overall. Only a few studies actually control the spoken text to equalize lexical and morphosyntactic fluency (as in Kalin and Rayko) in order to ascertain whether accent is the operative judgment criterion. An even smaller number directly test degree of accent as a factor in employability judgments. In the Rey study, Cubans with the strongest accents were rated lowest in terms of perceived social and educational background as well as employability. Also noteworthy is Carlson and McHenry (2006), which asked 60 human resource personnel to rate both comprehensibility and employability on a 7-point scale for 3 different groups of job applicants: Asian, Latino, and African American. All applicants read from a semi-guided text describing their qualifications for an entry-level position. There were no significant differences in employability judgments for the 'minimal' accent group, regardless of ethnicity, even though the Asian group was found significantly less comprehensible than the other two. Under the 'maximal' accent condition, there was a rank order preference: Spanish-accented speakers were found significantly more comprehensible *and* more employable than the others. This contradicts familiar references to the low status of Spanish-accented workers as compared to Asian Americans, but perhaps a familiarity advantage was at work here.

These studies suggest that accent-related discrimination at the hiring phase could well have long-term implications for professional advancement. This works for regional accents as it does for foreign ones, as shown by Markley (reported in Kolsti 2000), who found that hiring personnel prefer 'neutral' sounding American accents for positions that require technical expertise or customer contact, even when all (mock) applicants described similar qualifications for the job.

The accent–employability issue is unlikely to fade as the face of the American workforce rapidly changes. A 2011 report by the Brookings Institution[6] estimates that 1 in 7 US residents, and 1 in 6 US workers, is foreign born. Their level of education has been steadily increasing since the early 1990s, with about 30 percent now holding the equivalent of a bachelor's degree or greater. During the same period the immigrant population defined as "low-skilled," with a high-school diploma or less, has declined, from nearly 33 percent to nearly 28 percent, and is now outnumbered by the college-educated immigrant population by at least 25 percent. The vast majority speak English or transition to it relatively quickly (Crawford 1992; Tse 2001), whether because of education received before they arrived, the pressures of the US job market, citizenship laws requiring a basic knowledge of English (Piatt 1993: 16), or other motives related to assimilation.

Far more research is needed to carefully assess the connections between employability and accent, as most of these data are based on hypothetical situations, and the dynamics are complex, to say the least. First, language ability must be separated from accent when investigating the various criteria affecting employability judgments. Second, degree of accent must be taken into account, since it may be more salient than accent type. Third, detailed documentation is needed regarding job types, so that skill levels and qualifications associated with specific ethnic groups can be separated from accent-related criteria like comprehensibility and degree of accent. Most importantly, more awareness of these issues is needed among those who make hiring decisions. Such judgments presumably do not stop at the hiring phase but underlie promotion and retention decisions as well, with claims of incomprehensibility or insufficient language skills used as a defense. Tackling the legitimacy of such claims has proven to be a challenge, as the next section will show.

5.3 Challenges to accent in the workplace

Keeping in mind the question of whether some groups encounter more accent discrimination than others, we consider Lippi-Green's (1997) look at relevant complaints filed in the US federal and state courts from 1972–94. According to her tally, 10 cases were settled in court for Asian/Pacific Rim plaintiffs with a 40 percent success rate; but 11 others – 3 from Caribbean, 3 from Eastern European, 3 from African, and 2 from Central/South American plaintiffs – were

---

[6] The Geography of Immigrant Skills: Educational Profiles of Metropolitan Areas (2011). Retrieved from www.brookings.edu/papers/2011/06_immigrants_singer.aspx

far less successful, with just one finding among them in favor of the plaintiff. (It is curious that there are many more cases for Asian-accented employees, and that these have been much more successful, on balance.) Without a doubt, workplace claims of incomprehensibility can have devastating effects for the persons in question. A few actual cases illustrate this point:

- Chetankumar Meshram was raised speaking English in India and moved to Northampton, England as a 25-year-old. He landed a job at Talk Talk Direct in 2005 and was assigned two years later to provide technical expertise at their call center in New Delhi. Just three weeks later, Meshram told the *Northampton Chronicle*, "I was called into a meeting with my boss who told me I was going home because my accent wasn't English enough, and I was to be replaced with a better English speaker. I know I speak with an accent but my job out there was to give technical advice, not to give expertise on how to communicate. It was an embarrassing and humiliating experience."[7] The Bedford Employment Tribunal found that Meshram had suffered both direct and indirect racial discrimination, and awarded him £5,000 for emotional damages and travel expenses incurred.
- M. Chow was hired as a bilingual English and Cantonese interviewer for a California marketing research firm in 1992. For two years her reviews were favorable and she received regular raises. When a new supervisor was hired, he insisted she practice English pronunciation with him daily for half an hour because he did not like her "enunciation, tone, and the choppiness of her speaking" (Ni 1999). Chow's evaluations dropped to "less than satisfactory" and she quit six months later, filing a complaint with the Equal Employment Opportunity Commission (EEOC). Chow settled for $55,000 in lost wages and damages, citing the stress and shame that her supervisor's treatment caused her.
- Manuel Fragante, a Filipino resident of Honolulu, took the civil service exam and applied for a clerk position at the Honolulu Division of Motor Vehicles in 1981, a job that involved filing, processing mail, and providing information to customers. His application was denied despite impressive professional qualifications and the fact that he scored higher than any other applicant on the exam. One interviewer wrote: "Speaks with very pronounced accent which is difficult to understand. He has 37 years of experience in management administration and appears more qualified for professional rather than clerical work. However, because of his accent, I would not recommend him for this position."[8] Fragante was denied the position on grounds that his verbal skills were inadequate to deal with customers, especially over the telephone and under high stress conditions. In court, two linguists explained

---

[7] Retrieved from http://articles.timesofindia.indiatimes.com/2007-11-29/indians-abroad/27961309_1_discrimination-case-accent-racial-discrimination
[8] (P. Ex. A at 9; P. Ex. N). 888 F.2d 591; 1989 US App. LEXIS 2636.

that Fragante's accent was a matter of national origin and testified that his English was comprehensible and grammatically correct, but the judge ruled that Fragante's accent was not tied to national origin. Fragante lost on appeal as well, with the circuit court judge stating that an adverse employment decision may be predicated upon an individual's accent "when – but only when – it interferes materially with job performance."

As seen here, a range of possible negative actions toward the accented individual is possible: firing, poor evaluations, refusal to hire, and demotion. Such stories are undoubtedly common, though few are prosecuted in court, and those that are rarely find for the plaintiff (Lippi-Green 1997).

Other cases involve entire groups, with the real motive similarly dubious. In Arizona, the Department of Education recently instituted a policy for all public school teachers requiring fluency in English, which officially precludes having a 'heavy accent'. Teachers in Low English Proficiency (LEP) classes were warned that they would be subject to special scrutiny on the assumption that non-native students are disadvantaged by the teachers' 'bad' linguistic habits. Arizona imposed an English-only rule in 2000 to replace previous bilingual education initiatives, and Arizona's deputy superintendent of schools has pushed the school board to address the 'fluency problem' in the interest of maintaining federal funding under the No Child Left Behind Act (Jordan 2010).[9] Teachers who do not pass an evaluation by state auditors may take classes to improve their grammar or accent, but if their efforts to improve are deemed unsuccessful the school district has the authority to either fire or reassign them.

Faculty in the Department of Linguistics at the University of Arizona drafted an official response to this policy and submitted it to Governor Brewer and the superintendent of schools in May 2010.[10] The document lays out these important arguments (inter alia):

- There is no such thing as unaccented speech, so policies aimed at eliminating accented speech from the classroom are paradoxical.
- Heavily accented speech is not the same as unintelligible or ungrammatical speech, and those with a strong foreign accent may have nevertheless mastered grammar and idioms of English as well as native speakers.
- There are many different accents within English that can affect intelligibility, but the policy targets foreign accents and not dialects of English.
- Communicating to students that foreign accented speech is bad or harmful is counterproductive to learning, and affirms pre-existing patterns of linguistic bias and harmful linguistic profiling.

---

[9] About 13 percent of Arizona's 1.2 million public school students are considered English-language learners, mostly concentrated in lower grades according to the Arizona Department of Education.

[10] *Teachers' English Fluency Initiative in Arizona* (May 26, 2010). Department of Linguistics, University of Arizona. Retrieved from www.u.arizona.edu/~hammond/ling_statement_final.pdf

The statement further clarifies that accented speech is all around us, including from native speakers, and being able to communicate with others is thus a useful skill. By extension, practice doing so is a valuable educational experience. The TESOL organization (Teachers of English to Speakers of Other Languages) drafted a similar statement criticizing the "environment of fear and xenophobia being fostered by lawmakers in the state without consideration of the consequences upon student learning and achievement."[11] For its part, the state insists that the educational success of the child is its top priority, and a 'quick path' to English proficiency is the best guarantee of that. The school is a public institution, and the state has the right to set educational policy, but in this instance, that right is at odds with federal anti-discrimination law. Like the general immigration law recently passed in Arizona, State Bill 1070,[12] the new policy has simultaneously sparked vocal outrage as well as support, and it already faces challenges in court. (As of this writing, the US Department of Justice has filed suit to contest the constitutionality of the law.)

The prosecution of language-related discrimination in the US is supported by Title VII of the Civil Rights Act of 1964, Section 2000e [2] (and the following), which prohibits workplace discrimination on the basis of race, color, religion, sex, or national origin.[13] This applies to all workers in the US, citizen and non-citizen alike. Section 703 states that it is unlawful for an employer to discriminate on these criteria in the following ways:

- by failing to hire, or by discharging, any individual, or by otherwise discriminating against any individual with respect to compensation, terms, conditions, or privileges of employment;
- by limiting, segregating, or classifying employees in any way which would deprive or tend to deprive any individual of employment opportunities or otherwise adversely affect his status as an employee.

Plaintiffs sometimes invoke the 14th Amendment of the Constitution as well, which guarantees equal access and equal protection to all citizens under the law.[14]

---

[11] www.tesol.org/s_tesol/sec_document.asp?CID=33andDID=13249

[12] Signed into law April 23, 2010, SB 1070 has been called the broadest and strictest immigration measure in generations because it criminalizes the failure to carry immigration documents and allows police to detain anyone suspected of being in the country illegally (Archibold 2010). A US District judge blocked those provisions from taking effect in July 2010, and protests have taken place across the US despite apparently broad support for the law within and beyond Arizona. Retrieved from http://senatebill1070.com/arizona-senate-bill-1070/full-text-of-arizona-senate-bill-1070

[13] Title VI, 42 USC Section 2000d was also enacted to prohibit discrimination within programs and activities receiving federal funding. Retrieved from www.justice.gov/crt/about/cor/coord/titlevi.php

[14] The Canadian Human Rights Act (RSC, 1985, c. H-6) protects the same traits, and adds pardoned conviction, age, sexual orientation, and family or marital status, some of which are now protected in the US by subsequent statutes (see Munro 2003 for more on accent discrimination in the Canadian context). Retrieved from http://laws-lois.justice.gc.ca/eng/acts/H-6/page-18.html

The EEOC has clarified how Title VII is applied in practice, beginning with what is meant by 'national origin.' According to the EEOC Compliance Manual, Section13-III B 1, a national origin group (also referred to as an ethnic group) shares a common *language*, culture, ancestry, and/or similar social characteristics. Discrimination against such a group can be based on ethnicity or any "physical, *linguistic* or cultural traits" (my emphasis).

Accent per se is not protected under Title VII; it must be tied to national origin or another protected category like sex or race (black speakers of AAVE – African American Vernacular English – may have legal recourse in such cases) (Cunningham 1998). This means that regional accents are not covered because, unlike foreign accents, they are not considered a national origin characteristic. Another important distinction is that foreign accents are more likely to be seen as 'immutable' (as is sex, race, etc.) for first-generation immigrants who arrive as adults; regional speech patterns are not.

The adjudication of accent discrimination complaints sets a high standard for the plaintiff, who must show prima facie evidence for 'disparate treatment,' i.e., that discrimination was a motivating factor in the employer's actions.[15] A prima facie case requires the plaintiff to provide: (a) evidence of national origin; (b) evidence of application and qualifications for the job; (c) evidence that plaintiff was rejected despite adequate qualifications; (d) evidence that the job remained open after this rejection and that the employer continued to seek applicants with the plaintiff's qualifications. In some cases, the plaintiff must also prove that he is a member of a 'protected class'[16] and that employees who are not members of that class were treated more favorably, as in *In re Rodriguez* (2007), the case of FedEx employee Jose Rodriguez who was not selected for a higher-level position based on a supervisor's critique of his "Hispanic accent and speech patterns."[17]

Once a prima facie case has been made, the burden of proof shifts to the employer to provide a non-discriminatory explanation of the action. This bona fide defense must persuade the court that the candidate's ability to perform the job was in question, or that a certain accent was needed as a matter of workplace necessity, i.e., that discrimination was not the motive for the action. At that point, the burden of proof shifts back to the plaintiff to show why this argument is not credible. For Rodriguez, the initial decision found in favor of FedEx on

---

[15] For 'disparate impact' – actions that apply to all members of a protected group – this burden of proof is less stringent. Plaintiffs must show that a 'facially neutral' practice had a discriminatory effect, as opposed to proving that the employer intended to discriminate. A disparate impact claim applies to workplace language restrictions, e.g., English-only policies that prohibit employees from speaking other languages while on duty (usually Spanish). (Space does not permit discussion of this issue, but see Del Valle 2003.)
[16] A standard set forth in *McDonnell Douglas Corp* v. *Green*, 411 US 792, 802 (1973).
[17] 487 F.3d 1001; 2007 US App. LEXIS 15244.

the basis of its bona fide defense, but Rodriguez won on appeal. The 6th US Circuit Court concluded that the supervisor's comments were direct, not merely circumstantial, evidence of discrimination.[18]

Because the ability to communicate is essential to most jobs, the workplace necessity argument usually trumps the prohibition against discrimination, writes Matsuda (1991: 1332). A certain accent is needed, so the argument goes, for job safety or to attract customers. When accent is used as a measure of communicative ability, "how then, should Title VII squeeze between the walls of accent as a protected trait and speech as job requirement?" Matsuda asks (ibid.: 1348). This is perhaps why reversals of lower court decisions are common in these cases; workplace necessity is ultimately a subjective determination, and the judge must decide whether an employee's rights have actually been violated. Furthermore, if testimony from coworkers and customers is allowed, they may present biased impressions and the judge must then assess their credibility (Munro 2003).

In the cases mentioned, an understanding of accent itself is rarely apparent. A bona fide argument often confuses workplace necessity with customer preference, and accent with language ability. An example provided by the EEOC illustrates how accent is linked to customer preference, without reference to actual language ability:

> Example 17: Employment decision where accent is a material factor
> A major aspect of Bill's position as a concierge for XYZ Hotel is assisting guests with directions and travel arrangements. Numerous people have complained that they cannot understand Bill because of his heavy Ghanaian accent. Therefore, XYZ notifies Bill that he is being transferred to a clerical position that does not involve extensive spoken communication. The transfer does not violate Title VII because Bill's accent materially interferes with his ability to perform the functions of the concierge position.

Based on precedent, XYZ hotel would not have to provide evidence of actual complaints, but simply testify that customers and/or coworkers found Bill to be difficult to understand. This elevates preference to the more objective standard of comprehensibility, although no official definition – much less verification – thereof is required.

As a point of contrast, a hypothetical example (based on Nguyen 1993) indicates what would *not* be acceptable by Title VII standards: A television station in Upstate New York wants to hire a news anchor, and advertises for applicants who have that regional accent. This would preclude all foreign-accented speakers,

---

[18] 2008 US Dist. LEXIS 41422.

and thereby constitute prima facie evidence of discrimination on the basis of national origin. It would not matter whether the employer insisted that an Upstate New York accent was a workplace necessity to ensure comprehensibility or engender audience favorability; the requirement set out in the job ad is discriminatory on its face.

Commonly in such cases, language-based requirements were not specified up front for the job, and foreign-accented individuals were denied employment or promotion ad hoc on grounds of being hard to understand, even if professionally qualified. Because the burden of proof lies with the plaintiff, employers usually win with this defense. Accent is thus *not* protected in the same ways as other immutable traits, even though the definition of national origin actually references language characteristics.

To be sure, client or coworker preference is not an allowable defense in Title VII cases pertaining to race, sex, etc. (i.e., the television station in the above scenario would clearly violate Title VII protection if it overtly advertised for white male news anchors on the basis of audience preference). The EEOC guidelines actually warn employers not to "rely on coworker, customer, or client discomfort or preference as the basis for a discriminatory action." They urge employers to state job requirements up front, with as much specificity as possible to avoid ad hoc discrimination, but their own published examples contradict this statement, suggesting leeway through a workplace necessity loophole, in effect.

One category of employers has been granted special leniency: schools and universities. In the educational context, teaching effectiveness is at stake, and employers who claim that accent materially interferes with job performance have enjoyed the benefit of the doubt. Student evaluations are sometimes cited, as are the comments of colleagues – neither of which can be assumed devoid of bias. At the same time, a strong accent could legitimately interfere with teaching effectiveness. In *Tseng v. Florida A and M University* (2010),[19] the 11th Circuit court affirmed the finding of a district court that the university did not discriminate against Tseng, a visiting professor, when it promoted another visiting professor from mainland China to a tenure-track position instead of him. The university cited the other professor's "better communication skills and stronger record of collaboration with other faculty members." Because Tseng was passed over for another foreign national, also a non-native speaker of English, the prima facie case of discrimination on the basis of national origin was not successful; the other visiting professor also had a foreign accent, and no other discriminatory actions were identified. Both courts found that choosing between two candidates with similar qualifications was not unreasonable, even though

---

[19] 380 Fed. Appx. 908; 2010 US App. LEXIS 10909.

they acknowledged that Tseng was slightly more qualified.[20] The US Supreme Court refused Tseng's petition for review (writ of certiorari) in spring 2011.

An obvious concern raised by all of these cases is that accent is equated with general communicative skill. They are closely intertwined, but not equivalent. Lippi-Green writes that accent "cannot predict the level of an individual's communicative competence. In fact, communicative competence can often be so high as to compensate for strong L2 interference" (1994: 185). For many of the cases brought to court, it is clear that employers have assumed otherwise and made decisions accordingly. Smith (2005) discusses several cases where a company's policy toward accented speakers appears openly disparaging, yet plaintiffs have been unable to make a prima facie case because of this basic confusion.[21]

So how does the court decide when accent legitimately interferes with communicative ability and thus job performance? Rarely is any effort made to officially determine a plaintiff's language fluency beyond the court's or the employer's own impressions (Nguyen 1993; Smith 2005). Lippi-Green (1994) describes the unsuccessful suit brought by Mr. Xieng, a Cambodian-American who worked for Peoples National Bank of Washington. Xieng was repeatedly denied promotion despite an excellent work history and performance reviews, and despite having filled in on the position for which he was applying. The court conceded that he was qualified because he had already done the job satisfactorily, but no expert testimony was called to determine whether his accent in any way impeded communication. By contrast, a psychiatrist was asked to testify about the emotional distress caused by the discriminatory treatment he experienced (ibid.: 189). In Lippi-Green's view, this resistance to seek expert testimony in matters related to language reflects an ideology that discounts anything other than the dominant (Anglo, native speaker) standard. The courts are an institutional stronghold of this ideology, she argues, and judges have no 'personal investment' to act in a way that reflects today's multicultural realities (ibid.: 188ff.). A less politicized view holds that courts think of language as so commonplace a phenomenon that it requires no expertise to understand (Hall et al. 2011: 297).

In other well-known cases, linguists have been called to testify (e.g., *James Kahakua v. the National Weather Service in Honolulu* (1989)),[22] but to little effect. Kahakua, a meteorologist with an identifiably Hawaiian Creole accent was applying for a promotion that would have entailed broadcasting weather reports. The weather service passed him over, and the district judge found in its

---

[20] Similar cases include *Hou v. Dept. of Education, Slippery Rock State College* (1983), 573 F. Supp. 1539; 1983 US Dist. LEXIS 11939 (see Matsuda 1991; Smith 2005 for more examples).
[21] For example, *Ang v. Proctor and Gamble* (1991) and *Carroll v. Elliott Personnel Services* (1989).
[22] Unpublished disposition. Refer to 876 F.2d 896; 1989 US App. LEXIS 8253.

favor. The judge maintained that the linguist who testified on Kahakua's behalf was "not considered an expert in speech" and that Kahakua could have used standard pronunciation of his own volition (Matsuda 1991, quoting from the decision). Matsuda vehemently opposes this assertion:

In telling people they must abandon their native accent, we impede their ability to participate in the democratic process. . . . The way we talk, whether it is a life choice or an immutable characteristic, is akin to other attributes of the self that the law protects. In privacy law, due process law, protection against cruel and unusual punishment, and freedom from inquisition, we say the state cannot intrude upon the core of you, cannot take away your sacred places of the self. A citizen's accent, I would argue, resides in one of those places. (ibid.: 1391f.)

Matsuda recommends that courts fairly evaluate intelligibility by first separating social evaluations of accent from actual communicative abilities. By taking the perspective of a non-prejudiced customer/client, the employee's real communicative needs could be dispassionately assessed. Courts should also consider whether a coworker, boss or client is willing to accommodate the non-native employee, or has simply forfeited her share of the communicative burden by dismissing him as 'hard to understand' (see Chapter 4).

These suggestions are on the right track, but need to be fleshed out. At issue is how to best ascertain a plaintiff's communicative abilities in an objective way. Nguyen (1993) recommends using an external measure like the TSE (Test of Spoken English) that includes a number of tasks, including reading aloud, completing partial sentences, telling a story according to picture prompts, and answering questions about general topics. As the TSE has been discontinued as of 2010, other tests with a speaking component could be used, including TOEFL, which also verifies scores independently by expert raters, and any relevant Cambridge ESOL test for specific purposes, some of which require speaking with an examiner and/or other exam takers in a more conversational format.[23] Contrary to what Nguyen asserts, low scores would not establish a lack of discrimination on the employer's part (this could always influence employment decisions regardless of language skills), but a high score would raise the bar for a workplace necessity defense. Furthermore, by referencing an objective measure of communicative fluency, the connection between accent and language abilities would be effectively decoupled. In this way, the presence or absence of discriminatory intent would be more obvious.

The courts themselves must appreciate the dangers of arbitrariness and potential prejudice in their own judgments of accent-related cases. Several countermeasures can be undertaken, focused on the standards for bona fide evidence:

---

[23] See: www.cambridgeesol.org/exams/index.html

- Workplace impressions from coworkers or clients – if allowed at all – should be closely scrutinized.
- To tease apart bias from real communicative issues, the judge should require external validation of the plaintiff's language skills if accent is said to materially interfere with job performance. A low score on such a measure would strengthen the employer's claim, while a plaintiff who scores highly would have an impartial means to rebut the employer's bona fide claim.
- Expert testimony should be required to explain the social implications of accent and the dynamics of the communicative burden.
- The duties and environment of the job should be carefully documented, since extenuating factors might apply, e.g., urgency or safety concerns, or particular language skills that do constitute a workplace necessity, such as advanced literacy or oral communication.
- The employer should be required to discuss efforts undertaken to increase tolerance and accommodation among work staff, or otherwise address the comprehensibility issue, before the unfavorable action was taken.

In short, the judge should get a full account of the situation and avoid over-reliance on subjective evaluations.

As for the workplace itself, the fact that accent lawsuits are on the rise suggests a need for cooperative problem-solving, including awareness-raising for all employees and overt training on specific communicative strategies. In negotiations of language use in the workplace, an approach that emphasizes mutual responsibility and cooperation is more successful than unilateral dismissals or restrictive top-down policies that demoralize non-native speakers (e.g., as outlined Macias 1997).

Increasing immigration and multiculturalism will not eliminate discrimination – if anything, it predicts an increase in anti-foreigner sentiment, such as that seen in Arizona, and an increase in work-related accent discrimination cases. Courts, too, will find it hard to assume an unprejudiced listener stance, as advocated by Matsuda (1991). Too often, bias against accented individuals is considered socially acceptable, contradicting basic principles of fairness and legal protections against trait-based discrimination. "While Americans generally disavow race or gender discrimination, many accept accent discrimination as reasonable," Nguyen writes (1993: 1335). Thus far, the courts' actions have done little to show that they are rising above this long-standing trend. This is not simply a matter of prejudice, or arbitrariness, but a result of fundamental misunderstandings about the nature of accent itself.

5.4 Accent bias in the courtroom

Up to this point we have looked at accent as an explicit criterion in employment decisions, and as a factor in access to housing and other services. We now consider other legal applications, first looking at accent as a source of forensic evidence, then as a more subconscious factor in criminal prosecution. Given the paucity of empirical work on either point, only a few preliminary remarks are possible.

In order to identify witnesses, linguists are increasingly called to offer expertise in civil and criminal suits where language is a central consideration (Tiersma and Solan 2002). Their testimony is used most often for purposes of voice recognition, i.e., to verify 'earwitness' accounts of a suspect's voice, or to explain the linguistic features of certain speech acts, e.g., the intonational patterns typical of a threat, or the conversational sequences that constitute a bribe, etc. (Coulthard 2004; Eades 2010; Solan and Tiersma 2004). Because the field of forensic linguistics is relatively new and professional standards for evidence reliability are still evolving,[24] these kinds of analysis are not yet regarded as fully scientific (Hall et al. 2011; Solan and Tiersma 2004). Language behavior is also highly variable, and we all routinely alter how we utter any given word or sound sequence according to context, mood, and many other non-linguistic factors. Thus, on the most basic phonetic level, even a precise formant frequency analysis cannot provide irrefutable evidence of a speaker's identity. New approaches tend to combine several techniques to bolster accent-based identification, and as new technologies are developed, reliability should increase (Solan and Tiersma 2004).

Beyond accent as an evidential focus, there is little doubt that it is a relevant, if implicit, factor at every level of the judicial system. Police officers, lawyers, jurors and judges are all subject to accent-triggered perceptions of credibility and trustworthiness. An interesting question is therefore whether linguistic profiling is subconsciously at work in the hearing and sentencing of suspects. Several studies lend support to this idea. Dixon and Mahoney (2004) asked 199 college students to listen to a dialogue between a policeman and an accused perpetrator, using a matched guise technique. Dialogue was taken from an actual police transcript and read by actors. The accused (the guise) spoke in either British RP or Birmingham dialect. Accent did not figure significantly in the assignment of guilt, nor did it interact statistically with strength of evidence or crime type (blue vs. white collar). But in a similar experiment, Seggie (1983) manipulated crime type (embezzlement, property damage, assault) and accent type (RP, Broad Australian, and 'Asian') in suspects' proclamations of innocence. For Australian listeners, the Broad Australian (non-standard) accented suspect was perceived as most guilty when a blue-collar crime was committed. No

---

[24] The International Association for Forensic Phonetics and Acoustics (IAFPA) was established in 1991, in part to establish a code of professional ethics, conduct, and methodological standards for the field.

such interaction was found for the Asian (foreign) accented suspect. Taken together, these studies suggest that, to the extent that social class is a salient association, listeners draw conclusions about *type* of crime committed and the likelihood of guilt as a function of accent. This recalls Shuy's evidence for the salience of social class over ethnicity, mentioned earlier.

Even beyond credibility and guilt, accent may figure significantly in the kinds of punishment recommended by a jury. Frumkin (2007) compared the impressions of 6 groups of students (total N=174), each of whom watched a 3-minute videotape from a different (mock) eyewitness testifying about an armed robbery. The foreign-accented eyewitness was either German, Mexican, or Lebanese. These three nationalities had been verified by a pilot study as representing 'high,' 'middle,' and 'low' favorability, respectively, and each mock eyewitness referenced their ethnic/national origin in their testimony so that participants would not misattribute their background. Frumkin included an accent–no accent condition to clearly separate the significance of accent from ethnicity for four traits: credibility, deceptiveness, accuracy of testimony, and prestige. Based on her analysis of rating results and survey data, Frumkin reported the following relationships:

- regardless of ethnic origin, participants were significantly more likely to rate accented witnesses as less credible, less accurate, more likely to deceive, and less prestigious;
- *t*-tests revealed a hierarchy of preference for ethnicity, in line with the pilot study (German most favored, Lebanese least favored, Mexican in the middle) but *only* for those in the accent condition – unaccented testimonies demonstrated no such preference order;
- overall, accent and ethnicity interacted significantly in perceptions of guilt, and in the recommended punishments.

All of this suggests that foreign-accented witnesses are at a disadvantage whether or not their ethnicity is correctly identified. Determinations of credibility, guilt, and eventual punishment may ultimately hinge on degree of accent as a trigger for suspicion or doubt.

This evidence is provocative, but experimental investigations like these are too few and far between, and in future studies, populations more typical of a jury pool should be tested (i.e., beyond similarly aged college students). A range of ethnicities should be balanced in the mock witness line-up as well. Access to a real jury is forbidden, but perhaps more post hoc research could also be done. Finally, it would be helpful to provide some community or regional – if not national – context for understanding accent-credibility associations, such as an explication of race or class relations in the area and statistics about crime in relation to factors such as social class and ethnicity.

5.5 Conclusion: future empirical and legal challenges

This chapter set out to address the practical implications of sounding foreign, and in so doing, to show how accent can conjure up negative associations in the minds of employers, landlords, jurors, and others who serve as society's gatekeepers; in short, to show its potential reach into consequential realms of an L2 user's life. We have left aside the issue of harassment and ridicule (see Munro 2003) to concentrate on the ways in which attitudes toward foreign accent find more formal expression. This is not to suggest that all those who sound foreign encounter such treatment, nor that legitimate accent-related communication barriers do not exist. It is rather to bring attention to accent discrimination as a problem that, by all accounts, is more openly tolerated than other forms of disparate treatment. In some cases this affects hiring and retention, as well as earnings. The economic impact is far-reaching: Some foreign nationals are unfairly forced to take positions beneath their qualifications, and valuable resources are thereby wasted. On a more personal level, the psychological effects can be severe for the individual, to say nothing of long-term professional implications.

Acknowledging the scarcity of formal research in this area, these conclusions point out areas where more empirical work is needed:

- Accent and other noticeable traits of foreignness can move some employers to avoid hiring non-native speakers for various reasons, among them fear of legal, client-related, or coworker difficulties down the road. Firing, poor evaluations, failure to promote, and demotion are additional actions that could be related to accent. Such profiling is not uncommon, as seen in decisions regarding housing and other services. In gathering data about such phenomena, the role of demographic and political factors relevant to the region and the business itself should be measured and analyzed, and more direct measures of employer attitudes should be taken to better understand the motivations for such decisions.
- Negative judgments about accent may come down to degree more than origin; strongly accented speakers are consistently rated lowest for perceived employability, reliability, credibility, and likelihood to advance professionally, regardless of ethnic identity. It has yet to be established whether familiarity with a given foreign accent, or experience with non-native speakers overall, makes an important difference in this regard.
- The accent–ethnicity connection is a puzzle. It seems to be relevant for attitudes, stereotypes, and bias – both positive and negative. At the same time, ethnicity seems to recede when social class becomes more salient. Where accent is associated with the high end of the social spectrum, for example, prestige wins the day. The reverse is also true, as accented witnesses deemed to be less favorable socially are potentially viewed with

greater suspicion and are more likely to be found guilty of certain crimes, as indicated by the mock courtroom experiments mentioned. This means that accent could well be a factor in sentencing.

To summarize, accent, ethnicity, and social status are locked in a complex interrelationship in the legal domain, just as they are in less formal settings. Because the consequences are so serious, more research should address the attitudes of prospective employers, judges, jurors, and clients toward L2 users. The challenge is to ascertain the extent to which accent influences their thinking, and whether a legitimate comprehensibility issue can be effectively disentangled from a priori attitudes unrelated to speech itself.

This discussion has drawn attention to some critical misunderstandings apparent in professional and legal domains. Perhaps the most fundamental problem is the conflation of accent with language ability, more generally. Some employers have benefitted from the weak standards required for a business necessity defense against workplace discrimination, and the courts have not established the need to verify language ability through external means. Moreover, there is confusion about the nature of accent itself and whether it is truly immutable. Title VII does not explicitly mention accent as an immutable aspect of linguistic and cultural heritage, and individual judges therefore interpret this as they deem fit.

We have acknowledged that some non-native speakers do have difficulty communicating as a result of accent or low levels of language fluency, and not every claim of incomprehensibility is off the mark, nor is it necessarily racist in nature. Moreover, not all who sound foreign experience broad-based discrimination; many surely do not. On a broader level, however, accent discrimination is widespread – in immigrant nations, as well as those who do not consider themselves as such (e.g., Germany). Perhaps this is an expression of a general anti-foreigner sentiment or a kind of misguided, exclusionary patriotism.

As noted in Chapter 4, there is a classic battle cry heard in times of great upheaval: that all who come to the US should assimilate quickly to English and banish all traces of foreignness (like our forebears, it is presumed). In 1917, Theodore Roosevelt's wartime essay, "The Children of the Crucible," boasted of America's immigrant roots at the same time that it lambasted those who would eschew assimilation:

It has been our boast that out of the crucible, the melting pot of life in this free land, all the men and women of all the nations who come hither emerge as Americans and nothing else ... The crucible must melt all who are cast in it; it must turn them out in one American mold ... We must have but one flag. We must also have but one language ... The greatness of this nation depends on the swift assimilation of the aliens she welcomes to her shores. Any force which attempts to retard that assimilative process is a force hostile to the highest interests of our country. (excerpted in Crawford 1992: 84f.)

At times of great cultural and social volatility, a foreign accent is not "simply perceived as more or less exotic ... epitomizing cultural diversity as an asset of humankind," rather it is typically heard as a surrogate for ethnicity – a common basis for stigmatization (Rubio-Marin 2003: 63).

In the US, the majority white population will soon be the minority, as it already is in cities such as Miami and Phoenix. Accommodations will have to be made and attitudes will necessarily shift, as they have (to some extent) with regards to race, gender, and sexual orientation. Landmark legislation at the federal level, e.g., the Civil Rights Act of 1964, the Voting Rights Act of 1965, *Brown v. Board of Education* (1954), etc., as well as numerous state and local laws have helped to drive and/or solidify these attitudinal changes. With fundamental demographic changes underway, Title VII's protections will need to be renegotiated as the link between discrimination and various cultural traits is sorted out – speech and accent among them. This could have repercussions for those with regional accents who thus far have no defense unless they are members of a protected group.

In their desire to adapt, many newcomers feel pressure to quickly lose outward signs of their native language and culture (Smith 2005); in effect, accent becomes a proxy for assimilatory success, yet this pressure does not apply to all in equal measure. Raj Gupta, assistant to the EEOC commissioner in the early 1990s and author of its compliance guidelines, was quoted in a 1992 article as saying he had seen no cases of discrimination against immigrants from Western Europe: "Generally if an employer has an applicant who speaks with a French accent, they say 'How cute,' or with an English accent they say, 'How cute.' But if he speaks with a Hispanic accent they say, 'What's wrong with this guy?'" (Holmes 1992). Immigrants who come from countries with less economic and social capital are clearly subject to greater pressures to 'sound American,' be that because of ethnic or cultural associations. Those who actually feel shame, or fear professional or personal repercussions for the way they sound, may try to lose their accent through any means necessary. Chapter 6 takes up this issue with an eye toward how successful that quest is likely to be.

6 Accent and instruction

> WE WILL FIX YOUR ENGLISH PRONUNCIATION PROBLEMS PERMANENTLY IN MINUTES! Our approach is Simple, Easy, Painless and Fun!
>
> We GUARANTEE that people will begin COMPLIMENTING you in only 7 days, or we will REFUND your $9.95 during the first week! Try it NOW! You've got ABSOLUTELY NOTHING to LOSE but your Accent!
>
> *"I LOVE this course – it has opened a new door in my life! After only a few lessons of the Pronunciation Workshop program, my English has become clearer and I am already seeing fast and amazing results ... and the more I study, the more knowledge and skills I gain. People around me are becoming more open and I see that there are now many more possibilities in my life."* Emily D.[1]

Up to now we have highlighted the ways in which accent can be a particularly meaningful, and challenging, aspect of L2 performance. Having considered some of the social, psychological, communicative, and professional implications of accent, we turn to the issue of formal, instructed practice as a means to change it.

A cursory glance at accent reduction programs online gives the distinct impression that a non-standard accent is a professional, if not a personal, liability. Improve your accent, so the claim goes, and you will gain confidence and respect, and advance your professional profile. Non-native-speaking immigrants are surely susceptible to this promise, and even classroom L2 learners often express a desire to attain to that level, regardless of whether it is a realistic goal.

In this chapter, we explore how accent is treated in the FL classroom today, what we know about which instructional techniques and tools can improve it, and why teacher–student attitudes do not always coincide with the intelligibility principle so widely advocated in scholarly discussions of L2 phonology.

---

[1] Accessed August 10, 2012, from: www.pronunciationworkshop.com

6.1 Phonology's place in the FL classroom

Linguistically speaking, phonological fluency implies the ability to perceive and produce fine phonetic and phonemic distinctions, and master features like juncture, elision, stress, and assimilation, as well as prosodic patterns that convey meaning in contextually appropriate ways. Foreign language (FL) pedagogy traditionally assumed that classroom language learners would only master these skills with the help of explicit instruction. Phonological training concentrated on the segmental level, and more often than not, sounds were treated in isolation. These practices have come under much criticism amid a consensus that isolated drills are not enough, and that a 'one-size fits all' approach is inappropriate; it contradicts the pedagogical principle of learner-centeredness, not to mention the growing emphasis on individual differences in SLA.

In fact, phonological fluency has been largely ignored in pedagogical circles for several decades now, seen only as "a means to negotiate meaning in discourse," rather than as an end in itself (Dalton and Seidlhofer 1994: ix). The long-held 'nativeness' principle in SLA has given over to the notion that intelligibility is a more reasonable goal (Levis 2005), boosted by the focus on English as a global language. Many scholars insist that L2 users cannot, and should not, be held to a native-like standard because it is not necessary for communication to succeed. If intelligibility is the new benchmark, should teachers even worry about whether their students sound accurate or authentic?

Despite increasing interest in phonology among applied linguists, neither the cognitive nor the sociolinguistic paradigm offers much practical insight or advice for FL teachers. They must decide for themselves how vital accent is for their learners, and how to approach its treatment in formal terms. This is challenging on several levels. Developmentally speaking, acquiring a new accent is a laborious undertaking predicated on numerous cognitive and affective orientations, if not certain aptitudes – be they innate talents or learnable skills (discussed in Chapter 3, Section 3.1). At the level of performance, phonological authenticity implies some degree of flexibility since contextual appropriateness demands style-shifting and accommodation. These skills cannot be gained quickly or easily, and the classroom cannot guarantee their acquisition any more than informal target-language exposure can. Given what we know about the complexity of accent, and taking various viewpoints into consideration, we pose two fundamental challenges facing FL phonology instruction:

- If accent in a second language is such an individual skill, and much of what contributes to it lies beyond conscious practice, how consequential can explicit training be?
- Can the classroom address phonological fluency in a comprehensive way, providing enough contextualized practice to promote real authenticity?

Research has not sufficiently addressed either question; current FL pedagogical approaches have all but ignored both. Nevertheless, this chapter argues that the classroom is an opportune site for interactive practice and targeted feedback, and therefore offers some advantages over informal, immersion-style experience. Beyond actual skill building, the classroom is also an optimal forum to raise awareness of accent's broader significance and the realities of phonological variation.

We begin with an overview of pedagogical trends pertaining to accent, then consider what kinds of instruction help to advance phonological accuracy. Finally, we locate accent within current standards for language learning in the US and Europe. The conclusion returns to the questions above, summarizing the relevant empirical evidence and re-emphasizing the issue of intelligibility, which seems to hold different currency for learners as opposed to SLA scholars.

6.2 Classroom approaches to phonological instruction: past and present

Advocates of pronunciation instruction view accent as an important communicative skill because, above all, it helps to structure interaction – think of rising, flat, and falling intonation as signals for the speaker's intent to hold or give up the floor, for example. Socially and psychologically, it signals attitude and mood and offers clues about the speaker–hearer relationship (Pennington 1989: 20). Semantically, accent highlights vital distinctions within an utterance, such as topic/comment, or given vs. new information (see Low 2006). On the level of speech acts, one can further imagine how volume, articulation, and tempo are modulated in commands as opposed to apologies, and how meaningful these shifts can be as expressions of speaker authority and/or distance. Non-native speakers unaware of these many distinctions risk serious intercultural misunderstandings. The current thinking is therefore that pronunciation instruction should take an integrated, 'top-down' approach to include practice on voice quality, stress, rhythm, pitch, and even gesture, since all such features contribute to syntactic, semantic and pragmatic processing (Pennington 1989). This is a far cry from the traditional 'bottom-up' emphasis on segmental-level accuracy alone.

In its heyday during Audiolingualism in the 1950s and 1960s, pronunciation training delivered a prepackaged set of drills for imitation and repetition. Influenced by behaviorist psychology, Audiolingualism stressed the need to eradicate or even prevent errors before they had a chance to become entrenched 'bad habits'. To this end, aural/oral drills presented vowels and consonants in various environments (initial, medial, final) to highlight L1–L2 contrasts, often in the form of minimal word pairs (e.g., *car/cab*, *sheep/ship*, etc.) and brief, isolated sentences. Through consistent practice at this level, students ideally became aware of the new sounds, learned to produce them with some accuracy, and gained a certain degree of self-awareness, at least on the segmental level.

Many techniques found in today's classroom textbooks and commercial programs are recognizable as audiolingual in nature, others pre-date that method (adapted from Celce-Murcia et al. 1996: 8ff.):
- imitating teachers and/or pre-recorded native speakers as models;
- practicing phonemic contrasts via minimal pair drills;
- reading aloud and reciting words, sentences, and longer passages to focus on stress, rhythm, tempo, and intonation;
- recording and analyzing one's own speech and comparing it to a native speaker model;
- becoming familiar with the articulatory organs, e.g., through diagrams;
- practicing transcription with the International Phonetic Alphabet;
- using mirrors or other visual aids to observe how sounds are created;
- practicing tongue twisters.

The effectiveness of such techniques is rarely tested, however, and some may be inappropriate depending on the individual's proficiency level or learning style. But these techniques have remained consistent over the years; the only real innovation is their delivery through new technologies.

Perhaps more than any method before or since, Audiolingualism stressed the importance of sounding native-like (also essential to its predecessor, the Direct Method, popular in the early twentieth century). Audiolingualism centered its training around audiocassette recordings for the first time, and it is credited with ushering in the language lab concept, where students were expected to spend many hours honing their articulatory precision.

Pronunciation practice fell out of favor as Cognitivism took hold in the 1970s. Errors were now seen as a natural byproduct of the learning process, inherently sorting themselves out over time as long as sufficient input was available (as advocated in the Natural Approach) (Celce-Murcia et al. 1996). Experimental methods proliferated for a time (e.g., Total Physical Response, Community Language Learning, etc.), followed by Communicative Language Teaching (CLT) in the 1980s, which located accent as a feature of linguistic, but not communicative, competence (Chun 1988; Wong 1985). CLT is still the dominant paradigm today, arguably the last real method grounded in a theory about what it means to know a language. Expanding on Dell Hymes' (1971) notion of communicative competence as a function of knowing *how* to use language rather than knowing *about* language, Canale and Swain (1980) elaborated four fundamental components of communicative competence – grammatical, sociolinguistic, discursive, and strategic. This placed the emphasis squarely on the ability to appropriately negotiate the flow of an interaction *in context*. Their definition remains the foundation for communicative FL teaching.

CLT takes an integrated view of language, emphasizing global fluency rather than discrete-point accuracy (Pennington and Richards 1986: 207). To encourage the learner's ability to 'negotiate meaning,' tasks reflect the functions necessary to navigate specific situations (e.g., giving and receiving information to make hotel reservations). CLT does not prioritize how one sounds so much as whether one can appropriately, sufficiently convey meaning to complete a specific speech act. Accent is not seen as vital for that kind of competence; grammar and vocabulary are. Largely due to this change in priorities, few students these days receive the kind of focused accent training that used to be considered integral to language instruction, and few teachers acquire a formal phonetics background as in earlier times.

Against the backdrop of pedagogical paradigm shifts, one thing has not changed: Instructed environments still offer unique opportunities for phonological feedback and practice at the sound, word, sentence, *and* discourse levels, in order to advance discrete-point, and overall, fluency. Indeed, there is evidence that instruction can lead to short-term gains in perception and production (e.g., see Saito 2011), and that it makes a difference in long-term phonological attainment as well if it is communicative in nature (Elliott 1997; Moyer 1999); includes discourse-level training on suprasegmental features like stress, intonation, pitch, and rhythm (Akita 2006; Derwing and Rossiter 2003; Moyer 1999); and takes a form-focused approach (Couper 2006; see also Chapters 2 and 3). Moreover, it seems that perceptual training can actually aid production (Couper 2006; deBot and Mailfert 1982; Lambacher et al. 2005; see also Derwing et al. 1998; cf. Neufeld 1987 and 1988). Moreover, pronunciation training, especially focused on discourse features like pitch and intonation, may aid in the development of listening comprehension (Gilbert 1983).

Two experimental studies are noteworthy as they suggest short-term and long-term benefits of explicit practice. Elliott (1997) provided training sessions on Spanish phonemes to L2 Spanish learners over the course of a college semester. Practice incorporated word and sentence-level repetition after a native speaker model, targeting specific phonemes, and clarifying phoneme–grapheme mismatches (e.g. the /b/ phoneme represented by *v* orthographically). Couper's (2006) 'high-intermediate' learners of English retained the gains they made after explicit training on common errors of consonant deletion and vowel epenthesis to break up consonant clusters. Training took place in 12 sessions over a 2-week span, and the gains evident in the immediate post-test were only slightly diminished 12 weeks later. Taken together, these two studies suggest that explicit instruction can indeed become part of the learners' underlying phonological competence, even if they are at a point many would consider *fossilized*. Although McCandless and Winitz (1986) assert that instruction is not necessary for accurate pronunciation to develop so long as sufficient input is provided, but here we see that instruction can push pronunciation toward a closer-to-native target more quickly and effectively than exposure alone.

This evidence notwithstanding, little has changed since Leather (1983) decried the disconnect between L2 phonology research and practice some 25 years ago. Teachers today are on their own to integrate pronunciation training absent any specific guidelines. Leather called for intelligibility as a more realistic goal given how few adult L2 learners end up sounding native-like, yet intelligibility is relative; we have seen that it varies according to listener expectations and attitudes (Dalton and Seidlhofer 1994; Morley 1996a), as well as contextual factors, making it an amorphous goal. That being so, local decisions are most appropriate for deciding which accent features warrant explicit instruction, and which can be overlooked as less than critical.

However the individual teacher decides to proceed, Morley suggests that pronunciation instruction always advance from imitative speaking practice (e.g., isolated drills), to rehearsed speaking at the discourse level, to extemporaneous practice (1996a). Only by working through all three levels can the classroom ensure "an integration of modified speech patterns into naturally occurring creative speech" (ibid.: 150). The hope is that controlled practice will then lead to more automatic, authentic performance abilities (Pennington and Richards 1986).

Since the 1990s accent has been viewed as integral to "both referential and interactional meaning" (Pennington and Richards 1986: 219). Suprasegmentals therefore deserve far more treatment in the classroom. Phrasal pitch and stress features should be presented within entire conversational sequences to highlight the role they play in establishing contextual meaning (see Levis and Pickering 2004). For example, Dalton and Seidlhofer outline specific exercises to practice intonation as a way to establish topic prominence and flow, express social roles, and indicate turn-taking expectations. One such task asks students to practice dropping pitch to indicate a willingness to yield their conversational turn; another is structured to practice fall–rise patterns to signal doubt or contradiction, and learners are asked to 'try on' various speaker roles (1994: 91ff.). While such tasks are undoubtedly important, suprasegmental features are inherently difficult to isolate in terms of specific learning objectives and assessments.

Any holistic approach should include discourse-level training without overlooking the importance of segmental discrimination and articulation. Research can help advance a coherent approach by delineating the tools and techniques most useful for developing phonological fluency. Teachers would then have to tailor specific techniques to suit their students' needs. A logical progression would begin with a needs analysis, incorporate a range of contextualized and isolated practice techniques, and continually measure improvement through video/audio recordings, oral interviews, or even peer feedback on intelligibility and comprehensibility, as suggested by Derwing (2008).

It is fair to say that L2/FL research and teaching have taken divergent paths over the past few decades, both setting aside phonology for a time. On the research side, interest in interactional phonology is growing as prosody is seen as key to the negotiation of meaning and the control of interactional structures (Chun 1988; Couper-Kuhlen 2007; Field 2005; Jenkins 2004; Levis 1999; Riney et al. 2005 – see also Chapter 4). Even so, no unified teaching agenda has emerged to operationalize intelligibility, i.e., to specify instructional techniques in practical terms (see Derwing et al. 1998; Macdonald et al. 1994). Given this, and the fact that CLT and task-based learning – the dominant approaches today – all but dismiss the role of accent in communicative fluency, it is unsurprising that phonology instruction remains at a standstill.

6.3 The basis for instructional efficacy in L2 phonology

This relative inattention aside, the classroom offers a unique opportunity to teach awareness and self-monitoring strategies in addition to targeted practice (Morley 1996a, 1996b). Even if explicit instruction is not necessary for the acquisition of all L2 forms (Sanz and Morgan-Short 2005), the typical classroom learner enjoys limited exposure to authentic input. Instructed environments can structure formal input efficiently, by directing the learner's attention to form and meaning simultaneously to accomplish what Sharwood-Smith (1991) called consciousness-raising, or 'input enhancement'. At the same time, teachers can provide targeted feedback and correction (aka negative evidence). The classroom is also ideal because it can easily combine visual and auditory stimuli to raise metalinguistic awareness, which may increase the learnability and retention of new concepts. Below, we consider these potential advantages in turn.

6.3.1 Explicit practice, attention, and awareness

Explicit practice is understood to be metalinguistic in nature. In the 1980s, Krashen (1981) famously argued that the classroom could only be effective to the extent that it replicated the conditions of first language acquisition, i.e., loading the environment with authentic input and limiting corrective feedback. Although influential at the time, a Focus on Form (FonF) perspective has since emerged as a dominant research paradigm for instructed SLA, so that metalinguistic tasks are now considered useful. Counter to Krashen's claim that explicitly learned L2 knowledge never becomes automatic, it is widely assumed that explicit knowledge *can* become implicit through practice, and that both develop as a function of attention (Sanz and Morgan-Short 2005: 235). (Just how effective explicit vs. implicit learning is continues to fuel a lively debate in the SLA literature, with very little known about the long-term implications of either.)

The fundamental premise of FonF is that instruction is effective to the extent that the individual learner is aware of, or notices[2], the input available, and in some way attends to it. *Attention* is defined as a state of alertness and readiness that leads the learner to select and register the intended input (Tomlin and Villa 1994). It is thought to signify that all-important threshold of consciousness that allows input to become *intake*, i.e., available for the learner's use. Intake, in turn, is thought to be a precursor to hypothesis formation and testing (Schmidt 1992 and 2001). Of consequence here are frequency of occurrence and perceptual salience. Instruction can increase both to the extent that it structures and enhances the input while simultaneously focusing learners' attention (Skehan 1998: 48f.). FonF is also flexible; it can be structured around anything from direct teaching and rule-based explanations, to corrective feedback, to inductive tasks that encourage learners to notice forms for themselves (Doughty 2001: 210).

In an attempt to mimic conditions of first language acquisition, some researchers – and some methodologists – have experimented with an initial comprehension phase or 'silent period'. Schneiderman et al. (1988) presented an experimental group of learners of French with 6 hours of listening exercises, including graphic representation of intonation contours and rhythmic patterns. This comprehension phase was followed by 6 hours of imitation exercises, including short and long utterances, geared to segmental trouble spots in French. The subjects were pre- and post-tested for discrimination ability as well as production, and were rated by native speakers. While the experimental group did improve in discrimination, its pronunciation remained noticeably foreign. (The raters were instrumental in developing the discrimination training, so reliability is an issue here.)

In an interpretive twist, Neufeld posed the following question: Does targeted training have an *adverse* effect on production abilities? One can imagine a claim that overthinking a point of articulatory precision may obscure one's 'feel' for how it should sound. Neufeld's 1987 study was somewhat unusual in that it emphasized both segmental and suprasegmental features but allowed no reference to syntax or meaning for the phrases studied. Moreover, students were instructed not to attempt any mimicry until numerous lessons were completed, although they were asked to pay close attention during each lesson. They had therefore lost out on at least two counts: no matching behaviors were encouraged and no feedback was received. And not only was the training passive, it was purposely detached from meaning, which surely reduced its effectiveness.

On the whole, results for formal instruction have been mixed in L2 phonology studies, but when learners have extended access to instruction – for phonology, per se, or simply instruction in the target language – they tend to

---

[2] *Awareness* and *noticing* are used here synonymously, understanding that both connote detection, but with less effort and/or control than *attention* generally implies (see Skehan 1998).

sound more native-like (Bongaerts et al. 1995 and 1997; Moyer 1999). Piske (2007) theorizes that this is why early bilinguals end up sounding far more native-like than late bilinguals:

> [C]hild immigrants are usually enrolled in schools where they frequently interact with native speakers of the L2, whereas adult or adolescent immigrants hardly spend any time in schools where the L2 is the language of instruction. Adult or adolescent immigrants rather enter the workplace, where they often primarily interact with other non-native speakers of the L2. (307)

In other words, early bilinguals spend much more time in a high-quality input environment over a period of many years (ibid.), and this surely contributes to their edge, accent-wise, over those with a later exposure (Moyer's 2004 statistical analysis bears this out). It is impossible to know whether this advantage owes itself to the intensity, the quality, or the amount of their L2 experience (see Moyer 2004, 2009, 2011).

6.3.2 Self-monitoring

The value of phonological instruction is predicated on the learner's ability to detect the differences between their own output and the native(like) model provided to them. Schmidt and Frota (1986) describe this as 'noticing the gap' (cited in Swain 1998). "Evidence suggests that acquiring pronunciation is no different from acquiring syntax ... students need help noticing what they are doing," write Derwing and Munro (2005: 387). This is easier said than done, apparently. Couper (2006) had ESL learners record themselves and then identify the errors they made. This proved to be difficult even when they were given guidance. Asked to compare their own speech post hoc to a native speaker model reading the same passage, some could not hear the difference between "*baked a fish*" and "*baked fish*" (the former, their own version; the latter, that of the native speaker) (ibid.: 52). It is assumed, nonetheless, that if awareness is to transfer into articulation, the learner must be able to assess his or her own accent relative to the (modeled) input. This is how Yule et al. defined *self-monitoring* long ago (1987: 165).

Examples of self-monitoring instruction come from Smith and Beckmann (2010), who developed what they termed a 'noticing-reformulation' technique. Their 18 ESL learners in a weekly pronunciation class were periodically asked to record themselves reading a familiar text, after which they listened to the recording and analyzed their pronunciation. The next step involved listening to a native speaker read the text. Finally, they recorded the text again, listened to their revised versions, and reflected on any noticeable improvements. While listening skills and learner confidence in speaking were reported to have improved, no pre- or post-test measures validated the effects on actual pronunciation. Similar studies directed at awareness-raising include Acton (1984) and Aufderhaar (2004), but neither presents data directly supporting the effectiveness of implicit self-monitoring techniques. Others, however, have demonstrated significant effects for a range of techniques (Hanlon 2005; Lord 2005; Lambacher et al. 2005).

Of special interest is Ramirez Verdugo's (2006) experimental study of an audiovisual approach to self-monitoring. She incorporated computer-generated visual speech contours during read-aloud activities. Those in the experimental group exhibited a wider range of intonation patterns than the control group during subsequent, spontaneous speech tasks, an important indicator that the observed improvements had a potentially lasting effect.

This evidence notwithstanding, little is known about how self-monitoring becomes routine practice without formal prompting. Another question is whether self-monitoring techniques take on different qualities for different tasks. The classic treatment of self-monitoring in the phonology literature initially had to do with task effects, namely, whether L2 learners self-monitor more when tasks are presumably focused on form, such as when they read decontextualized word lists. Some evidence contradicts this premise, with phonological accuracy actually improved on conversational and extemporaneous speaking tasks (Oyama 1976; Sato 1987; Snow and Hoefnagel-Höhle 1982; cf. Dickerson 1975; Tarone 1982). Any relevant underlying mechanisms (e.g., selective attention) were not directly measured, so no conclusions can be drawn about how self-monitoring shifts as a function of task.

A fundamental issue is thus whether learners really do self-monitor as they speak extemporaneously. Osburne's (2003) 50 adult ESOL learners were asked to speak freely following a thematic prompt, then repeat the same task while monitoring their pronunciation (the interviewer said, *"Can you say that again and make your pronunciation as perfect as possible?"*). Both versions were recorded. After the second attempt, participants were asked what they did regarding pronunciation as they spoke. According to their self-reports, they focused on segmental precision, tempo, intonation, volume, and voice quality settings (e.g., one participant reminded herself to open her mouth widely when speaking English). Some even attempted to accommodate the regional variety of their interviewer. Osburne herself analyzed both sets of recordings and discovered that, indeed, all had adjusted at least two of the following while speaking: pause length, intonation, and tempo. Most had adjusted all three. But what would they have done without a prompt to self-monitor? Derwing and Rossiter (2002) present a further puzzle: Their 100 ESL learners reported that their comprehensibility problems were segmental in nature, yet their self-initiated repairs during interaction targeted the discourse level instead, e.g., using paraphrase and repetition, and less frequently adjusting volume and tempo. This casts doubt on how effectively learners match their self-monitoring techniques to their actual phonological difficulties.

Acknowledging the preliminary state of the research, it appears that self-monitoring instruction is more effective when it takes a two-pronged approach. Step one is discrimination training to learn how to *hear* target-language sound patterns. For this, Lambacher et al. (2005) suggest presenting L2 sound patterns taken from natural speech samples so that learners adapt their newfound awareness to novel contexts and voices. Explicit instruction on how to gauge one's own speech patterns against those of native speakers should then follow. Statistical analyses verify that over the long term, self-monitoring practices like repeating after native speakers and seeking out feedback on pronunciation do correlate to a closer-to-native accent (Moyer 2004). Thus, self-monitoring instruction may work best in conjunction with socially directed strategies beyond the classroom, such as limiting the use of L1 and actively seeking ways to use the target language informally.

6.3.3 The role of feedback

Learners are surely better adept at self-monitoring when they receive external feedback and instruction on how to notice the gap, as mentioned above. Communicative and humanistic teaching approaches largely de-emphasized corrective feedback for fear that it increases anxiety and discourages a focus on meaning, which could negatively affect speaking. But even naturalistic approaches acknowledge that *interactive* feedback is legitimate, so long as it mimics the kinds common in child language acquisition. Recasts – the immediate reformulation of a learner's inaccurate utterance to demonstrate its correct form – are one such technique. Mackey et al. (2000) provide an example of a phonology-directed recast:

NNS: *The rear, rear **legs*** (pronounced: [rleks])
NS: *The rear what?* ***Legs?***
NNS: ***Legs*** (pronounced [rɛgs]). *Yeah.*

The assumption is that recasts do not stifle interaction, and thus, are ideal for an implicit focus on form (Doughty and Varela 1998: 117). Yet one central question is whether students actually notice the feedback offered, especially in communicative classrooms "where interactional exchanges are motivated by a variety of purposes and foci" (Lyster 1998: 185). Furthermore, feedback can be ambiguous, as teachers employ recast techniques following well-formed sentences just as they do after ill-formed ones. Explicit corrections have generally been found to occur far less frequently in language classrooms compared to recasts, clarification requests, and various metalinguistic clues, e.g., questions related to the well-formedness of an utterance ("*Is that how you say . . . ?*") (Lyster 1998).

Feedback can take many forms, some more intrusive than others. Havranek and Cesnik's 2001 study on corrective feedback highlighted the importance of a practice effect, requiring the learner to repeat the corrected form. Another way to provide natural feedback is through an interrogative style recast, such as when the teacher repeats the student's incorrect utterance with rising intonation (likely also raised eyebrows, or other facial expressions indicating that revision is needed). Doughty and Varela (1998) found this technique to be highly effective for grammar repairs when the teacher followed it immediately with a correct reformulation. The effectiveness of any technique depends in part on the learner's attitude toward the correction (Havranek and Cesnik 2001) and her perception of the error's gravity (Kormos 2006). Regardless of which form it takes, feedback must be transparent in order to be effective, defined as leading to *uptake* – evidenced by an immediate repair or attempt at repair (Neri et al. 2002).

The issue of corrective feedback in interlanguage grammar has inspired much investigation (see Russell and Spada 2006 for meta-analysis), but studies of phonological feedback are all but nonexistent. A handful of quasi-experimental studies compare phonological, grammatical and lexical feedback. Lyster (1998) pursued two questions in a French immersion class: (a) whether teachers offered different kinds of feedback depending on error type (grammatical, lexical, or phonological); (b) whether any feedback type predictably led to immediate repair by the learner. He found that lexical errors elicited the most feedback from the teachers, followed by phonology, then grammar. Teachers did not react to these error types with the same techniques, however: Phonology elicited the greatest percentage of recasts and explicit correction. As for the second question, phonological feedback was most likely to result in self-correction compared to grammatical and lexical feedback, thus phonological recasts were assumed to be more effective. In Sheen's study (2006) from a college-level ESL classroom, nearly 92 percent of phonological recasts resulted in uptake, evidenced by (attempted) repair. This significantly exceeds the uptake observed for either grammatical or lexical recasts (cf. Mackey et al. 2000).

Why would phonological recasts be repaired more frequently and/or effectively than recasts directed at grammar and lexicon? Lyster's hypothesis is that phonological recasts are comparatively short, highly salient, and often take place as the student is reading aloud, making the focus of the correction unambiguous. Neri et al. (2002) further note that unlike grammatical and lexical feedback, phonological feedback does not force learners to go through a complex reanalysis (448); oftentimes one simple change such as a vowel substitution is all that is needed (Sheen 2006). Another possibility is that students perceive phonology to be critical to the communicative value of their utterance (ibid.: 385).

More experiments are needed to compare the effectiveness of various feedback types for phonology, but at an even more basic level, observational data are needed on how classroom teachers attune their students to accent. Do they address segmental and syllable- and/or word-level stress errors more so than rhythm, intonation, and the like? Another important question is how learners at various stages respond to explicit vs. implicit feedback. Perhaps explicit feedback is more effective at the very beginning stages of learning, and implicit feedback is more readily accessible as students' intuitions and sensitivities to the sounds of the language increase.

Given the preliminary nature of the work in this area, it is fair to say that no one really knows how feedback works; perhaps it helps to redirect attention (as Lyster 1998 speculates), to narrow down working hypotheses, to fine-tune cue weighting (see Chapter 2), or to consolidate memory traces (Sanz and Morgan-Short 2005: 246f.). Thus, two fundamental questions drive the inquiry: first, whether and how feedback really benefits acquisition over time, and second, which conditions are conducive to self-correction. The best way to address these questions is to compare experimental and control groups, and to include delayed post-tests to ascertain long-term effects, as Doughty and Varela (1998) did. Only if the group differences are significant can any confident claims be made about the effects of a specific type of feedback; after all, students typically improve over time, given sufficient practice.

6.4 Computer-assisted pronunciation training

Several decades ago, experimental work on visual graphics and recorded auditory stimuli made it possible to highlight discrepancies between native and non-native speech in new ways, including real-time spectrograms and waveforms, among other tools (deBot 1980 and 1983; see Erdener and Burnham 2005 for review). Photographs, film, laryngographs, and X rays have also been used to create pictures of articulators and waveforms of vocal cord vibration, but these are usually limited to specialists and laboratories. As deBot stresses, the effectiveness of such tools for teaching was not the main impetus for their initial development. Even today, with many more such tools in existence, e.g., ultrasound and magnetic resonance imaging (MRI) techniques, their practical use is relatively circumscribed. Perhaps the most influential advance for classroom learning is the digitization of audio, which permits the storage of great quantities of spoken data and a micro-level analysis of acoustic features, both segmental and suprasegmental (Chun 2007). Above all, digitization allows the user to easily access visual and auditory stimuli at the same time, and its costs are not prohibitive like many of the tools mentioned.

In the context of the second language classroom, two applications of technology commonly address accent, usually delivered by CD-ROM or online: (a) pre-recorded audio clips of a native speaker, e.g., modeling minimal pairs or reading a short text, in some cases accompanied by a video or other 2-D or 3-D figure showing how to enunciate certain words or sounds; (b) visual representations of intonation curves and/or formant frequencies (spectrograms), sometimes comparing a stored native speaker-generated utterance with the user's own version (see Chun 2007, Levis 2007 for review and examples). The aim is to raise awareness of contrasts and improve discrimination of features like voicing, stress, syllable duration, etc. For some programs, the user simply imitates what is pre-recorded, or eyes the visual display without feedback; other programs allow the user to record her own version which may be scored for fitness to a native speaker model.[3] In most cases, however, it is up to the learner how to interpret the feedback and modify output accordingly (Neri et al. 2002).

Pennington (1999) and Levis (2007) assess the respective benefits and drawbacks of computer-aided pronunciation training (CAPT), and what stands out from their reviews is the potential for unlimited practice on sounds, speech rate, pitch, and intonation. A secondary benefit is that such tools may enhance learner motivation or interest in phonological training. Moreover, CAPT is less psychologically loaded than spontaneous conversation with native speakers, or even classroom talk; learners can experiment with articulation at their leisure and with as much repetition as necessary. On the negative side, many programs are not adaptable, and they have limited interactive capacity. The learner's output is typically transcribed via Automatic Speech Recognition (ASR) so that feedback can address specific sounds, but only a few closed responses are pre-stored as 'correct'; even normal variation in learners' voices can result in false negatives. Delmonte (2000) therefore supports ASR for targeted segmental and prosodic training only; he cautions that such programs cannot adequately evaluate open-ended speech input. Pennington (1999), however, contends that ASR is reliable, consistent, "authoritative," and highly salient insofar as it can analyze an individual's errors based on past trials (429). If nothing else, ASR outdoes a human teacher in terms of patience (ibid.). Simply put, "CAPT is tireless" (Levis 2007: 197).

The potential of a computer vs. a teacher to provide effective, individualized training and feedback is another sore point. Human listeners can often understand a heavily accented speaker, in part because not all pronunciation errors are of equal weight, as Derwing et al. (2000) rightly point out. If this is indeed a "crucial characteristic of native listeners' processing of L2 speech," then an ASR program has limited relevance, in their estimation (ibid.: 594). To underscore their point, they compared a software program's responses to native

---

[3] The fact that this model is almost exclusively based on a single, regionally neutral standard is also problematic, given that a learner may (intend to) live in a region with a distinctively non-standard accent, not to mention the fact that developing an awareness of accent variation has its own educational and communicative merits. An exception in this regard is the program Streaming Speech which offers training by regional variety (e.g., for English: US, British, Irish, Canadian, and Australian) using unscripted speech samples.

listeners' intelligibility scores for a group of L2 users and found no significant overlap between them. "The properties of ESL speech that adversely affect the software tend not to interfere with comprehensibility and intelligibility for human listeners," they note, adding that their accented participants were very proficient in English, deemed to be just slightly less intelligible to the human listeners than were the native speaker controls (ibid.: 601). The software was far less judicious. For this reason, teachers should consider whether ASR tools actually correspond well with programmatic goals for either micro-level accuracy or global intelligibility.

There are few studies exploring the effects of CAPT, and they often incorporate just small numbers of participants undergoing very brief training phases. One exception comes from Tanner and Landon (2009), whose experimental group of ESL learners undertook 11 weeks of self-directed CAPT using cued pronunciation readings. Comparing pre-test and post-test performance on both perception and production, the authors document statistically significant improvements in pausing, word stress, and sentence-final intonation curves (cf. Abuseileek 2006). Bratu (2002) also found significant improvements for the perception and production of vowels among beginning and intermediate learners of French after just 6 hours of computer-based training, but, here, the instructor's feedback significantly enhanced that provided by the computer (see Neri et al. 2002 for similar findings). Of real interest is the preliminary evidence that CAPT's effects are long lasting. In fact, Schwartz and Brogan (1997) found much longer-term retention for CAPT than for traditional one-on-one tutoring (cited in Ferrier et al. 1999; see also Hirata 2004; Wang and Munro 2004).

One noteworthy pattern has been evident since the early days of experimental research: Audiovisual feedback is more effective than auditory feedback alone (deBot 1983), and learners who receive it opt for more repetition and practice, replaying and revising their pronunciation more than those who receive auditory feedback only (ibid.). Indeed, both perception and production appear to benefit (Knoerr and Weinberg 2005), especially when learners can see accompanying waveforms or simultaneously watch close-up video of native speakers talking (deBot 1980 and 1983; Hirata 2004; Seferoglu 2005). According to Hardison (2005), seeing video of native speakers' faces as they articulated words made a significant difference for her Japanese and Korean learners practicing difficult phonetic English contrasts (e.g., /ɹ/–/l/). Hardison's analysis suggests that a multimodal approach is more effective for perceiving phonetic contrasts in all word positions (initial, medial, final), but that initial position is most positively impacted. There is other evidence that L2 learners can best identify new and familiar words when they have a view of the speaker's head, or at least the mouth and jaw area. This recalls the idea that speech processing is audiovisual by nature, i.e., that audio and visual information are processed in overlapping areas of the brain (see Erdener and Burnham 2005; Hardison 2007).

A multimodal approach may enhance attention and working memory by reinforcing stimuli along multiple pathways, possibly maximizing retention over the long term (see Wang and Munro 2004).

Several conditions maximize the potential benefits of CAPT, based on the evidence cited here: First, students should first be instructed on the phonetics and phonology of the target language to set the stage for what is about to be practiced – what deBot calls 'feed-forward' – and both students and teachers must be able to use the software and understand the feedback it provides. Second, stimuli should represent multiple models – not just one voice (Levis 2007) – and embed targeted features within entire sentences and passages in addition to isolated environments. This sets up tasks to be more meaningful and engaging in order to maximize learning. To the extent possible, students should get close-up visual representations of real-time speaking, concentrating on the face. In general, technology must be integrated well within the overall pedagogical approach, and be introduced early before perception and production are well established (Hincks 2003).

CAPT has perhaps not fulfilled its potential due to the fact that users make different demands on it (Levis 2007). A legitimate concern is that most ASR programs do not actually teach learners how to modify or improve their pronunciation (Chun 2007), however, and CAPT activities can look suspiciously like "traditional, drill-oriented pedagogy," as Levis describes it (2007). To the extent that only the segmental level is treated, students will not get a full appreciation of phonology as it conveys discursive, social, and pragmatic meaning. Of further concern is that these programs are not well grounded theoretically or pedagogically, and thus may be difficult to incorporate into a communicative or task-based syllabus (Chun 2007). On a purely practical level, technological tools can be prohibitive in terms of cost and the teacher preparation required to utilize them well. This is surely aggravated by the ever-changing nature of such technologies (Ferrier et al. 1999), but some accessible, inexpensive tools can also be employed, e.g., podcasts and video diaries to emphasize collaborative communicative tasks (Lord 2008).

6.5 Effects of orthographic input

Given the likely cross-over in the underlying representation of visual and auditory stimuli (Hardison 2007), some scholars remind us that orthography can interfere with pronunciation, if not perception in the target language. Relevant here is the degree to which sound–symbol correspondences are transparent, namely, whether there is one-to-one correspondence between a phoneme and a grapheme (or cluster of graphemes). Transparency does not affect the acquisition of native language phonology because speaking is already well developed before the acquisition of reading and writing. FL learners, on the other hand, have a writing system in mind, and inevitably refer to L1 sound–symbol correspondences when learning to hear and speak L2 (Piske 2008). Compounding the potential for confusion, universal phonetic symbols found in instructional materials make it appear as if vowels and consonants in the target language are pronounced exactly as they are in the native language. "This means that students may not pronounce L2 sounds in a target-like way, because the similarities and differences ... are insufficiently represented" (Piske 2008: 163).

Bassetti (2009) documents several error types among L2 learners of English she attributes to a lack of orthographic transparency, leading them to pronounce the *b* in *debt* or the *l* in *walk*, for example, or insert segments based on L1 orthographical patterns (Italian learners of English often pronounce special as [spɛtʃəl] because the written symbol combination *ci* in Italian is pronounced as [tʃ]). Another error type associated with orthographic interference is substitution, an example of which occurs among Spanish learners of English for the onset /j/ as in *you*, inaccurately pronounced by some as [dʒuː] because of a word-initial pattern for the letter *y* in Spanish.

What evidence is there that such errors are really due to orthographic input, and not simply to universal strategies of simplification, deletion, substitution, etc.? Bassetti asserts that some observed pronunciation errors cannot be attributed to either L1 or L2, nor are they heard from children during the early stages of L1 acquisition (ibid.: 198f.). She also points to learner versions of L2 phonemes that are more marked than their actual (correct) version, thus defying the Markedness Differential Hypothesis (see Chapter 2, Section 2.4.3). She suggests that orthographic interference is to blame, but more data are needed to delineate the various potential sources of interference.

An interesting hypothesis is that naturalistic L2 learners are surrounded by (mostly) spoken input, putting them at less risk for such interference than their classroom learner counterparts. Young-Scholten (2002) found preliminary evidence in support of this idea as she tracked the progress of three Americans studying in Germany with no previous exposure to the language. Over 11 months, the learner with the greatest exposure to the written language had the least native-like pronunciation of new phonemes, e.g., /ç and x/, producing both as [k] possibly because they are both spelled *ch*. Further studies should be carried out with larger numbers of learners, accounting closely for spoken and written input.

Taking the opposite perspective, is it possible that orthography can actually help a learner to hear and/or produce a phonemic distinction that does not exist in L1? Steele (2005, cited in Bassetti 2009) showed that Chinese learners of French more accurately produced /ʁ/ in a consonant cluster (*traîneau*) when they saw and heard the word at the same time, as compared to those who only heard the word. In this case, orthography could have reinforced the realization that /ʁ/ and /t/ occur together initially, leading them away from the assumption that /ʀ/ is simply an aspirated /t/. In Bassetti's words, "orthographic input provides a visual and permanent analysis of the auditory input, which may complement a defective perception and thus enable learners to produce phonemes they have difficulty perceiving" (ibid.: 193).

Orthography is not the only valuable type of visual input, of course, and it can be combined with other forms to good effect. Erdener and Burnham (2005) compared the production abilities of L1 Turkish (transparent) and L1 Australian (opaque) participants asked to repeat nonce words based on Spanish (transparent) and Irish (opaque) phonology. The conditions for input were as follows: (a) audio only; (b) audiovisual display – a video of native speakers' lower faces modeling the word; (c) audiovisual + orthography; (d) audio only + orthography. Conditions (c) and (d) – those that included orthography – correlated to a significantly better performance than those without, and the combination of orthography with video yielded the best results (condition c). (Interestingly, the Turkish participants appeared to rely more on orthographic input than did the Australian participants.) The authors conclude that all visual stimuli are helpful, but orthographic information is helpful in very specific ways, possibly because it provides a working memory advantage. It should be noted, however, that they did not provide an orthography-only condition to compare its effects with the other conditions.

Few would argue that orthography does not affect the mental representations of new (L2) sounds given that orthography and phonology interact during the learning process. These sound–symbol mappings are likely retained even in the absence of written input, leading the learner to 'see' the word mentally while speaking or hearing it later on (see Perfetti and Liu 2005). Hardison's (2007) review of the first language acquisition research affirms that matched auditory–visual correspondences are a part of normal attentional and linguistic development. Evidence for the relationship between literacy development and phonetic/phonological awareness lends further support for this idea (see Erdener and Burnham 2005; Perfetti and Bolger 2004; Piske 2008).

6.6 Accent within current standards models

With the potential benefits of instruction as a backdrop, we now consider how phonology stacks up against other skills according to current standards for L2 proficiency. The need to establish standards is clear, given that bilingualism and multilingualism are fundamental to the everyday reality of so many nations worldwide. Accent should be front and center in any model of L2 learning standards since it is the central criterion of mutual intelligibility between speakers – not just in native–non-native interactions, but for non-native speakers who must communicate across language boundaries (Sifakis and Sougari 2005). It also figures in mutual perceptions of identity (ibid.: 469f.), which is particularly relevant for lingua franca contexts, where 'accent addition' is a feature of additive bilingualism (Jenkins 2004: 115). How authentic and accurate should one sound to communicate effectively in various contexts? With increasing immigration globally, this question is being considered not only by scholars, but also by professional organizations and government agencies.

In Europe, the Common European Framework (CEF) details standards for L2 learning, intended to apply to various educational sectors, language regions, and nations. Adopted by the Committee of Ministers in July 2008, the CEF details traditional reading, speaking, listening, and writing skills in new ways. Specific examples for communication strategies include: "reading for information and argument," "writing for correspondence," and "thematic development in speaking," and "listening to radio and audio recordings," among others. Within the broad area of communicative language competence, linguistic competence is one subdomain (alongside sociolinguistic and pragmatic competencies), and phonology is just one of six further subdivisions.[4] Those interested in adopting this framework are advised to consider what level of phonological skills are required of the learner given the context, to judge the relative importance of prosody vs. segments or sounds, and to assess whether phonological fluency is best prioritized early on in the process, or developed as a longer-term objective.[5]

The CEF establishes five metrics for assessing language skills qualitatively, in terms of range, accuracy, fluency, interaction, and coherence. These are intended to refer primarily to lexicon and discourse strategies, not accent. Dividing skill types into three proficiency levels 'basic,' 'independent,' and 'proficient,' phonological abilities are only mentioned as follows (Table 6.1):

To their credit, these descriptors underscore the communicative relevance of accent, but they are disproportionately sparse compared to other skill sets. It is also interesting to note the considerable gap within the *independent user* category from "occasional mispronunciations" and evident "foreign accent" at level B1 to "clear, natural pronunciation and intonation" for B2 – quite a range of ability for just one proficiency category – leaving the impression that accent is almost coincidental to overall fluency, or that it magically develops as a by-product of gains in other skill sets.

The US has two dominant frameworks for assessing second/foreign language ability, from the American Council on the Teaching of Foreign Languages (ACTFL) and the government's Interagency Language Roundtable (ILR). Their histories are intertwined: The ILR began its work in the 1950s as a response to the government's realization that foreign language preparation in the US was sorely lacking.[6]

---

[4] See overview of learning, teaching, and assessment scales at: www.coe.int/t/DG4/Portfolio/?L=E&M=/documents_intro/Data_bank_descriptors.html
[5] See Framework guidelines at : www.coe.int/t/dg4/linguistic/cadre_en.asp
[6] See www.govtilr.org

Table 6.1 *Phonological control – CEF descriptors per proficiency level*

Proficient user	C2	No descriptor available
	C1	Can vary intonation and place sentence stress correctly in order to express finer shades of meaning
Independent user	B2	Has a clear, natural pronunciation and intonation
	B1	Pronunciation is clearly intelligible even if a foreign accent is sometimes evident and occasional mispronunciations occur
Basic user	A2	Pronunciation is generally clear enough to be understood despite a noticeable foreign accent, but conversational partners will need to ask for repetition from time to time
	A1	Pronunciation of a very limited repertoire of learnt words and phrases can be understood with some effort by native speakers used to dealing with speakers of his/her language group

Source: Table 'Phonological Control', p. 117, in Council of Europe, *Common European Framework for Languages: Learning, teaching, assessment* (2001), Cambridge University Press.

The Civil Service Commission was directed to assess government employees' language skills, and working with the Foreign Service Institute, came up with a six-point scale (0 = no functional ability; ... 5 = equivalent to an educated native speaker). Descriptions of listening, reading, speaking, and writing came later, and ACTFL then developed a similar scale and designed its Oral Proficiency Interview (OPI) based on the ILR version.

Because the ACTFL Oral Proficiency Guidelines (1985) were modeled on those of the ILR, the basic ILR ability description per level is given here for pronunciation, specifically (Table 6.2):

These descriptions are limited, to be sure, but the ACTFL Guidelines are even less detailed within their scale of *novice, intermediate, advanced, superior*, and *distinguished* (corresponding roughly to 0, 1, 2, 3, 4 on the ILR scale). For example, novice and intermediate descriptions say only, "pronunciation is highly influenced by L1." It is not until the advanced level that the ACTFL scale mentions accent as a meaningful communicative skill: "differentiated intonation is effectively used to communicate fine shades of meaning"; and at the superior level, "the ability to distinguish main ideas from supporting information through ... suprasegmental features (pitch, stress, intonation)." (Speech rate is also mentioned at the advanced level as a communicative strategy.)

The ACTFL Guidelines are widely referenced, if not directly employed through OPI-type assessments at various agencies and universities. Although not all FL instructors adopt them, their influence is widely felt. Teachers would be hard-pressed to develop more detailed rubrics based on these vague descriptions. They must therefore determine their own objectives for phonological fluency ad hoc (Derwing and Munro 2005; Morley 1991).

Table 6.2 *ILR descriptions of speaking ability*

Scale number	Scale description	General ability	Pronunciation ability
0+	Memorized proficiency	Able to satisfy immediate needs using rehearsed utterances	Stress, intonation, tone, etc. are usually quite faulty
1	Elementary proficiency	Able to satisfy minimum courtesy requirements and maintain very simple face-to-face conversations on familiar topics	Pronunciation, stress, and intonation are generally poor, often heavily influenced by another language
1+	Elementary proficiency plus	Can initiate and maintain predictable face-to-face conversations and satisfy limited social demands	Pronunciation is understandable to natives used to dealing with foreigners. Can combine most significant sounds with reasonable comprehensibility, but has difficulty in producing certain sounds in certain positions or in certain combinations. Speech will usually be labored
2	Limited working proficiency	Able to satisfy routine social demands and limited work requirements. Can handle routine work-related interactions that are limited in scope	[no mention of accent]
3	General professional proficiency	Able to speak the language with sufficient structural accuracy and vocabulary to participate effectively in most formal and informal conversations in practical, social, and professional topics	Pronunciation may be obviously foreign. Individual sounds are accurate: but stress, intonation and pitch control may be faulty
4	Advanced professional proficiency	Able to use the language fluently and accurately on all levels normally pertinent to professional needs	[No mention of accent except 'occasional weaknesses in pronunciation']
5	Functionally native proficiency	Speaking proficiency is functionally equivalent to that of a highly articulate well-educated native speaker	Pronunciation is typically consistent with that of well-educated native speakers of a non-stigmatized dialect

Levis argues that pronunciation should not be formally assessed, at least not in terms of accuracy (2006). "How many errors are too much? It is impossible to know since pronunciation is only one part of a spoken message and interlocutors have many clues to meaning available beyond phonetic form" (ibid.: 252). It is true that phonology overall is less about right and wrong and more about whether one is effectively understood. (Then again, listener difficulties can arise for many different reasons, some linguistic, others contextual or personal.) Perhaps the ambiguity evident in current standards is a reflection of this realization; most of the descriptions downplay accent except where it concerns comprehensibility. In the American context, this coincides with a lack of pedagogical emphasis on phonology, as discussed. The dominant approaches of the day – Communicative Language Teaching and Task-Based Language Teaching – have not reassessed accent relative to other communicative skills, and the National Standards movement does not mention it at all. In the European context, perhaps the brevity of description reflects the everyday realities of multilingualism. After all, having a foreign accent is normal in multilingual contexts, and does not necessarily affect fluency or intelligibility in a second language.

6.7 Conclusions: the potential of phonological instruction

We began this chapter by posing two challenges to the notion that instruction in phonology is an effective means to improve accent:
- If accent in a second language is such an individual skill, and much of what contributes to it lies beyond conscious practice, how consequential can explicit training be?
- Can the classroom address phonological fluency in a comprehensive way, i.e., provide enough contextualized practice to promote real authenticity?

The various efforts to gauge the efficacy of phonological instruction have delivered mixed results. Evidence in favor suggests that instruction and explicit practice can speed up the acquisition of some features, and eradicate some errors and points of confusion, but this is not to say that it will work for everyone in all circumstances. Nor can we claim that classroom input alone is sufficient for high-level attainment, although it can certainly set learners on the path to noticing, and possibly emulating, essential qualities that characterize native speech. Instruction's impact depends on the conditions under which it is offered, the consistency of its availability over time, and the individual's receptivity to it.

Assuming that targeted phonological training makes a real difference – and we have cited some evidence that it can – the greatest puzzle is whether the benefits of practice and feedback relate to specific cognitive mechanisms such as attention and memory, or to specific metacognitive learning strategies like self-monitoring and repair. All would presumably facilitate hypothesis formation and knowledge restructuring – the bases for acquisition. Along the way, however, learners also have to maintain an interest in improving their accent, and this cannot be assumed (Moyer 1999).

Researchers interested in the particulars of implicit and explicit learning are up against mostly unobservable processes and idiosyncratic orientations of both a cognitive and a psychological nature. This makes it far more difficult to isolate which tasks and feedback types reliably affect outcomes. Having acknowledged this, a few tentative conclusions can be made about how to ensure the efficacy of phonological instruction:

(1) Approach: A holistic approach is presumed most effective, not only because it appeals to a range of learning styles, but also because it represents phonology as an essential part of overall fluency. 'Holistic' here refers to a combination of isolated and contextualized practice; a transition from controlled to extemporaneous tasks to promote meaningful learning; and the incorporation of both discrimination and production practice, so that students must learn to hear new L2 sounds as distinct from L1 sounds before they are expected to produce them accurately. A holistic approach necessarily stresses the communicative import of accent as well. This requires an overt treatment of suprasegmentals at the word and sentence levels as well as within entire passages. Listening tasks should incorporate different voices and practice 'noticing' how accent is used to provide social cues, negotiate interaction, and control discursive flow. In cognitive terms, this increases salience by accentuating the connections between forms and various types of meaning; in psychological terms, it may increase interest and motivation toward accuracy and authenticity. Furthermore, a holistic approach combines explicit and implicit practice and feedback, raising awareness as much as it provides direct explanations. It also implies an overt discussion of regional and social variation so that learners understand the connections between accent and identity in the target language.

(2) Techniques and tools: Some tried-and-true things do seem to work, e.g., mimicry of native speaker models, by whatever means available. Practice 'noticing the gap' is an essential part of this. Visuals and cross-modal training can be employed to enhance learning through multiple, overlapping pathways. (They also serve to raise interest and engagement for some.) Technology can deliver cross-modal training in a package, and boost learner interest as well, but it should be accessible and offer something unique in terms of learning, for example, by providing immediate audio-visual feedback on self-generated recordings. To the extent that techniques and tools are learner-centered, i.e., self-paced and individualized, they seem to be especially effective.

A few important stipulations accompany these recommendations. The first is that any such practice should be consistent and ongoing; training that is overly brief or episodic is far less effective, and does seem to not last. Second, this list is not meant to be prescriptive. If anything, the previous discussion indicates that some experimentation is in order. Absent any formal method or detailed set of assessment standards, teachers should proceed according to well-informed principles and tailor their programs as they see fit, cognizant of their learners' intentions for how, and with whom, they will use the target language. To this end, accent should not be treated solely as an aspect of structural accuracy, devoid of any social or communicative value.

As for the extent to which instruction facilitates the acquisition of a more authentic-sounding accent, this is a matter of time and focus. FL classrooms tend to be short on time, and necessarily devoted to many learning objectives at once. Phonology typically takes a backseat to grammar, lexicon, and culture as a result. Anecdotally, many would say that accent is best 'picked up' in the target-language country, and yes, a typical FL classroom cannot compete in terms of providing a culturally and socially rich learning environment. Diaz-Campos (2004) indicates that immersion experience is not necessary for phonetic fluency to develop (his 'stay home' Spanish learners actually outperformed his study abroad group for specific phonetic contrasts). A reasonable position is that a combination of instruction and immersion best supports oral fluency (Segalowitz and Freed 2004) and a closer-to-native accent (Moyer 2004 and 2007a). In particular, this may be most noticeable when immersion *follows* phonological instruction, i.e., after the foundation for noticing has been laid (Lord 2010).

In this chapter we have noted the now-popular stance that intelligibility is a reasonable, more realistic benchmark for phonological attainment among FL learners, but we have also noted how difficult it is to pin this down in specific terms. Moreover, teachers and students may not be warming up to the idea yet. Students, regardless of L1 background, seem to prefer having a native-speaking FL teacher (Lasagabaster and Sierra 2005), and many hold on to the goal of a native-like accent for themselves (Simon 2005). Teachers adhere to similar normative attitudes, including those in the Expanding Circle who are non-native speakers themselves (Sifakis and Sougari 2005). In other words, even international contexts with their own regional varieties of English are 'enmeshed' in nativeness ideologies (ibid.), and students and teachers alike are susceptible to preconceptions and stereotypes about the desirability of a 'standard' accent (Cenoz and Garcia Lecumberri 1999; Dalton-Puffer et al. 1997). Jenkins' (2005) qualitative study of eight non-native, international ESL teachers found numerous contradictions in terms of accent attitudes. For example, many felt conflicted about whether it is right to teach a pronunciation model based on the local ESL accent. Most were not inclined to do so, attributing their reluctance to *others'* perceptions that it would not be a valid standard. (Of interest here is Zhang's (2004) finding that teachers tend to rate native speech more positively than accented speech. He therefore recommends pre-service training to address covertly negative attitudes among teachers – see also Haddon 1991; Munro et al. 2006.)

Those likely to interact with other non-native speakers in lingua franca settings may warrant a different set of standards than those hoping to integrate into the target-language community (Derwing and Munro 2005; Levis 2005). Let us also remember that native and non-native speakers do not necessarily prioritize the same features when judging accent, as shown by Riney et al. (2005), with suprasegmentals making a great difference for lingua franca-type speech, as segmental accuracy does for native–non-native interactions (see also Jenkins 2000).

The default classroom approach these days is to let non-egregious errors go and assume that students will eventually work things out for themselves. After all, "having an accent is a normal aspect of second language learning, particularly for adult learners" (Munro 2003: 48). Yet teachers are the primary resource for most learners to gain meaningful practice, assuming access to target-language input beyond the classroom is lacking, and online lab activities offer only minimal phonology training. Lefkowitz and Hedgcock (2002) verify that learners are aware of the impressions accent can make but they are not the most astute judges of how they themselves sound. Teachers can help learners to realistically assess this, and to realize how significant accent is, socially and communicatively. Such efforts acknowledge the sociolinguistic realities that all language learners face when they step beyond the classroom. Decisions on how rigorously to pursue the native ideal will effectively be in their hands at that point, armed with an understanding of how and why accent matters.

7 Conclusions

7.1 Accent in a second language: viewpoints and expectations

This book has endeavored to describe accent in all its complexity. Accent conveys our linguistic meaning and our communicative intent, at the same time that it controls the flow of a conversation and situates us socially and psychologically vis-à-vis our interlocutors. Because of our human propensity to judge one another on the basis of easily identifiable categories, the salience of accent is immediate and perhaps even greater than other signals of 'in-group' vs. 'out-group' status, including physical appearance (see Chapter Four, Section 4.4).

The preceding chapters have investigated foreign accent from a number of angles – as a neurobiological, a cognitive, a social, a psychological, and a communicative phenomenon. We have examined the ways that phonology uniquely challenges language learners beyond early childhood, and considered what it means to sound foreign in this age of globalization, multiculturalism and 'expanding circles' of L2 users. This is a matter of some debate in the current literature. We have thus counterposed prescriptive notions about accent standards with *intelligibility*, cognizant of the fact that 'the nativeness principle' has been called into question as an outdated, and essentially unfair, benchmark for acquisition. For phonology it appears especially difficult to achieve anything approaching nativeness.

From the researcher's perspective, nativeness is an important reference point for perception and production abilities – not just for decontextualized discrimination tasks, but also for measures that allow for a speaker's full range of segmental and suprasegmental fluency to emerge. In the pedagogical realm, teachers commonly reinforce nativeness as a goal, even if an unspoken one, and learners may not see this as an unwelcome imposition; many consider it their target whether or not they are likely to reach it. From the standpoint of communication, a native ideal can serve as a baseline for mutual comprehensibility in native/non-native interactions (as for non-native/non-native ones). American and British English standards may retain their preferred status in this regard, at least for now, but this will surely change with shifts in population and the concomitant redistribution of economic, social, and political power.

Considering that many L2 users have fewer linguistic resources at hand with which to make communicative adjustments and accommodations, *intelligibility* seems to present a more reasonable standard from which to view non-native speech, but it has proven difficult to pin down. Linguistically, many criteria affect perceptions of intelligibility, including segmental precision, pitch, intonation, speech rate, rhythm, and stress (morphosyntax and lexicon are obviously critical as well). At the same time, listener expectations and experiences also determine whether a non-native speaker is 'heard,' literally and figuratively. And let us not forget that even beyond the immediate context, there is inevitably some broader consensus about the value associated with specific foreign accents. Any biases present surely influence the negotiation of the communicative burden between interlocutors. Native speakers are arguably well equipped to work around gaps in phonological fluency, and non-native errors are frequently tolerated no matter who is listening. But in trying to understand how all of this affects communicative dynamics, we have barely scratched the surface, research-wise. Too much is assumed, and too little verified, when it comes to the factors that guide actual communicative behaviors.

Despite a rapidly changing linguistic landscape, many who speak with a foreign accent will no doubt continue to encounter negative reactions at times, even within so-called 'immigrant' nations like the US. Beyond constraining interaction – with all the consequences for phonological attainment that implies – accent-related attitudes play out in the workplace, and in our schools, neighborhoods, and judicial system. There is not yet a clear indication whether *degree* of accent is at the heart of this phenomenon. The research is clearly challenged in this regard: It is difficult to extrapolate real-life experiences of foreign-accented individuals from mock judicial procedures or employment scenarios, and study participants may avoid claiming prejudice, in any case. What is clear is that overall language proficiency should be disambiguated from accent, especially in cases where there is a legitimate concern about comprehensibility (e.g., in the workplace).

The adjudication of accent discrimination is on the rise in the US and the UK, suggesting that foreign accents do not enjoy a more positive reception these days, i.e., as an aspect of cultural diversity. If anything, times of great social and cultural change predict harsher reactions toward those who sound or appear foreign. So while some immigrants take pride in accent as an emblem of their heritage, others may feel pressured to lose it as quickly as possible. The deeply personal side of having a foreign accent is rarely discussed, much less closely studied.

7.2 Remaining questions and methodological recommendations

Much ground has been covered in the preceding chapters from many empirical perspectives. Throughout, we have endeavored to point out questions still to be addressed within the various realms of phonology research. A few considerations for future work are summarized here:

7.2.1   Neurocognitive processing

The neurocognitive realm is something of a black box, but research is beginning to offer intriguing insights on language processing differences between early and late bilinguals. Many areas pertaining specifically to phonological acquisition need clarification:

- Does bilateral processing imply greater perceptual acuity, especially for suprasegmental features of language? And, if so, are those who are naturally bilateral processors (e.g., females) inherently advantaged in this regard?
- If beginning language learning is characterized by bilateral processing, does this imply a *stage*-related window of greater openness to features like tone and rhythm?
- Does the learning environment affect bilateral processing, so that immersion-type experiences naturally activate both hemispheres while classroom instruction promotes LH (left hemisphere) processing? This is a logical, but mostly speculative, assumption at this point.
- How does perception connect to production? Specifically, can perceptual training aid the production of new sounds and sound patterns? If so, how much is enough, and at what point in the learning process is it most efficacious?
- What are the respective roles played by selective attention, repetition, imitation, and practice for restructuring phonological knowledge? Are such skills learnable, so that learners not predisposed to certain strategies can effectively target phonological fluency through conscious effort?
- What is the nature of the cognition-affect interface? As an example, is there a connection between selective attention, the enjoyment of sound pattern mimicry, and sensitivity to suprasegmental features, as has been suggested (Rota and Reiterer 2009)?

Isolated, lab-based studies are the primary means by which language processing is examined, but more natural, communicative tasks should be incorporated to discover what L2 learners actually do during negotiated interaction. There are obvious limits inherent to neural imaging techniques – they are quick snapshots of processing activity but give no view of long-term acquisition. More experiments could include instructional conditions to look for training effects, as seen in Sereno and Wang (2007). Additional lines of research could compare male and female language learners across a span of ages and proficiency levels to determine whether bilateral processing correlates to gender throughout the learning process, and at what point in the acquisition continuum bilateral processing of certain features (tone, rhythm, stress) becomes LH-dominant for all learners, regardless of gender or age.

7.2.2 Socio-psychological concerns

A simplistic, yet reasonable assumption is that a positive attitude and strong motivation lead to higher levels of attainment in the target language; however, affective factors are dynamic, complex, and sometimes conflicted. Gardner and Lambert (1972) remind us that negative attitudes can be just as powerful as positive ones. Some learners approach language learning out of a sense of resentment: resentment towards the mother tongue where it is seen as a detriment to upward mobility, and resentment towards the second language if there is no choice but to learn it. In the first case, the target language will be pursued with enthusiasm, in the second case it will not – it may even be avoided. This underscores another important reality: While various psychological forces collectively termed *affect* play a role in SLA, none operates in isolation: All such influences converge within the broader, highly individualized learning context, which makes them unpredictable (see Dörnyei 2003a). For this reason, instruments must be more inclusive to capture these interrelationships and to outline a fuller framework for understanding the learner's dynamic orientation toward the target language.

The socio-psychological factors relevant to accent have been presented here as a reflection of both *investment* and *self-regulation*. Successful learners, regardless of their stage of learning, take a consistently active, reflective role in their own learning. Their beliefs about the value of the target language have a great deal to do with how they utilize resources for language contact and interaction. If we think of language learning as a very long-term endeavor, it makes sense that the consistency of one's approach, and one's motivation over time, are key. At the same time, language learning is dynamic, so flexibility is needed to reorient oneself to changing conditions, achievements, and also setbacks. Those who do end up sounding native-like are those who reliably initiate cognitive and social strategies to increase meaningful interaction in the target language. Some relevant questions are thus:

- Does an integrative orientation predispose the learner to a sense of openness that benefits phonological learning by way of noticing, reflection, self-initiated efforts to improve, etc.?
- Is empathy the key to both outward approach and internal processes such as noticing and attention? Specifically, do empathic learners attend to features that signify emotion, stance, and intent in special ways? Could this give them an edge in phonological fluency given the importance of suprasegmentals for perceptions of accentedness? Moreover, does empathy encourage specific accommodation types or other behaviors that result in beneficial practice, e.g., through imitation, repetition, etc.?
- Do episodes of passing eventually become routinized, developing into real fluency? Are they some kind of precursor to nativeness in the sense that they constitute a *practice*?

- Can full acculturation and foreign accent peacefully coexist, and how is this decision negotiated internally, even as social networks are established and the target language takes on deeply symbolic significance in the learner's life?

Studies of a qualitative nature are needed to explore the mutual development of accent and identity in the target language, yet these are rarely undertaken in phonological research. Introspective, longitudinal data are the best way to understand how the development of social networks opens opportunities to use the target language in meaningful ways. Diary studies of phonological development, such as Pawlak (2011) describes, can further substantiate the conscientious efforts of self-aware learners, especially with regards to their goal-setting, self-monitoring, and self-evaluation.

Hansen Edwards (2008) has written that "access – or lack thereof – to various communities may affect what elements of the L2 are targeted for acquisition and use, as well as the extent to which L2 learners use or avoid using (or avoid acquiring) certain features" if they symbolize an identity that is uncomfortable or not viable (ibid.: 273). Accordingly, we should not assume that all deviations from standard language forms are mistakes or errors (ibid.) – they may be purposeful aspects of performance rather than competence.

SLA research has long been skewed toward a 'less-than' viewpoint when it comes to performance data, and this is partly a byproduct of a rigorous analytical focus. As we aim to understand what learners do, it is perhaps more efficient to emphasize what they (apparently) cannot do. One way to open up this outdated approach is to focus on learner agency, as Hansen suggests, but this is still quite rare in the phonology research. A starting point would be to explore in depth why some learners make a conscious choice to hold on to their accent in the face of 'acceptability' concerns? This question turns upside down the notion that all learners hope, and intend, to sound native-like. An equally important task is to observe socio-psychological factors as interrelated pieces of a puzzle, not as stand-alone influences on phonological acquisition.

7.2.3 Experience, learning context, and age

Many immigrants live for years in their host country without progressing beyond rudimentary linguistic skills, and many children have overheard, or otherwise been passively exposed to, a second language without developing any real competence in it. Mere exposure is no guarantee of the opportunity – or inclination – to turn input into intake. We have therefore defined experience as *meaningful* language practice, characterized by consistent interaction with native speakers. Accordingly, future phonological research should advance the following themes:

- the relative balance of L1–L2 use, and how that affects long-term phonological acquisition
- quantity vs. quality of language use, measured by specific contexts and interlocutors, to gain a fuller picture of whom L2 users interact with, and to what purpose
- long-term processing effects of immersion vs. classroom-type exposure. Those with the benefits of intense exposure seem to have a more native-like (neural) representation of the target language (Muñoz 2008). (An additional question is whether those processing effects pertain more to perception or production.)

Time spent in the target-language environment manifests a special convergence of intrinsic and extrinsic factors, and as such, deserves more nuanced examination overall. In-country experience essentially connects language use and *investment*, and allows us to better understand phenomena like passing, language shift, and even attrition.

Experience is something of a new frontier in L2 phonology research, which is exciting, but it is inextricably connected to the age issue, and that complicates the researcher's task considerably. Young immigrants clearly have the advantage in terms of input and practice because they are typically schooled in the target language itself and have plentiful opportunities to create new social networks. Adults must strive to structure language contact in optimal ways. All of these foundational issues must be taken into account methodologically, through both instruments and analysis procedures (Moyer 2007b).

A paradigm shift is in order, and may be well underway when it comes to understanding age effects in L2 phonology. Up to now, studies on the effects of AO (age of onset) have too often described the age at which *insignificant* exposure begins, Muñoz argues, rather than providing crucial information on amounts of, and contexts for, L2 input (2008: 585). Furthermore, the *younger is better* adage does not apply equally to all learning contexts, because "when younger learners attain a state of cognitive development that is similar to that of older learners with whom they are being compared, and are given the same conditions of time and exposure (and instruction), the [age] differences should disappear" (ibid.: 34; see DeKeyser 2000). For this reason, Muñoz (2008) questions the appropriateness of comparing classroom foreign language learners not living in the target-language environment to those who are immersed. A classroom cannot meet 'optimal' conditions, so attributing "low achievement solely to starting age does not seem to be justified" (ibid.: 580).

The Barcelona Age Factor Project (Muñoz 2006a) provides rare insight into age effects across a span of AO for instructed learners of English in Spain – all bilingual speakers of Spanish and Catalan. Via a longitudinal approach, Muñoz and colleagues track the progress of various age groups while controlling for learning context. The data from a range of tests across language levels point to a faster rate of learning and higher scores for adolescent and adult learners. The most significant factor throughout (with the exception of listening comprehension) is L1 proficiency, which Muñoz (2006b) associates with cognitive development. Extracurricular exposure is also moderately influential within the first 200 instructional hours. This is a reminder that the learning environment surely activates different mechanisms, with explicit learning and declarative memory likely dominating instructed contexts and implicit mechanisms guiding uninstructed ones. The BAF project is an important model for how to address learning context while accounting for age at the same time.

There is a longstanding notion in the pedagogical literature that classroom language learners unwittingly reinforce one another's 'bad habits'. Such a debate has never taken off in the phonology research (but see Flege 2009), and no hard evidence exists to verify such a claim, to this author's knowledge. Here again though, the particulars of experience are important. Classroom learners are typically exposed to many different phonological models, including non-native teachers (Bohn and Bundgaard-Nielsen 2009; Muñoz 2008). The immersion learner likely encounters a more consistent phonological model by comparison. The result is that those who get no immersion experience could be limited to an 'ill-defined' target for the new sound system (Bohn and Bundgaard-Nielsen 2009: 209). This is another reason to clearly detail the instructional background of study participants and contextualize the conditions under which they are approaching new target-language sounds.

The emphasis on experience throughout this book underscores a fundamental reality for language acquisition, namely that sufficient input and practice are necessary for fluency to develop. Regardless of his age, a learner needs plentiful opportunities to engage with, not simply be exposed to, the target language if procedural knowledge is to develop. For classroom learners, the rarity of unstructured, authentic practice with native speakers can present an insurmountable obstacle to phonological fluency, even if instruction begins early. Research suggests that this kind of communicative engagement with native speakers has great significance for accent, perhaps even more so than does AO.

7.3   The unique challenge of L2 accent

While detailing the various ways that phonology can be a challenge for L2 learners, we have aimed to portray it as a fluid and dynamic phenomenon, emphasizing the learner's role in the process. No one is subject to language acquisition processes and outcomes as a passive participant. In many ways, traditional SLA research has promoted a deterministic message, however: *These are the limits, this is the boundary you will experience despite your best efforts, and only a few exceptional ones among you will cross over this boundary to sound native-like.* For phonology, more than any other subdomain of language, that sense of inevitable foreignness still prevails. But an analysis by Moyer (2012) suggests that exceptional learners do not have extraordinary talents. Instead, they employ an *adaptive* approach – cognitively, socially, and psychologically. They respond with flexibility and a great measure of self-reflection, continuing to direct their efforts toward accent even after achieving solid fluency overall. Some even initiate painful trade-offs, such as avoiding contact with other speakers of their mother tongue to prioritize immersion in the new language. Few among us are willing to go to such extremes, leaving our linguistic (and emotional) comfort zone for the sake of fully adopting the sounds of a different culture.

In her essay, "Speaking in Tongues," (2009) Zadie Smith recalls George Bernard Shaw's *Pygmalion* and its main character, Eliza Doolittle, a Cockney-speaking flower girl from working-class London who is the guinea pig for Professor Higgins' accent-altering experiment. Smith's premise is that "something's got to give" – a person can have only "one voice or the other" (41), and acquiring a new accent is bound to change a person – not necessarily in positive ways:

> By the end of his experiment, Professor Higgins has made Eliza an awkward, in-between thing, neither flower girl nor lady, with one voice lost and another gained, at the steep price of everything she was, and everything she knows ... How persistent this horror of the middling spot is, this dread of the interim place ... [like] the contemporary immigrant, tragically split between two worlds, ideas, cultures, voices – whatever will become of them? (41)

Some learners deemed 'exceptional' for accent may have pushed through that predicted boundary to land in a Doolittle-like place, at least temporarily, before settling into a comfortable L2 identity. This is what sets accent apart from other aspects of language; only for phonology would our core sense of self be so thoroughly challenged. (The neuro-muscular basis of phonology is another unique layer to contend with, of course.)

In his original definition of language attitudes, decades back now, Gardner (1979) emphasized *desire plus effort sustained over the long term*. That is to say, an individual must be willing to invest deeply in the target language to reach the advanced level since the effort required is so substantial. Phonology is arguably the greatest test of this effort. Any relevant aptitudes aside, most late learners struggle with the sounds, the rhythm, the intonation, and the stress patterns of a new language. Individuals can only negotiate this struggle commensurate with their views of the target-language's value, their attitudes about its speakers, and their views on the value of language learning in general.

Glossary

accentedness	is another way of describing *degree of foreign accent*, often measured on a scale of five or more points.
accommodation	is the process by which interlocutors adjust aspects of their own speech, typically to indicate social convergence, neutrality, or divergence with one another. Accommodation is evident on any level (lexical, grammatical, discursive), including the segmental and suprasegmental aspects of phonology (see Giles and Coupland 1991).
acculturation	is the ongoing process of adopting certain values and traits of the target-language culture while simultaneously maintaining ties to the native language group (Schumann 1978).
age of onset	is generally the age at first exposure to the target language. In some studies this refers to meaningful use, in others simply exposure through informal means, such as through a trip abroad, overhearing native speakers in some context, or formal instruction. The differences in the nature of such levels of experience, not to mention the implications for acquisition, are sometimes addressed empirically by separating age of immersion from age of instruction.
attention	is defined as a state of alertness and readiness that leads the learner to select and register the intended input (Tomlin and Villa 1994). It is thought to signify that all-important threshold of consciousness that allows input to become *intake*, i.e., available for the learner's use (see Chapter Six, Section 6.3.1).

Glossary

authenticity — in the phonological realm implies more than segmental and word- or phrase-level accuracy; it includes the ability to modulate prosody, rhythm and intonation for pragmatic, social, and communicative effect.

comprehensibility — refers to the perceived ease with which a listener understands a speaker's meaning at a global level (see also *intelligibility*). Comprehensibility is bidirectional, not solely dependent on the speaker's accent for example, given that interlocutors necessarily come to any interaction with expectations for general, as well as phonological, fluency.

critical period — denotes a specific neurobiological window, after which language acquisition is thought to be incomplete. Age effects are apparent as early as 9–10 years according to Lenneberg's research on language recovery among aphasics, but others maintain that the critical period for phonology closes even earlier, by the age of 5 or 6 years, if not before (see *plasticity*).

declarative knowledge — has to do with the rule-based, grammatical aspects of a language while *procedural knowledge* refers to know-how, or the contextual applications of such rules (generally acquired through contextualized practice).

fluency — is generally defined as the ability to process language in real time, as opposed to understanding language as an object of knowledge, i.e., it reflects an automatic, procedural level of skill (Schmidt 1992: 358).

fossilization — refers to the presumed cessation of learning at some point in the SLA developmental continuum. Those who learn language beyond early childhood are said to inevitably stop short of nativeness for phonology in particular, but potentially for morphology and syntax as well (Selinker 1972; see Han 2004).

intelligibility — describes the extent to which a word or longer utterance is understood at the acoustic-phonetic level, but also depends on expectations about the speaker's intended meaning (discussed at length in Chapter 4). Intelligibility is commonly invoked in discussions of English as an International Language as a more reasonable and relevant target for L2 accent, as opposed to nativeness or near-nativeness.

Glossary

Language Acquisition Device (LAD)	is Chomsky's term for an innate and uniquely human faculty responsible for the acquisition of language despite primary linguistic data (input) that is 'impoverished' in various ways, especially as it lacks negative evidence, or evidence of what is *not* possible in a language. It is an ongoing theoretical debate in the SLA literature whether the LAD is still accessible for late language learning (see Gregg 1996).
lateralization	see *plasticity*
matched guise	is a technique developed by Lambert and colleagues working in bilingual and multilingual communities, as a way to test listener evaluations of dialects and accents somewhat surreptitiously (see Lambert et al. 1960). A speaker records the same speech passage more than once, using a different regional or social dialect for each recording, and listeners rate the personal and social attributes of the 'guise' – matched for linguistic content – along the lines of education, physical attractiveness, reliability, friendliness, etc.
nativeness	is not a well-defined term, but generally indicates a speaker's ability to produce or perceive some (or all) aspects of a language on par with its native speakers, i.e., those who are raised within that language environment and whose language use is consistent and ongoing through time (e.g., not limited to episodic use in childhood). Whether an L2 user must perform as a native in all levels to be considered native-like (e.g., phonology, morphology, etc.), or simply on specific tasks within one level, is a matter of some debate.
passing	is the purposeful attempt to sound native in a language other than one's mother tongue, usually confined to a specific context and/or episode (see Piller 2002).
phonetics	refers to the system of discrete speech sounds in a language – their articulatory, auditory, and acoustic properties and classification.
phonology	is the system of sounds in a language and their distributional rules. Phonological rules explain language-specific phenomena such as segmental

	assimilation, elision, deletion, coarticulation, etc., as well as phrasal rhythm and stress patterns. (NB: The term *phonology* is often used in a general way to refer to both phonetics and phonology, unless specific learning phenomena are the subject of discussion, such as the acquisition of phonetic contrasts like /ɪ/ v. /ɛ/) (see *phonetics*).
plasticity	describes the flexibility of neural structures associated with *lateralization*, the assignment of specific functions (e.g., auditory processing, visual processing) to a specific neural area located in either the right or left hemisphere. Lenneberg's *Critical Period Hypothesis* predicted that plasticity begins to decline around puberty, and that this accounts for the difficulty experienced by many adult language learners with regards to phonology, which is based partly on neuro-muscular skill. Any age-based cessation of neural plasticity is still a matter of debate in the scientific literature.
prescriptivism	is the term given to the common view that one variety of language has an inherently higher value than others, and that this 'standard' should be imposed on the entire *speech community* (Crystal 1987: 2).
procedural knowledge	see *declarative knowledge*.
processing	is a general term that encompasses the mental activities involved in real-time language use. For the native speaker, language processing is automatic (Herschensohn 2007: 193).
segments/segmentals	are individual sounds usually represented by a single grapheme or symbol in the International Phonetic Alphabet. For example, the word *then* contains 3 segments or sounds (in graphemes or letters: *th, e, n*), rendered in IPA symbols as /ðɛn/ (see *suprasegmentals*).
social class	is defined as a measure of economic wealth or position, but functions as a proxy variable for lifestyle, attitudes, and beliefs, all of which affect language behavior (see Brown and Fraser 1979; Robinson 1979).

Glossary

speech community	is a group of people who share a common language variety based on geography, ethnicity, religion, gender, citizenship, etc. *Speech community* can be further described in terms of *social networks* (Milroy and Milroy 1985b) and *communities of practice* (Meyerhoff 2002), which highlight both the degree to which individuals are personally connected, and the (co)construction of identity through interaction.
style-shifting	is a communicative phenomenon by which a speaker adjusts certain features for effect, to indicate personal stance and/or to reflect contextual appropriateness, e.g., adopting a more careful enunciation and avoiding slang in a formal environment such as a job interview.
suprasegmentals	are features that extend beyond the level of the individual sound, or segment, including syllable and word stress, pitch, rhythm, intonation, loudness, juncture, and length or duration of syllables.
ultimate attainment	refers to the purported 'end-state' of learning. Han (2004) maintains that this term implies 'global' interlanguage fossilization, but for our purposes here it refers more generally to outcomes in long-term phonological acquisition.
universal grammar (UG)	is a theoretical concept that assumes a specialized language acquisition module to account for the fact that infants are remarkably adept at processing speech sounds and acquiring the complexities of language despite faulty and 'impoverished' input (see Müller 1996). Some SLA scholars assert that such a module is no longer available after early childhood, thereby accounting for age effects. Others maintain that UG is partially or even fully available, but is overwhelmed by cognitive-analytic processes once puberty is reached (see Hancin-Bhatt 2008; O'Grady 2003; White 2003).
voice onset time (VOT)	is the time elapsed between the release of airflow, or burst, from a closure and the beginning of vocal cord vibration. Measured in milliseconds, it can distinguish phonemes, e.g., /b/ and /p/.

References

Abraham, L. (2003). Media stereotypes of African Americans. In P. Lester and S. Ross (eds.), *Images that injure: Pictorial stereotypes in the media* (87–92). Westport, CN: Praeger.

Abuhamdia, Z. (1987). Neurobiological foundations for foreign language. *International Review of Applied Linguistics*, 25, 203–11.

Abuseileek, A. (2006). An evaluation of a computer-assisted pronunciation training program for EFL learners. *Grazer Linguistische Studien*, 66, 1–24.

Abutalebi, J. (2008). Neural aspects of second language representation and language control. *Acta Psychologica*, 128, 466–78.

ACTFL (1985). *ACTFL proficiency guidelines*. American Council for the Teaching of Foreign Languages. Hastings-on-Hudson, NY: ACTFL Materials Center.

Acton, W. (1984). Changing fossilized pronunciation. *TESOL Quarterly*, 18, 71–85.

Adamson, H. and Regan, V. (1991). The acquisition of community speech norms by Asian immigrants learning English as a second language: A preliminary study. *Studies in Second Language Acquisition*, 13, 1–22.

Akita, M. (2006). Global foreign accent and classroom input in L2 perception and production. *Proceedings of the Annual Boston Conference on Language Development*, 30, 1–14.

Albrechtsen, D., Henriksen, B., and Faerch, C. (1980). Native speaker reactions to learners' spoken interlanguage. *Language Learning*, 30, 365–96.

Alford, R. and Strother, J. (1990). Attitudes of native and nonnative speakers toward selected regional accents of US English. *TESOL Quarterly*, 24, 479–95.

Altenberg, E. and Vago, R. (1987). Theoretical implications of an error analysis of second language phonology production. In G. Ioup and S. Weinberger (eds.), *Interlanguage phonology* (148–64). Cambridge, MA: Newbury House.

Anderson, B. (1983). *Imagined communities: Reflections on the origin and spread of nationalism*. London: Verso.

Anderson, J. (1987). The markedness differential hypothesis and syllable structure difficulty. In G. Ioup and S. Weinberger (eds.), *Interlanguage phonology* (279–91). Cambridge, MA: Newbury House.

Anderson-Hsieh, J., Johnson, R., and Koehler, K. (1992). The relationship between native speaker judgments of nonnative pronunciation and deviance in segmentals, prosody, and syllable structure. *Language Learning*, 42, 529–55.

Anderson-Hsieh, J. and Koehler, K. (1988). The effect of foreign accent and speaking rate on native speaker comprehension. *Language Learning*, 38, 561–613.

References

Aoyama, K., Guion, S., Flege, J., Yamada, T., and Akahane-Yamada, R. (2008). The first years in an L2-speaking environment: A comparison of Japanese children and adults learning American English. *IRAL*, 46, 61–90.

Archibald, J. (1998). *Second language phonology*. Amsterdam: John Benjamins.

Archibold, R. (2010, April 23). Arizona enacts stringent law on immigration. *New York Times*. Retrieved from http://www.nytimes.com/2010/04/24/us/politics/24immig.html

Asher, J. and Garcia, R. (1969). The optimal age to learn a foreign language. *Modern Language Journal*, 53, 334–41.

Atkinson, D. (2010). Sociocognition: What it can mean for second language acquisition. In R. Batstone (ed.), *Sociocognitive perspectives on language use and language learning* (24–53). Oxford, UK: Oxford University Press.

Aufderhaar, C. (2004). Learner views of using authentic audio to aid pronunciation: "You can just grab some feelings." *TESOL Quarterly*, 38, 735–46.

Azaria, H. (2004, Dec. 6). Interview with Terry Gross. *Fresh Air*, WHYY, Philadelphia: National Public Radio. Retrieved from http://www.npr.org/player/v2/mediaPlayer.html?action=1&t=1&islist=false&id=4679119&m=4679120

Bailey, R. (2004). American English: Its origins and history. In E. Finegan and J. Rickford (eds.), *Language in the USA* (3–17). Cambridge: Cambridge University Press.

Bakanic, V. (2009). *Prejudice. Attitudes about race, class, and gender*. Upper Saddle River, NJ: Pearson/Prentice Hall.

Baker, C. (1992). *Attitudes and language*. Clevedon, UK: Multilingual Matters.

Baker, W. and Trofimovich, P. (2005). Interaction of native- and second-language vowel system(s) in early and late bilinguals. *Language and Speech*, 48, 1–27.

Baker, W., Trofimovich, P., Flege, J., Mack, M., and Halter, R. (2008). Child–adult differences in second language phonological learning: The role of cross-language similarity. *Language and Speech*, 51, 317–42.

Baron, D. (1982). *Grammar and good taste*. New Haven, CT: Yale University Press.

Bassetti, B. (2009). Orthographic input and second language phonology. In M. Young-Scholten and T. Piske (eds.), *Input matters in SLA* (191–206). Bristol, UK: Multilingual Matters.

Battistella, E. (2005). *Bad language: Are some words better than others?* Oxford, UK: Oxford University Press.

Baugh, J. (2003). Linguistic profiling. In S. Makoni, G. Smitherman, A. Ball, and A. Spears (eds.), *Black linguistics: Language, society, and politics in Africa and the Americas* (155–68). London: Routledge.

Beebe, L. (1984.) Myths about interlanguage phonology. In S. Eliasson (ed.), *Theoretical issues in contrastive phonology* (51–61). Heidelberg: Julius Groos.

Beebe, L. and Giles, H. (1984). Speech-accommodation theories: A discussion in terms of second-language acquisition. *International Journal of the Sociology of Language*, 46, 5–32.

Bender, J. (1943). *NBC handbook of pronunciation*. New York: Thomas Y. Crowell.

Benson, B. (1988). Universal preference for the open syllable as an independent process in interlanguage phonology. *Language Learning*, 38, 221–42.

Bent, T. and Bradlow, A. (2003). The interlanguage speech intelligibility benefit. *Journal of the Acoustical Society of America*, 114, 1600–10.

Bent, T., Bradlow, A., and Smith, B. (2007). Segmental errors in different word positions and their effects on intelligibility of non-native speech. In O. Bohn and M. Munro (eds.), *Language experience in second language speech learning* (331–47). Amsterdam: John Benjamins.

Bent, T., Bradlow, A., and Wright, B. (2006). The influence of linguistic experience on the cognitive processing of pitch in speech and nonspeech sounds. *Journal of Experimental Psychology: Human Perception and Performance*, 32, 97–103.

Berkowitz, D. (1989). The effect of cultural empathy on second-language phonological production. In M. Eisenstein (ed.), *The dynamic interlanguage* (101–14). New York: Plenum Press.

Best, C. and Tyler, M. (2007). Non-native and second language speech perception. Commonalities and complementarities. In O.-S. Bohn and M. Munro (eds.), *Language experience and second language speech learning: In honor of James E. Flege* (13–34). Amsterdam: John Benjamins.

Best, C., McRoberts, G., and Sithole, N. (1987). Examination of perceptual reorganization for nonnative speech contrasts: Zulu click discrimination by English-speaking adults and infants. *Haskins Laboratories Status Report on Speech Research* 91, 1–29.

Bever, T. (1981). Normal acquisition processes explain the critical period for language learning. In K. Diller (ed.), *Individual differences and universals in language learning aptitude* (176–98). Rowley, MA: Newbury House.

Bever, T. and Chiarello, R. (1974). Cerebral dominance in musicians and non-musicians. *Science*, 185, 537–9.

Bialystok, E. and Hakuta, K. (1994). *In other words: The science and psychology of second language acquisition*. New York: Basic Books.

Bialystok, E., Majumder, S., and Martin, M. (2003). Developing phonological awareness: Is there a bilingual advantage? *Applied Psycholinguistics*, 24, 27–44.

Bielska, J. (2008). Gender differences in strategy use and classroom task preferences of Polish EFL learners. *Linguistic Insights: Studies in Language and Communication*, 78, 113–27.

Birdsong, D. (2005). Interpreting age effects in second language acquisition. In J. Kroll and A. De Groot (eds.), *Handbook of bilingualism: Psycholinguistic perspectives* (109–27). Oxford, UK: Oxford University Press.

  (2006). Age and L2 acquisition and processing. *Language Learning*, 56, 9–49.

Birdsong, D. and Molis, M. (2001). On the evidence for maturational effects in second language acquisition. *Journal of Memory and Language*, 44, 235–49.

Bley-Vroman, R. (1989). What is the logical problem of foreign language learning? In S. Gass and J. Schachter (eds.), *Linguistic perspectives on second language acquisition* (41–68). New York: Cambridge University Press.

Block, D. (2007). *Second language identities*. New York: Continuum.

Bohn, O. (2005). A fond farewell to the critical period hypothesis for non-primary language acquisition. In A. Saleemi, O. Bohn, and A. Gjedde (eds.), *In search of a language for the mind-brain* (285–310). Aarhus, Denmark: Aarhus University Press.

Bohn, O. and Bundgaard-Nielsen, R. L. (2009). Second language speech learning with diverse inputs. In M. Young-Scholten and T. Piske (eds.), *Input matters in SLA* (207–18). Bristol, UK: Multilingual Matters.

Bongaerts, T. (2005). Introduction: Ultimate attainment and the critical period hypothesis for second language acquisition. *IRAL*, 43, 259–67.

Bongaerts, T., Planken, B., and Schils, E. (1995). Can late starters attain a native accent in a foreign language? A test of the critical period hypothesis. In D. Singleton and

Z. Lengyel (eds.), *The age factor in second language acquisition* (30–50). Clevedon: UK: Multilingual Matters.

Bongaerts, T., Summeren, C., Planken, B., and Schils, E. (1997). Age and ultimate attainment in the production of foreign language. *Studies in Second Language Acquisition*, 19, 447–65.

Bourhis, R., Giles, H., and Lambert, W. (1975). Social consequences of accommodating one's style of speech: A cross-national investigation. *Linguistics*, 166, 55–71.

Bowden, H., Sanz, C., and Stafford, C. (2005). Individual differences: Age, sex, working memory, and prior knowledge. In C. Sanz (ed.), *Mind and context in adult second language acquisition: Methods, theory and practice* (105–40). Washington, DC: Georgetown University Press.

Bradlow, A. and Bent, T. (2008). Perceptual adaptation to non-native speech. *Cognition*, 106, 707–29.

Bratu, R. (2002). The role of computer software in the phonological development of students enrolled in university courses of French as a second language. Unpublished doctoral dissertation, University of Alberta.

Bresnahan, M., Ohashi, R., Nebashi, R., Liu, W., and Shearman, S. (2002). Attitudinal and affective responses toward accented English. *Language and Communication*, 22, 171–85.

Broselow, E. (1988). An investigation of transfer in second language phonology. In D. Nehls (ed.), *Interlanguage studies* (77–93). Heidelberg: Groos.

Broselow, E., Chen, S., and Wang, C. (1998). The emergence of the unmarked in second language phonology. *Studies in Second Language Acquisition*, 20, 261–80.

Broselow, E., Hurtig, R., and Ringen, C. (1987). The perception of second language prosody. In G. Ioup and S. Weinberger (eds.), *Interlanguage phonology* (350–61). Cambridge, MA: Newbury House.

Brown, B., Giles, H., and Thakerar, J. (1985). Speaker evaluations as a function of speech rate, accent and context. *Language and Communication*, 5, 207–20.

Brown, H. D. (2007). *Principles and practice of language learning and teaching*, 5th edn. New York: Pearson Longman.

Brown, P. and Fraser, C. (1979). Speech as a marker of situation. In K. Scherer and H. Giles (eds.), *Social markers in speech* (33–62). Cambridge, UK: Cambridge University Press.

Brown, P. and Levinson, S. (1979). Social structure, groups and interaction. In K. Scherer and H. Giles (eds.), *Social markers in speech* (291–342). Cambridge, UK: Cambridge University Press.

Bucholtz, M. and Hall, K. (2005). Identity and interaction: A sociocultural linguistic approach. *Discourse Studies*, 7, 585–614.

Burman, D., Bitan, T., and Booth, J. (2008). Sex differences in neural processing of language among children. *Neuropsychologia*, 46, 1349–62.

Burnham, D. and Mattock, J. (2007). The perception of tones and phones. In O. Bohn and M. Munro (eds.), *Language experience in second language speech learning* (259–80). Amsterdam: John Benjamins.

Burnham, D., Tyler, M., and Horlyck, S. (2002). Periods of speech perception development and their vestiges in adulthood. In P. Burmeister, T. Piske, and A. Rohde (eds.), *An integrated view of language development: Papers in honor of Henning Wode* (281–300). Trier, Germany: Wissenschaftlicher Verlag.

Burns, T., Yoshida, K., Hill, K., and Werker, J. (2007). The development of phonetic representation in bilingual and monolingual infants. *Applied Psycholinguistics*, 28, 455–74.
Callan, D., Jones, J., Callan, A., and Akahane-Yamada, R. (2004). Phonetic perceptual identification by native- and second-language speakers differentially activates brain regions involved with acoustic phonetic processing and those involved with articulatory auditory/orosensory internal models. *Neuroimage*, 22, 1182–94.
Callan, V., Gallois, C., and Forbes, P. (1983). Evaluative reactions to accented English: Ethnicity, sex role, and content. *Journal of Cross-Cultural Psychology*, 14, 407–26.
Cameron, D. (2000). Styling the worker: Gender and the commodification of language in the globalized service economy. *Journal of Sociolinguistics*, 4, 323–47.
  (2001). Language: Designer voices. *Critical Quarterly*, 43, 81–5.
Campbell-Kibler, K. (2011). The sociolinguistic variant as a carrier of social meaning. *Language Variation and Change*, 22, 423–41.
Canale, M. and Swain, M. (1980). Theoretical bases of communicative approaches to second language teaching and testing. *Applied Linguistics*, 1, 1–47.
Canto, M. (2006, June 12). Striking an ethnicity/assimilation balance. *Television Week*. Retrieved from http://web.ebscohost.com
Cargile, A. (2000). Evaluations of employment suitability: Does accent always matter? *Journal of Employment Counseling*, 37, 165–77.
Cargile, A. and Giles, H. (1998). Language attitudes toward varieties of English: An American–Japanese context. *Journal of Applied Communication Research*, 26, 338–56.
Carlisle, R. (2001). Syllable structure universals and second language acquisition. *International Journal of English Studies*, 1, 1–19.
Carlson, H. and McHenry, M. (2006). Effect of accent and dialect on employability. *Journal of Employment Counseling*, 43, 70–83.
Carranza, M. and Ryan, E. (1975). Evaluative reactions of bilingual Anglo and Mexican-American adolescents toward speakers of English and Spanish. *International Journal of the Sociology of Language*, 6, 83–104.
Carroll, J. and Sapon, S. (1959.) *Modern Language Aptitude Test*. New York: Psychological Corporation.
Celce-Murcia, M., Brinton, D., and Goodwin, J. (1996). *Teaching pronunciation: A reference for teachers of English to speakers of other languages*. Cambridge: Cambridge University Press.
Cenoz, J. and Garcia Lecumberri, M. (1999). The acquisition of English pronunciation: Learners' views. *International Journal of Applied Linguistics*, 9, 3–17.
Cesar-Lee, B. (2000). Quantification of accented pronunciation by American-English speakers in French as a foreign language. Unpublished doctoral dissertation, University of Florida, Gainesville, FL.
Chambers, J. K. (2009). *Sociolinguistic theory*, rev. edn. Malden, MA: Wiley-Blackwell.
Chand, V. (2009). [V]at is going on? Local and global ideologies about Indian English. *Language in Society*, 38, 393–419.
Chiarello, C. (2003). Parallel systems for processing language: Hemispheric complementarity in the normal brain. In M. Banich and M. Mack (eds.), *Mind, brain and language: Multidisciplinary perspectives* (229–47). Mahwah, NJ: Lawrence Erlbaum.
Chiarello, C. and Beeman, M. (1998). Right hemisphere linguistic decoding – More than meets the eye and ear? In M. Beeman and C. Chiarello (eds.), *Right hemisphere*

comprehension: Perspectives from cognitive neuroscience (133–7). Mahwah, NJ: Lawrence Erlbaum.
Chipman, K. and Kimura, D. (1999). An investigation of sex differences on incidental memory for verbal and pictorial material. *Learning and Individual Differences*, 10, 259–72.
Chuang, H. (2010). Undergraduates' perceptions and attitudes toward the foreign accentedness of international teaching assistants in the USA. Unpublished master's thesis, Southern Illinois University, Carbondale, IL.
Chun, D. (1988). The neglected role of intonation in communicative competence and proficiency. *Modern Language Journal*, 72, 295–303.
 (2007). Technological advances in phonology. In M. Pennington (ed.), *Phonology in context* (274–99). New York: Palgrave Macmillan.
Clément, R. and Kruidenier, B. (1983). Orientations in second language acquisition: The effects of ethnicity, milieu, and target language on their emergence. *Language Learning*, 33, 273–91.
Clements, A., Rimrodt, S., Blankner, J., Mostofsky, S., Pekar, J., Denckla, M., and Cutting, L. (2006). Sex differences in cerebral laterality of language and visuospatial processing. *Brain and Language*, 98, 150–8.
Colantoni, L. and Steele, J. (2008). Integrating articulatory constraints into models of second language phonological acquisition. *Applied Psycholinguistics*, 29, 489–534.
Conrey, B., Potts, G., and Niedzielski, N. (2005). Effects of dialect on merger perception: ERP and behavioral correlates. *Brain and Language*, 95, 435–49.
Cook, V. (2002). Background to the L2 user. In V. Cook (ed.), *Portraits of the L2 user* (1–28). Clevedon, UK: Multilingual Matters.
Coulthard, M. (2004). Author identification, idiolect and linguistic uniqueness. *Applied Linguistics*, 25, 431–47.
Council of Europe (2001). Common European *Framework for Languages: Learning, teaching, assessment*. Cambridge, UK: Cambridge University Press.
Couper, G. (2006). The short and long-term effects of pronunciation instruction. *Prospect*, 21, 46–66.
Couper-Kuhlen, E. (2007). Situated phonologies: Patterns of phonology in discourse contexts. In M. Pennington (ed.), *Phonology in context* (186–218). New York: Palgrave Macmillan.
Coupland, N. (1984.) Accommodation at work: Some phonological data and their implications. *International Journal of the Sociology of Language*, 46, 49–70.
Coupland, N. and Bishop, H. (2007). Ideologised values for British accents. *Journal of Sociolinguistics*, 11, 74–93.
Cowie, C. (2007). The accents of outsourcing: The meanings of "neutral" in the Indian call center industry. *World Englishes*, 26, 316–30.
Crawford, J. (1992). What's behind Official English? In J. Crawford (ed.), *Language loyalties: A source book on the Official English controversy* (171–7). Chicago: University of Chicago Press.
Crowley, T. (2003). *Standard English and the politics of language*, 2nd edn. New York: Palgrave Macmillan.
Crystal, D. (1987). *Cambridge encyclopedia of language*. Cambridge, UK: Cambridge University Press.

(2003) *The Cambridge encyclopedia of the English language*, 2nd edn. Cambridge, UK: Cambridge University Press.
Cukor-Avila, P. (1988). The effect of accent on speech and personality judgments. *PALM*, 3, 1–20.
Cunningham, E. (1998). The rise of identity politics I: The myth of the protected class in Title VII disparate treatment cases. *Connecticut Law Review*, 30, 441, 32–75.
Dabrowska, E. (2004). *Language, mind and brain*. Washington, DC: Georgetown University Press.
Dai, Y. (2006). The effects of language aptitude on second language acquisition. *Foreign Language Teaching and Research*, 38, 451–9.
Dailey, R., Giles, H., and Jansma, L. (2005). Language attitudes in an Anglo-Hispanic context: The role of the linguistic landscape. *Language and Communication*, 25, 27–38.
Dalton-Puffer, C., Kaltenboeck, G., and Smit, U. (1997). Learner attitudes and L2 pronunciation in Austria. *World Englishes*, 16, 115–28.
Dalton, C. and Seidlhofer, B. (1994). *Pronunciation*. Oxford, UK: Oxford University Press.
Daly, N. and Warren, P. (2001). Pitching it differently in New Zealand English: Speaker sex and intonation patterns. *Journal of Sociolinguistics*, 5, 85–96.
Davies, A. (2000). What second language learners can tell us about the native speaker. In R. Cooper, E. Shoshamy, and J. Walters (eds.), *New perspectives and issues in educational language policy* (91–112). Amsterdam: John Benjamins.
Davies, B. (2004). The gender gap in modern languages: A comparison of attitude and performance in year 7 and year 10. *Language Learning Journal*, 29, 53–8.
Dávila, A., Bohara, A., and Saenz, R. (1993). Accent penalties and the earnings of Mexican Americans. *Social Science Quarterly*, 74, 902–16.
deBot, K. (1980). The role of feedback and feedforward in the teaching of pronunciation: An overview. *System*, 8, 35–45.
 (1983). Visual feedback of intonation: Effectiveness and induced practice behavior. *Language and Speech*, 26, 331–51.
deBot, K. and Mailfert, K. (1982). The teaching of intonation: fundamental research and classroom applications. *TESOL Quarterly*, 16, 71–7.
DeKeyser, R. (2000). The robustness of critical period effects in second language acquisition. *Studies in Second Language Acquisition*, 22, 499–533.
DeKlerk, V. and Bosch, B. (1995). Linguistic stereotypes: Nice accent – nice person? *International Journal of the Sociology of Language*, 116, 17–37.
Del Valle, S. (2003). *Language rights and the law in the United States*. Clevedon, UK: Multilingual Matters.
DeLeeuw, E., Schmid, M., and Mennen, I. (2010). The effects of contact on native language pronunciation in an L2 migrant setting. *Bilingualism: Language and Cognition*, 13, 33–40.
Delmonte, R. (2000). SLIM prosodic automatic feedback tools for self-learning instruction. *Speech Communication*, 30, 145–66.
Derwing, T. (2003). What do ESL students say about their accents? *Canadian Modern Language Review*, 59, 547–66.
 (2008). Curriculum issues in teaching pronunciation to second language learners. In J. Hansen Edwards and M. Zampini (eds.), *Phonology and second language acquisition* (347–60). Amsterdam: John Benjamins.

References

Derwing, T. and Munro, M. (1997). Accent, intelligibility, and comprehensibility. *Studies in Second Language Acquisition*, 20, 1–16.
  (2005). Second language accent and pronunciation teaching: A research-based approach. *TESOL Quarterly*, 39, 379–97.
Derwing, T. and Rossiter, M. (2002). ESL learners' perceptions of their pronunciation needs and strategies. *System*, 30, 155–66.
  (2003). The effects of pronunciation instruction on the accuracy, fluency and complexity of L2 accented speech. *Applied Language Learning*, 13, 1–17.
Derwing, T., Munro, M., and Carbonaro, M. (2000). Does popular speech recognition software work with ESL speech? *TESOL Quarterly*, 34, 592–603.
Derwing, T., Munro, M., and Thomson, R. (2007). A longitudinal study of ESL learners' fluency and comprehensibility development. *Applied Linguistics*, 29, 359–80.
Derwing, T., Munro, M., and Wiebe, G. (1998). Evidence in favor of a broad framework for pronunciation instruction. *Language Learning*, 48, 393–410.
Derwing, T., Rossiter, M., Munro, M., and Thomson, R. (2004). Second language fluency: Judgments on different tasks. *Language Learning*, 54, 655–79.
Devine, P. and Sharp, L. (2009). Automaticity and control in stereotyping and prejudice. In T. Nelson (ed.), *Handbook of prejudice, stereotyping, and discrimination* (61–110). New York: Psychology Press, Taylor & Francis Group.
Dewey, M. and Jenkins, J. (2010). English as a lingua franca in the global context: Interconnectedness, variation and change. In M. Saxena and T. Omoniyi (eds.), *Contending with globalization in world Englishes* (72–92). Bristol, UK: Multilingual Matters.
Diaz-Campos, M. (2004). Context of learning in the acquisition of Spanish second language phonology. *Studies in Second Language Acquisition*, 26, 249–73.
Dick, F., Dronkers, N., Pizzamiglio, L., Saygin, A., Small, S., and Wilson, S. (2005). Language and the brain. In M. Tomasello and D. Slobin (eds.), *Beyond nature–nurture: Essays in honor of Elizabeth Bates* (237–60). Mahwah, NJ: Lawrence Erlbaum.
Dickerson, L. (1975). The learner's interlanguage as a system of variable rules. *TESOL Quarterly*, 9, 401–7.
Dixon, J. and Mahoney, B. (2004). The effect of accent evaluation and evidence on a suspect's perceived guilt and criminality. *Journal of Social Psychology*, 144, 63–73.
Dörnyei, Z. (2003a). Attitudes, orientations, and motivations in language learning: Advances in theory, research and applications. *Language Learning*, 53, 3–32.
  (2003b). *Questionnaires in second language research*. Mahwah, NJ: Lawrence Erlbaum.
  (2005). *Psychology and the language learner*. Mahwah, NJ: Lawrence Erlbaum.
  (2006). Individual differences in SLA. *AILA Review*, 19, 42–68.
Doughty, C. (2001). Cognitive underpinnings of focus on form. In P. Robinson (ed.), *Cognition and second language instruction* (206–57). Cambridge, UK: Cambridge University Press.
Doughty, C. and Varela, E. (1998). Communicative focus on form. In C. Doughty and J. Williams (eds.), *Focus on form in classroom second language acquisition* (114–38). Cambridge, UK: Cambridge University Press.

Dudley, B. (2004, Aug. 16). Microsoft's call-center business in India gets an American accent. *Seattle Times.* Retrieved from http://seattletimes.nwsource.com

Dupoux, E. (2003, October). Plasticity and non-plasticity in speech processing: Late learners and early forgetting. Paper presented to Linguistics Department, University of Maryland, College Park, MD.

Eades, D. (2010). *Sociolinguistics and the legal process.* Bristol, UK: Multilingual Matters.

Eckman, F. (1977). Markedness and the contrastive analysis hypothesis. *Language Learning*, 27, 315–30.

Eisenstein, M. (1983). Native reactions to non-native speech: A review of empirical research. *Studies in Second Language Acquisition*, 5, 160–76.

Elliott, A. (1995). Field independence/dependence, hemispheric specialization, and attitude in relation to pronunciation accuracy in Spanish as a foreign language. *Modern Language Journal*, 79, 356–71.

(1997). On the teaching and acquisition of pronunciation within a communicative approach. *Hispania*, 80, 95–108.

Elliott, D. (2003). Moral responsibilities and the power of pictures. In P. Lester and S. Ross (eds.), *Images that injure: Pictorial stereotypes in the media* (7–14). Westport, CN: Praeger.

Ensz, K. (1982). French attitudes toward typical speech errors of American speakers of French. *Modern Language Journal*, 66, 133–9.

Enteman, W. (2003). Stereotyping, prejudice and discrimination. In P. Lester and S. Ross (eds.), *Images that injure: Pictorial stereotypes in the media* (15–22). Westport, CN: Praeger.

Erdener, V. and Burnham, D. (2005). The role of audiovisual speech and orthographic information on nonnative speech production. *Language Learning*, 55, 191–228.

Escudero, P. (2007). Second language phonology: The role of perception. In M. Pennington (ed.), *Phonology in context* (109–34). New York: Palgrave Macmillan.

Escudero, P. and Boersma, P. (2004). Bridging the gap between L2 speech perception research and phonological theory. *Studies in Second Language Acquisition*, 26, 551–85.

Faerch, C. and Kasper, G. (1987). Perspectives on language transfer. *Applied Linguistics*, 8, 111–36.

Fathman, A. (1975). The relationship between age and second language productive ability. *Language Learning*, 25, 245–53.

Ferguson, C. (1971). Absence of copula and the notion of simplicity: A study of normal speech, baby talk, foreigner talk, and pidgins. In D. Hymes (ed.), *Pidginization and creolization of languages.* New York: Cambridge University Press.

Ferrier, L., Reid, L., and Chenausky, K. (1999). Computer-assisted accent modification: A report on practice effects. *Topics in Language Disorders*, 19, 35–48.

Field, J. (2005). Intelligibility and the listener: The role of lexical stress. *TESOL Quarterly*, 39, 399–423.

Finegan, E. (1980). *Attitudes toward English usage: The history of a war of words.* New York: Teachers College Press.

(2004). American English and its distinctiveness. In E. Finegan and J. Rickford (eds.), *Language in the USA* (18–38). Cambridge, UK: Cambridge University Press.

References

Fiske, S., Harris, L., Lee, T., and Russell, A. (2009). The future of research on prejudice, stereotyping and discrimination. In T. Nelson (ed.), *Handbook of prejudice, stereotyping, and discrimination* (525–34). New York: Psychology Press, Taylor & Francis Group.

Flege, J. (1995). Second language speech learning: Theory, findings and problems. In W. Strange (ed.), *Speech perception and linguistic experience: Issues in cross-language research* (229–73). Timonium, MD: York Press.

(2009). Give input a chance! In T. Piske and M. Young-Scholten (eds.), *Input matters in SLA* (175–90). Bristol, UK: Multilingual Matters.

Flege, J., Birdsong, D., Bialystok, E., Mack, M., Sung, H., and Tsukada, K. (2006). Degree of foreign accent in English sentences produced by Korean children and adults. *Journal of Phonetics*, 34, 153–75.

Flege, J. and Fletcher, K. (1992). Talker and listener effects on degree of perceived foreign accent. *Journal of the Acoustical Society of America*, 91, 370–89.

Flege, J., Frieda, E., and Nozawa, T. (1997). Amount of native language (L1) use affects the pronunciation of an L2. *Journal of Phonetics*, 25, 169–86.

Flege, J. and Hillenbrand, J. (1987). Limits on phonetic accuracy in foreign language speech production. In G. Ioup and S. Weinberger (eds.), *Interlanguage phonology* (176–203). Cambridge, MA: Newbury House.

Flege, J. and Liu, S. (2001). The effect of experience on adults' acquisition of a second language. *Studies in Second Language Acquisition*, 23, 527–52.

Flege, J., MacKay, I., and Piske, T. (2002). Assessing bilingual dominance. *Applied Psycholinguistics*, 23, 567–98.

Flege, J., Munro, M., and MacKay, I. (1995b). Factors affecting strength of perceived foreign accent in a second language. *Journal of the Acoustical Society of America*, 97, 3125–34.

Flege, J., Takagi, N., and Mann, V. (1995a). Japanese adults can learn to produce English /r/ and /l/ accurately. *Language and Speech*, 38, 25–55.

Flege, J., Yeni-Komshian, G., and Liu, S. (1999). Age constraints on second-language acquisition. *Journal of Memory and Language*, 41, 78–104.

Frumkin, L. (2007). Influences of accent and ethnic background on perceptions of eyewitness testimony. *Psychology, Crime and Law*, 13, 317–31.

Fullana, N. (2006). The development of English (FL) perception and production skills: Starting age and exposure effects. In C. Muñoz (ed.), *Age and the rate of foreign language learning* (41–64). Clevedon, UK: Multilingual Matters.

Gallois, C. and Callan, V. (1981). Personality impressions elicited by accented English speech. *Journal of Cross-Cultural Psychology*, 12, 347–59.

Galloway, L. and Scarcella, R. (1982). Cerebral organization in adult second language acquisition: Is the right hemisphere more involved? *Brain and Language*, 16, 56–60.

Garcia Lecumberri, M. and Gallardo, F. (2003). English FL sounds in school learners of different ages. In M. Garcia Mayo and M. Garcia Lecumberri (eds.), *Age and the acquisition of English as a foreign language* (115–35). Clevedon, UK: Multilingual Matters.

Gardner, R. (1979). Social psychological aspects of second language acquisition. In H. Giles and R. Sinclair (eds.), *Language and social psychology* (193–220). Baltimore, MD: University Park Press.

Gardner, R. and Lambert, W. (1972). *Attitudes and motivation in second language learning*. Rowley, MA: Newbury House.

Gardner, R., Masgoret, A. and Tremblay, P. (1999). Home background characteristics and second language learning. *Journal of Language and Social Psychology*, 18, 419–37.

Garrett, P. (1992). Accommodation and hyperaccommodation in foreign language learners: Contrasting responses to French and Spanish English speakers by native and non-native recipients. *Language and Communication*, 12, 295–315.

(2010). *Attitudes to language*. Cambridge, UK: Cambridge University Press.

Gass, S. and Varonis, E. (1984). The effect of familiarity on the comprehensibility of non-native speech. *Language Learning*, 34, 65–89.

Gatbonton, E., Trofimovich, P., and Magid, M. (2005). Learners' ethnic group affiliation and L2 pronunciation accuracy: A sociolinguistic investigation. *TESOL Quarterly*, 39, 489–511.

Gilbert, J. (1983). Pronunciation and listening comprehension. *Cross Currents*, 10, 53–61.

Giles, H. (1979). Ethnicity markers in speech. In K. Scherer and H. Giles (eds.), *Social markers in speech* (251–90). Cambridge, UK: Cambridge University Press.

Giles, H. and Coupland, N. (1991). *Language: Contexts and consequences*. Pacific Grove, CA: Brooks/Cole Publishing Co.

Giles, H., Coupland, N. and Coupland, J. (1991). Accommodation theory: Communication, context and consequence. In H. Giles, J. Coupland, and N. Coupland (eds.), *Contexts of accommodation: Developments in applied sociolinguistics* (1–68). Cambridge, UK: Cambridge University Press.

Gill, M. (1994). Accent and stereotypes: Their effect on perceptions of teachers and lecture comprehension. *Journal of Applied Communication Research*, 22, 348–61.

Goldstein, L. (1998). Hollywood now plays cowboys and Arabs. *New York Times*, November 1. Retrieved from http://www.nytimes.com/1998/11/01/movies/film-hollywood-now-plays-cowboys-and-arabs.html

Golestani, N., and Zatorre, R. (2009). Individual differences in the acquisition of second language phonology. *Brain and Language*, 109, 55–67.

Golombek, P. and Jordan, S. (2005). Becoming "black lambs" not "parrots": A post-structuralist orientation to intelligibility and identity. *TESOL Quarterly*, 39, 513–33.

Gonzalez, V. and Schallert, D. (1999). An integrative analysis of the cognitive development of bilingual and bicultural children and adults. In V. Gonzalez (ed.), *Language and cognitive development in second language learning* (19–55). Boston, MA: Allyn & Bacon.

Gonzalez-Bueno, M. (1997). Voice-onset-time in the perceptions of foreign accent by native listeners of Spanish. *IRAL*, 35, 251–67.

Gottfried, T. (2008). Music and language learning. Effects of musical training on learning L2 speech contrasts. In O. Bohn and M. Munro (eds.), *Language experience in second language speech learning* (221–37). Amsterdam: John Benjamins.

Grabe, E., Rosner, B., Garcia-Albea, J., and Zhou, X. (2003). Perception of English intonation by English, Spanish and Chinese listeners. *Language and Speech*, 46, 375–401.

Granena, G. (2006). Age, proficiency level and interactional skills: Evidence from breakdowns in production. In C. Muñoz (ed.), *Age and the rate of foreign language learning* (183–207). Clevedon, UK: Multilingual Matters.

References

Grazia Busa, M. (2010). Effects of L1 on L2 pronunciation: Italian prosody in English. *Linguistic Insights – Studies in Language and Communication*, 96, 207–28.

Gregg, K. (1996). The logical and developmental problems of second language acquisition. In W. Ritchie and T. Bhatia (eds.), *Handbook of second language acquisition* (49–81). New York: Academic Press.

Guion, S. and Pederson, E. (2007). Investigating the role of attention in phonetic learning. In O. Bohn and M. Munro (eds.), *Language experience in second language speech learning* (57–77). Amsterdam: John Benjamins.

Guiora, A., Acton, W., Erard, R., and Strickland, F. (1980). The effects of Benzodiazepine (valium) on permeability of language ego boundaries. *Language Learning*, 30, 351–63.

Guiora, A., Beit-Hallami, B., Brannon, R., Dull, C., and Scovel, T. (1972). The effects of experimentally-induced changes in ego states on pronunciation ability in second language: An exploratory study. *Comprehensive Psychiatry*, 13, 421–8.

Guiora, A. and Schonberger, R. (1990). Native pronunciation of bilinguals. In J. Leather and A. James (eds.), *New sounds 90*. Amsterdam: University of Amsterdam.

Gupta, A. (2005). Inter-accent and inter-cultural intelligibility: A study of listeners in Singapore and Britain. In D. Deterding, A. Brown, and E. Low (eds.), *English in Singapore: Phonetic research on a corpus* (138–52). New York: McGraw-Hill.

Gynan, S. (1985). Comprehension, irritation and error hierarchies. *Hispania*, 68, 160–5.

Haddon, B. (1991). Teacher and nonteacher perceptions of second language communication. *Language Learning*, 41, 1–24.

Hahn, L. (2004). Primary stress and intelligibility: Research to motivate the teaching of suprasegmentals. *TESOL Quarterly*, 38, 201–23.

Hall, C., Smith, P., and Wicaksono, R. (2011). *Mapping applied linguistics: A guide for students and practitioners*. London: Routledge.

Hamers, J. and Blanc, M. (2000). *Bilinguality and bilingualism*, 2nd edn. Cambridge, UK: Cambridge University Press.

Hammarberg, B. (1993). The course of development in second language phonology acquisition: A natural path or strategic choice? In K. Hyltenstam and A. Viberg (eds.), *Progression and regression in language: Sociocultural, neuropsychological and linguistic perspectives* (439–62). Cambridge, UK: Cambridge University Press.

Han, Z. (2004). Fossilization: Five central issues. *International Journal of Applied Linguistics*, 14, 212–42.

Hancin-Bhatt, B. (1994). Segment transfer: A consequence of a dynamic system. *Second Language Research*, 10, 241–69.

  (2008). Second language phonology in optimality theory. In J. Hansen-Edwards and M. Zampini (eds.), *Phonology and second language acquisition* (117–46). Amsterdam: John Benjamins.

Hanlon, E. (2005). The role of self-judgment and other-perception in English pronunciation attainment by adult speakers of Spanish. Unpublished doctoral dissertation, New York: City University of New York.

Hansen, D. (1995). A study of the effect of the acculturation model on second language acquisition. In F. Eckman, D. Highland, P. Lee, J. Mileham, and R. Rutkowski-Weber (eds.), *Second language acquisition theory and pedagogy* (305–16). Mahwah, NJ: L. Erlbaum Associates.

Hansen, J. (2001). Linguistic constraints on the acquisition of English syllable codas by native speakers of Mandarin Chinese. *Applied Linguistics*, 22, 338–65.

(2004). Developmental sequences in the acquisition of English L2 syllable codas. *Studies in Second Language Acquisition*, 26, 85–124.
Hansen Edwards, J. (2008). Social factors and variation in production in L2 phonology. In J. Hansen Edwards and M. Zampini (eds.), *Phonology and second language acquisition* (251–79). Amsterdam: John Benjamins.
Hardison, D. (2005). Second-language spoken word identification: Effects of perceptual training, visual cues, and phonetic environment. *Applied Psycholinguistics*, 26, 579–96.
  (2007). The visual element in phonological perception. In M. Pennington (ed.), *Phonology in context* (135–58). New York: Palgrave Macmillan.
Havranek, G. and Cesnik, H. (2001). Factors affecting the success of corrective feedback. *EUROSLA Yearbook*, 1, 99–122.
Hayes-Harb, R., Smith, B., Bent, T., and Bradlow, A. (2008). The interlanguage speech intelligibility benefit for native speakers of Mandarin: Production and perception of English word-final voicing contrasts. *Journal of Phonetics*, 36, 664–79.
Hecht, B. and Mulford, R. (1987). The acquisition of a second language phonology: interaction of transfer and developmental factors. In G. Ioup and S. Weinberger (eds.), *Interlanguage phonology* (213–28). Cambridge, MA: Newbury House.
Heinzmann, S. (2009). "Girls are better at language learning than boys": Do stereotypic beliefs about language learning contribute to girls' higher motivation to learn English in primary school? *Bulletin suisse de linguistique appliquée*, 89, 19–36.
Henry, A. and Apelgren, B. (2008). Young learners and multilingualism: A study of learner attitudes before and after the introduction of a second foreign language to the curriculum. *System*, 36, 607–23.
Herschensohn, J. (2007). *Language development and age*. Cambridge, UK: Cambridge University Press.
Hincks, R. (2003). Speech technologies for pronunciation feedback and evaluation. *ReCALL*, 15, 3–20.
Hing, L. and Zanna, M. (2010). Individual differences. In J. Dovidio, M. Hewstone, P. Glick, and V. Esses (eds.), *The Sage handbook of prejudice, stereotyping and discrimination* (163–78). London: Sage Publications.
Hirata, Y. (2004). Computer assisted pronunciation training for native English speakers learning Japanese pitch and durational contrasts. *Computer Assisted Language Learning*, 17, 357–76.
Hoffman, E. (1990). *Lost in translation: A life in a new language*. New York: Penguin.
Hogg, M. and Rigoli, N. (1996). Effects of ethnolinguistic vitality, ethnic identification, and linguistic contacts on minority language use. *Journal of Language and Social Psychology*, 15, 76–89.
Holm, S. (2006). The relative contribution of intonation and duration to degree of foreign accent in Norwegian as a second language. Lund University, Centre for Languages and Literature, Dept. of Linguistics and Phonetics, Working Papers, 52, 61–4.
Holmes, S. (1992). US sues over dismissal for accent. *New York Times*, January 18. Retrieved from http://www.nytimes.com/1992/01/18/us/us-sues-over-dismissal-for-accent.html
Honey, J. (1997). Sociophonology. In F. Coulmas (ed.), *The handbook of sociolinguistics* (92–106). Malden, MA: Blackwell.
House, J. (1999). Misunderstanding in intercultural communication: Interactions in English as a *lingua franca* and the myth of mutual intelligibility. In C. Gnutzmann (ed.),

References

Teaching and learning English as a global language (73–89). Tübingen, Germany: Stauffenburg Verlag.

Hu, G. and Lindemann, S. (2009). Stereotypes of Cantonese English, apparent native/non-native status, and their effect on non-native English speakers' perception. *Journal of Multilingual and Multicultural Development*, 30, 253–69.

Hu, X. and Reiterer, S. (2009). Personality and pronunciation talent in second language acquisition. In G. Dogil and S. Reiterer (eds.), *Language talent and brain activity* (97–129). Berlin: Mouton de Gruyter.

Hummel, K. (2007). Aptitude, phonological memory, and second language proficiency in non-novice adult learners. *Applied Psycholinguistics*, 30, 225–49.

Hyltenstam, K. and Abrahamsson, N. (2001). Comments on Stefka H. Marinova-Todd, D. Bradford Marshall, and Catherine E. Snow's "Three misconceptions about age and L2 learning". *TESOL Quarterly*, 35, 151–76.

(2003). Maturational constraints in SLA. In C. Doughty and M. Long (eds.), *Handbook of second language acquisition* (539–88). Malden, MA: Blackwell.

Hyltenstam, K., Bylund, E., Abrahamsson, N., and Park, H.-S. (2009). Dominant-language replacement: The case of international adoptees. *Bilingualism: Language and Cognition*, 12, 121–40.

Hyman, H. (2002). *Foreign-accented adult ESL learners: Perceptions of their accent changes and employability qualifications*. Unpublished doctoral dissertation, New York University, New York.

Hymes, D. (1971). *On communicative competence*. Philadelphia, PA: University of Pennsylvania Press.

Imai, T. (2005). *Vowel devoicing in Tokyo Japanese: A variationist approach*. Unpublished doctoral dissertation, Michigan State University, East Lansing, MI.

Imaizumi, S., Homma, M., Ozawa, Y., Maruishi, M., and Muranaka, H. (2004). Gender differences in emotional prosody processing – an fMRI study. *Psychologia*, 47, 113–24.

Ioup, G., Boustagi, E., El Tigi, M., and Moselle, M. (1994). Re-examining the critical period hypothesis: A case study of successful adult SLA in a naturalistic environment. *Studies in Second Language Acquisition*, 16, 73–98.

Isaacs, T. (2008). Towards defining a valid assessment criterion of pronunciation proficiency in non-native English-speaking graduate students. *Canadian Modern Language Review*, 64, 555–80.

Iverson, G. and Kuhl, P. (1996). Influences of phonetic identification and category goodness on American listeners' perception of /r/ and /l/. *Journal of the Acoustical Society of America*, 99, 1130–40.

James, A. (1987). The acquisition of phonological representation: A modular approach. In A. James and J. Leather (eds.), *Sound patterns in second language acquisition* (225–49). Dordrecht: Foris.

Janicki, K. (1990). Native speakers' perceptions of foreigner's language: Some preliminary findings. *Sociolinguistics*, 19, 53–67.

Jarvis, S. and Pavlenko, A. (2008). *Crosslinguistic influence in language and cognition*. New York: Routledge.

Jenkins, J. (2000). *The phonology of English as an international language*. Oxford, UK: Oxford University Press.

(2002). A sociolinguistically-based, empirically-researched pronunciation syllabus for English as an International Language. *Applied Linguistics*, 23, 83–103.
  (2004). Research in teaching pronunciation and intonation. *Annual Review of Applied Linguistics*, 24, 109–25.
  (2005). Implementing an international approach to English pronunciation: The role of teacher attitudes and identity. *TESOL Quarterly*, 39, 535–50.
Jia, G. and Aaronson, D. (2003). A longitudinal study of Chinese children and adolescents learning English in the United States. *Applied Psycholinguistics*, 24, 131–61.
Jia, G., Strange, W., Wu, Y., Collado, J., and Guan, Q. (2006). Perception and production of English vowels by Mandarin speakers: Age-related differences vary with amount of L2 exposure. *Journal of the Acoustical Society of America*, 119, 1118–30.
Jilka, M. (2009). Talent and proficiency in language. In G. Dogil and S. Reiterer (eds.), *Language talent and brain activity* (1–16). Berlin: Mouton de Gruyter.
Johnson, J. and Newport, E. (1989). Critical period effects in second language learning: The influence of maturational state on the acquisition of English as a second language. *Cognitive Psychology*, 39, 215–58.
Jones, E., Gallois, C., Barker, M., and Callan, V. (1994). Evaluations of interactions between students and academic staff: Influence of communication accommodation, ethnic group and status. *Journal of Language and Social Psychology*, 13, 158–91.
Jordan, M. (2010). Arizona grades teachers on fluency. *Wall Street Journal*, April 30. Retrieved from http://online.wsj.com/article/SB10001424052748703572504575213883276427528.html
Joseph, J. (1987). *Eloquence and power: The rise of language standards and standard languages*. London: Frances Pinter.
Kachru, B. and Nelson, C. (1996). World Englishes. In S. McKay and N. Hornberger (eds.), *Sociolinguistics and language teaching* (71–102). Cambridge, UK: Cambridge University Press.
Kahane, H. (1992). American English: From a colonial substandard to a prestige language. In B. Kachru (ed.), *The other tongue: English across cultures* (211–19). Chicago, IL: University of Illinois Press.
Kalin, R. and Rayko, D. (1978). Discrimination in evaluative judgments of foreign-accented job candidates. *Psychological Reports*, 43, 1203–9.
Kaltenbacher, E. (1994). Der deutsche Wortakzent im Zweitspracherwerb: Zur Rolle von Ausgangssprache, Zielsprache und Markiertheit. *Linguistische Berichte*, 150, 91–117.
Kang, O. (2008). Ratings of L2 oral performance in English: Relative impact of rater characteristics and acoustic measures of accentedness. Spaan Fellow Working Papers in Second or Foreign Language Assessment, 6, 181–205.
  (2010). Relative salience of suprasegmental features on judgments of L2 comprehensibility and accentedness. *System*, 38, 301–15.
Kang, O. and Rubin, D. (2009). Reverse linguistic stereotyping: Measuring the effect of listener expectations on speech evaluation. *Journal of Language and Social Psychology*, 28, 441–56.
Kaplan, A. (1994). On language memoir. In A. Bammer (ed.), *Displacements: Cultural identities in question* (59–70). Bloomington, IN: Indiana University Press.
Kellerman, E. (1983). Now you see it, now you don't. In S. Gass and L. Selinker (eds.), *Language transfer in language learning* (112–29). Rowley, MA: Newbury House.

References

Kelman, M. (2007). An investigation of preschool children's primary literacy skills. Unpublished doctoral dissertation, Wichita State University, Wichita, KS.

Kennedy, S. and Trofimovich, P. (2008). Intelligibility, comprehensibility, and accentedness of L2 speech: The role of listener experience and semantic context. *Canadian Modern Language Review*, 64, 459–89.

Kerswill, P. and Shockey, L. (2007). The description and acquisition of variable phonological patterns: Phonology and sociolinguistics. In M. Pennington (ed.), *Phonology in context* (51–75). New York: Palgrave Macmillan.

King, K. (1998). Mandating English proficiency for college instructors: States' responses to "the TA problem." *Vanderbilt Journal of Transnational Law*, 31, 203–56.

Kinzler, K. (2008). The native language of social cognition: Developmental origins of social preferences based on language. Unpublished doctoral dissertation, Harvard University, Cambridge, MA.

Kissau, S. (2007). Is what's good for the goose good for the gander? The case of male and female encouragement to study French. *Foreign Language Annals*, 40, 419–32.

Knightly, L., Jun, S., Oh, J., and Au, T. (2003). Production benefits of childhood overhearing. *Journal of the Acoustical Society of America*, 114, 465–74.

Knoerr, H. and Weinberg, A. (2005). Teaching pronunciation in French as a second language: From cassette to CD-Rom. *Canadian Modern Language Review*, 61, 383–405.

Kolsti, N. (2000). Accents speak louder than words. North Texan Online, winter. Retrieved from http://www.unt.edu/northtexan/archives/w00/accents.htm

Kormos, J. (2006). *Speech production and second language acquisition*. Mahwah, NJ: Lawrence Erlbaum.

Krashen, S. (1981). *Second language acquisition and second language learning*. New York: Pergamon Press.

(1982). *Principles and practice in second language acquisition*. New York: Pergamon.

Krashen, S., Long, M., and Scarcella, R. (1982). Age, rate and eventual attainment in second language acquisition. In S. Krashen, R. Scarcella and M. Long (eds.), *Child–adult differences in second language acquisition* (161–72). Rowley, MA: Newbury House.

Kuhl, P. (2007). Cracking the speech code: How infants learn language. *Acoustical Science and Technology*, 28, 71–83.

Kuhl, P., Conboy, B., Coffey-Corina, S., Padden, D., Rivera-Gaxiola, M., and Nelson, T. (2008). Phonetic learning as a pathway to language: New data and Native Language Magent Theory Expanded (NLM-e). *Philosophical Transactions: Biological Sciences*, 363, 979–1000.

Kuhl, P. and Iverson, P. (1995). Linguistic experience and the "perceptual magnet effect." In W. Strange (ed.), *Speech perception and linguistic experience: Issues in cross-language research* (121–54). Timonium, MD: York Press.

Labov, W. (2006). American accent undergoing Great Vowel Shift. Interview by Robert Siegal, February, 16. Retrieved from http://www.npr.org

Labrie, N. and Clément, R. (1986). Ethnolinguistic vitality, self-confidence and second language proficiency: An investigation. *Journal of Multilingual and Multicultural Development*, 7, 269–82.

Lado, R. (1957). *Linguistics across cultures*. Ann Arbor, MI: University of Michigan Press.

Lakoff, R. (2001). *The language war.* Berkeley, CA: University of California Press.

Lambacher, S., Martens, W., Kakehi, K., Marasinghe, C., and Molholt, G. (2005). The effects of identification training on the identification and production of American English vowels by native speakers of Japanese. *Applied Psycholinguistics,* 26, 227–47.

Lambert, W. (1967). The social psychology of bilingualism. *Journal of Social Issues,* 23, 91–109.

(1977). The effects of bilingualism on the individual: Cognitive and sociocultural consequences. In P. Hornby (ed.), *Bilingualism: Psychological, social and educational implications* (15–27). New York: Academic Press.

Lambert, W., Giles, H., and Albert, G. (1976). Language attitudes in a rural community in Northern Maine. *Monda Lingvo-Problemo,* 5, 129–44.

Lambert, W., Hodgson, R., Gardner, R., and Fillenbaum, S. (1960). Evaluational reactions to spoken language. *Journal of Abnormal and Social Psychology,* 60, 44–51.

Larsen-Freeman, D. (1997). Chaos/complexity science and second language acquisition. *Applied Linguistics,* 18, 141–65.

(2009). Adjusting expectations: The study of complexity, accuracy and fluency in second language acquisition. *Applied Linguistics,* 30, 579–89.

(2011). A complexity theory approach to second language development/acquisition. In D. Atkinson (ed.), *Alternative approaches to second language acquisition* (48–72). New York: Routledge.

Lasagabaster, D. and Sierra, D. (2005). The nativeness factor: An analysis of students' preferences. *ITL, Review of Applied Linguistics,* 147–8, 21–43.

Leather, J. (1983). Second-language pronunciation learning and teaching. *Language Teaching Abstracts,* 16, 198–219.

(1987). F0 pattern inference in the perceptual acquisition of second language tone. In A. James and J. Leather (eds.), *Sound patterns in second language acquisition* (59–80). Dordrecht: Foris.

Leather, J. and James, A. (1996). Second language speech. In W. Ritchie and T. Bhatia (eds.), *Handbook of second language acquisition* (269–316). New York: Academic Press.

Lee, B., Guion, S., and Harada, T. (2006). Acoustic analysis of the production of unstressed English vowels by early and late Korean and Japanese bilinguals. *Studies in Second Language Acquisition,* 28, 487–513.

Lefkowitz, N. and Hedgcock, J. (2002). Sound barriers: Influences of social prestige, peer pressure and teacher (dis)approval on FL oral performance. *Language Teaching Research,* 6, 223–44.

(2006). Sound effects: Social pressure and identity negotiation in the Spanish language classroom. *Applied Language Learning,* 16, 13–38.

Lehtonen, J. and Sajavaara, K. (1984). Phonology and speech processing in cross-language communication. In S. Eliasson (ed.), *Theoretical issues in contrastive phonology* (85–99). Heidelberg: Julius Groos.

Lenneberg, E. (1967). *Biological foundations of language.* New York: Wiley.

LePage, R. and Tabouret-Keller, A. (1985). *Acts of identity: Creole-based approaches to language and ethnicity.* Cambridge, UK: Cambridge University Press.

Lev-Ari, S. and Keysar, B. (2010). Why don't we believe non-native speakers? The influence of accent on credibility. *Journal of Experimental Social Psychology,* 46, 1093–6.

Levis, J. (1999). Intonation in theory and practice revisited. *TESOL Quarterly,* 33, 37–63.

References

(2005). Changing contexts and shifting paradigms in pronunciation teaching. *TESOL Quarterly*, 39, 369–77.

(2006). Pronunciation and the assessment of spoken language. In R. Hughes (ed.), *Spoken English, TESOL and applied linguistics* (245–70). New York: Palgrave Macmillan.

(2007). Computer technology in teaching and researching pronunciation. *Annual Review of Applied Linguistics*, 27, 184–202.

Levis, J. and Pickering, L. (2004). Teaching intonation in discourse using speech visualization technology. *System*, 32, 505–24.

Lewis, J. (2003). Social influences on female speakers' pitch. Unpublished doctoral dissertation, University of California, Berkeley, CA.

Lim, T. and Kim, S. (2007). Many faces of media effects. In R. Preiss, B. Gayle, N. Burrell, M. Allen, and J. Bryant (eds.), *Mass media effects research* (315–25). Mahwah, NJ: Lawrence Erlbaum.

Lin, Y. (2003). Interphonology variability: Sociolinguistic factors affecting L2 simplification strategies. *Applied Linguistics*, 24, 439–64.

Lindell, A. and Lum, J. (2008). Priming vs. rhyming: Orthographic and phonological representations in the left and right hemispheres. *Brain and Language*, 68, 193–203.

Lindemann, S. (2002). Listening with an attitude: A model of native-speaker comprehension of non-native speakers in the United States. *Language in Society*, 31, 419–41.

(2003). Koreans, Chinese or Indians? Attitudes and ideologies about non-native English speakers in the United States. *Journal of Sociolinguistics*, 7, 348–64.

(2005). Who speaks "broken English"? US undergraduates' perceptions of non-native English. *International Journal of Applied Linguistics*, 15, 187–212.

Lippi-Green, R. (1994). Accent, standard language ideology, and discriminatory pretext in the courts. *Language in Society*, 23, 163–98.

(1997). *English with an accent: Language, ideology and discrimination in the United States*. London: Routledge.

Locke, J. (1997). A theory of neurolinguistic development. *Brain and Language*, 58, 265–326.

Long, M. (2005). Problems with supposed counter-evidence to the *Critical Period Hypothesis*. *IRAL*, 43, 287–317.

Lord, G. (2005). (How) Can we teach foreign language pronunciation? On the effects of a Spanish phonetics course. *Hispania*, 88, 557–67.

(2008). Podcasting communities and second language pronunciation. *Foreign Language Annals*, 41(2), 364–79.

(2010). The combined effects of immersion and instruction on second language pronunciation. *Foreign Language Annals*, 43, 488–503.

Low, E. (2006). A cross-varietal comparison of de-accenting and given information: Implications for international intelligibility and pronunciation teaching. *TESOL Quarterly*, 40, 739–61.

Lowie, W., Verspoor, M., and DeBot, K. (2009). A dynamic view of second language development across the lifespan. In K. DeBot and R. Schrauf (eds.), *Language development over the lifespan* (125–45). New York: Routledge.

Lybeck, K. (2002). Cultural identification and second language pronunciation of Americans in Norway. *Modern Language Journal*, 86, 174–91.

Lyster, R. (1998). Negotiation of form, recasts, and explicit correction in relation to error types and learner repair in immersion classrooms. *Language Learning*, 48, 183–218.

McCandless, P. and Winitz, H. (1986). Test of pronunciation following one year of comprehension instruction in college German. *Modern Language Journal*, 70, 355–62.

Macdonald, D., Yule, G., and Powers, M. (1994). Attempts to improve English L2 pronunciation: The variable effects of different types of instruction. *Language Learning*, 44, 75–100.

Macias, R. (1997). Bilingual workers and language use rules in the workplace: A case study of a nondiscriminatory language policy. *International Journal of the Sociology of Language*, 127, 53–70.

MacIntyre, P., Baker, S., Clément, R., and Donovan, L. (2003). Sex and age effects on willingness to communicate, anxiety, perceived competence, and L2 motivation among junior high school French immersion students. In Z. Dörnyei (ed.), *Attitudes, orientations and motivations in language learning* (137–65). Malden, MA. Blackwell.

MacKay, I., Flege, J., and Imai, S. (2006). Evaluating the effects of chronological age and sentence duration on degree of perceived accent. *Applied Psycholinguistics*, 27, 157–83.

McKay, J. (2004). All day, all night, the phone calls come in. Outsourcing the future? Part Three. *Pittsburgh Post-Gazette*, November 1. Retrieved from http://www.post-gazette.com

Macken, M. and Ferguson, C. (1987). Phonological universals in language acquisition. In G. Ioup and S. Weinberger (eds.), *Interlanguage phonology* (3–22). Cambridge, MA: Newbury House.

Mackey, A., Gass, S., and McDonough, K. (2000). How do learners perceive interactional feedback? *Studies in Second Language Acquisition*, 22, 471–97.

Mackie, D. and Devos, T. (2000). Intergroup emotions: Explaining offensive action tendencies in an intergroup context. *Journal of Personality and Social Psychology*, 79, 602–16.

McLaughlin, B. (1990). The relationship between first and second languages: Language proficiency and language aptitude. In B. Harley et al. (eds.), *The development of second language proficiency* (158–74). Cambridge, UK: Cambridge University Press.

McLaughlin, B. and Heredia, R. (1996). Information-processing approaches to research on second language acquisition and use. In W. Ritchie and T. Bhatia (eds.), *Handbook of second language acquisition* (213–28). New York: Academic Press.

McLean, M. (1927). *Good American speech*. New York: E.P. Dutton.

MacLeod, A. and Stoehl-Gammon, C. (2010). What is the impact of age of second language acquisition on the production of consonants and vowels among childhood bilinguals? *International Journal of Bilingualism*, 14, 400–21.

Major, R. (1992). Losing English as a first language. *Modern Language Journal*, 76, 190–208.

(1993). Sociolinguistic factors in loss and acquisition of phonology. In K. Hyltenstam and A. Viberg (eds.), *Progression and regression in language: Sociocultural, neuropsychological and linguistic perspectives* (463–78). Cambridge, UK: Cambridge University Press.

(2001). *Foreign accent: The ontogeny and phylogeny of second language phonology*. Mahwah, NJ: Lawrence Erlbaum.

References

(2004). Gender and stylistic variation in second language phonology. *Language Variation and Change*, 16, 169–88.
(2007). Identifying a foreign accent in an unfamiliar language. *Studies in Second Language Acquisition*, 29, 539–56.
(2008). Transfer in second language phonology. In J. Hansen-Edwards and M. Zampini (eds.), *Phonology and second language acquisition* (63–94). Amsterdam: John Benjamins.
(2010). First language attrition in foreign accent perception. *International Journal of Bilingualism*, 14, 163–83.
Major, R., Fitzmaurice, S., Bunta, F., and Balasubramanian, C. (2005). The effects of nonnative accents on listening comprehension: Implications for ESL assessment. *TESOL Quarterly*, 36, 173–90.
Markham, D. (1997). Phonetic imitation, accent, and the learner. *Travaux de l'Institut de Linguistique de Lund*, 33, 3–269.
Martohardjono, G. and Flynn, S. (1995). Is there an age factor for universal grammar? In D. Singleton and Z. Lengyel (eds.), *The age factor in second language acquisition* (135–53). Clevedon, UK: Multilingual Matters.
Marx, N. (2002). Never quite a "native speaker": Accent and identity in the L2 – and the L1. *Canadian Modern Language Review*, 59(2), 264–81.
Masgoret, A. and Gardner, R. (2003). Attitudes, motivation and second language learning: A meta-analysis of studies conducted by Gardner and associates. *Language Learning*, 53, 123–63.
Matsuda, M. (1991). Voices of America: Accent, antidiscrimination law, and a jurisprudence for the last reconstruction. *Yale Law Journal*, 100, 1329–1407.
Melchers, G. and Shaw, P. (2003). *World Englishes*. London: Arnold.
Merskin, D. (2011). *Media, minorities, and meaning*. New York: Peter Lang.
Meyerhoff, M. (2002). Communities of practice. In J. Chambers and P. Trudgill (eds.), *Handbook of language variation and change* (475–99). Malden, MA: Blackwell.
Miller, J. (2003). *Audible difference: ESL and social identity in school*. Clevedon, UK: Multilingual Matters.
Milroy, J. (1998). Children can't speak or write properly any more. In L. Bauer and P. Trudgill (eds.), *Language myths* (58–65). London: Penguin.
(1999). The consequences of standardisation in descriptive linguistics. In T. Bex and R. Watts (eds.), *Standard English: The widening debate* (16–39). Routledge: London.
Milroy, J. and Milroy, L. (1985a). *Authority in language. Investigating language prescription and standardization*. London: Routledge & Kegan Paul.
(1985b). Linguistic change, social network and speaker innovation. *Journal of Linguistics*, 21, 339–84.
Milroy, L. (1999). Standard English and language ideology. In T. Bex and R. Watts (eds.), *Standard English: The widening debate* (173–206). London: Routledge.
Moag, R. (1992). The life cycle of non-native Englishes: A case study. In B. Kachru (ed.), *The other tongue: English across cultures* (233–52). Chicago, IL: University of Illinois Press.
Molnár, H. (2010). Der Einfluss des Faktors Alter auf die Aussprachekompetenz in der L2. Ergebnisse einer Pilotstudie mit DaZ-Lernern. *Zeitschrift für Interkulturellen Fremdsprachenunterricht*, 15, 42–60.

Morley, J. (1991). The pronunciation component in teaching English to speakers of other languages. *TESOL Quarterly*, 25, 481–520.
  (1996a). Second language speech/pronunciation: Acquisition, instruction, standards, variation and accent. *Georgetown University Round Table on Languages and Linguistics*, 1996, 140–60. Washington, DC: Georgetown University Press.
  (1996b). A multidimensional curriculum design for speech-pronunciation instruction. In J. Morley (ed.), *Pronunciation pedagogy and theory: New views, new directions* (64–91). Alexandria, VA: TESOL.
Moyer, A. (1999). Ultimate attainment in L2 phonology: The critical factors of age, motivation and instruction. *Studies in Second Language Acquisition*, 21, 81–108.
  (2004). *Age, accent and experience in second language acquisition. An integrated approach to critical period inquiry.* Clevedon, UK: Multilingual Matters.
  (2005). Formal and informal experiential realms in German as a foreign language: A preliminary investigation. *Foreign Language Annals*, 38, 377–87.
  (2006). Language contact and confidence in L2 listening comprehension: A pilot study of advanced learners of German. *Foreign Language Annals*, 39, 255–75.
  (2007a). Do language attitudes determine accent? A study of bilinguals in the US. *Journal of Multilingual and Multicultural Development*, 28, 1–17.
  (2007b). Empirical considerations on the age factor in L2 phonology. *Issues in Applied Linguistics*, 15, 109–27.
  (2008). Conceptions of L2 phonology: Integrating cognitive and sociolinguistic approaches to research and teaching. In S. Katz and J. Watzinger-Tharp (eds.), *Conceptions of L2 grammar: Theoretical approaches and their application in the L2 classroom* (51–67). Boston, MA: Heinle Cengage Learning.
  (2009). Input as a critical means to an end: Quantity and quality of experience in L2 phonological attainment. In M. Young-Scholten and T. Piske (eds.), *Input matters in SLA* (159–174). Clevedon, UK: Multilingual Matters.
  (2010). Do gender differences in L2 accent really exist? Paper presented to the meeting of American Association for Applied Linguistics (AAAL), March, Atlanta, GA.
  (2011). An investigation of experience in L2 phonology. *Canadian Modern Language Review*, 67, 191–216.
  (2012). The exceptional learner: Legend or myth? Paper presented to the meeting of American Association for Applied Linguistics (AAAL), March, Boston, MA.
Mugglestone, L. (2003). *Talking proper: The rise of accent as a social symbol.* Oxford, UK: Oxford University Press.
Müller, R. (1996). Innateness, autonomy, universality? Neurobiological approaches to language. *Behavioral and Brain Sciences*, 19, 611–75.
Mumhall, K., Jones, J., Callan, D., Kuratate, T., and Vatikiotis-Bateson, E. (2004). Visual prosody and speech intelligibility: Head movement improves auditory speech perception. *Psychological Science*, 15, 133–7.
Muñoz, C. (2008). Symmetries and asymmetries of age effects in naturalistic and instructed L2 learning. *Applied Linguistics*, 29, 578–96.
  (2011). Input and long-term effects of starting age in foreign language learning. *IRAL* 49, 113–33.
  (ed.) (2006a). *Age and the rate of foreign language learning.* Clevedon, UK: Multilingual Matters.

References

(ed.) (2006b). The effects of age on foreign language learning: The BAF project. In C. Muñoz (ed.), *Age and the rate of foreign language learning* (1–40). Clevedon, UK: Multilingual Matters.

Muñoz, C. and Singleton, D. (2007). Foreign accent in advanced learners: Two successful profiles. *EUROSLA Yearbook*, 7, 171–90.

(2011). A critical review of age-related research on L2 ultimate attainment. *Language Teaching*, 44, 1–35.

Munro, M. (2003). A primer on accent discrimination in the Canadian context. *TESL Canada Journal*, 20, 38–51.

(2008). Aptitude for novel speech sounds and sound sequences: Implications for second-language pronunciation. Unpublished doctoral dissertation, University of California, Irvine, CA.

Munro, M. and Derwing, T. (1998). The effects of speaking rate on listener evaluations of native and foreign-accented speech. *Language Learning*, 48, 159–82.

(1999). Foreign accent, comprehensibility, and intelligibility in the speech of second language learners. In J. Leather (ed.), *Phonological issues in language learning* (285–310). Malden, MA: Blackwell.

(2001). Modeling perceptions of the accentedness and comprehensibility of L2 speech. *Studies in Second Language Acquisition*, 23, 451–68.

Munro, M. and Mann, V. (2005). Age of immersion as predictor of foreign accent. *Applied Psycholinguistics*, 26, 311–41.

Munro, M., Derwing, T., and Morton, S. (2006). The mutual intelligibility of L2 speech. *Studies in Second Language Acquisition*, 28, 111–31.

Munro, M., Derwing, T., and Sato, K. (2006). Salient accents, covert attitudes: Consciousness-raising for pre-service second language teachers. *Prospect*, 21, 67–79.

Mutz, D. and Goldman, S. (2010). Mass media. In J. Dovidio, M. Hewstone, P. Glick, and V. Esses (eds.), *The Sage handbook of prejudice, stereotyping and discrimination* (241–57). London: Sage Publications.

Nakamura, S. (2011). Characteristics of contrast between the stressed and the unstressed in rhythm units observed in duration structure in English speech by Japanese learners. *Journal of Pan-Pacific Association of Applied Linguistics*, 15, 177–89.

Nardo, D. and Reiterer, S. (2009). Musicality and phonetic language aptitude. In G. Dogil and S. Reiterer (eds.), *Language talent and brain activity* (213–55). Berlin: Mouton de Gruyter.

Nemiroff, G. (2000). No language to die in. In K. Ogulnick (ed.), *Language crossings: Negotiating the self in a multicultural world* (13–20). New York: Teachers College Press.

Neri, A., Cucchiarini, C., Strik, H., and Boves, L. (2002). The pedagogy–technology interface in computer assisted pronunciation training. *Computer Assisted Language Learning*, 15, 441–67.

Nesdale, D. and Rooney, R. (1996). Evaluations and stereotyping of accented speakers by pre-adolescent children. *Journal of Language and Social Psychology*, 15, 133–54.

Neufeld, G. (1987). On the acquisition of prosodic and articulatory features in adult language learning. In G. Ioup and S. Weinberger (eds.), *Interlanguage phonology* (321–32). Cambridge, MA: Newbury House.

(1988). Phonological asymmetry in second-language learning and performance. *Language Learning*, 38, 531–59.

Newport, E. (1991). Contrasting conceptions of the critical period for language. In S. Carey and R. Gelman (eds.), *The epigenesis of mind* (111–30). Hillsdale, NJ: Lawrence Erlbaum.
Nguyen, B. (1993). Accent discrimination and the test of spoken English: A call for an objective assessment of the comprehensibility of nonnative speakers. *California Law Review*, 81, 1325–61.
Ni, P. (1999). Accent discrimination claim costs company $55,000. *Asian Week Online*, (20)42, June 17. Retrieved from http://www.asianweek.com/061799/news_settlement.html
Niedzielski, N. (1999). The effect of social information on the perception of sociolinguistic variables. *Journal of Language and Social Psychology*, 18, 62–85.
Niedzielski, N. and Preston, D. (2003). *Folk linguistics*. Berlin: Mouton de Gruyter.
Nielsen Company (2009). Americans watching more TV than ever; mobile and web up too, May, retrieved from http://blog.nielsen.com/nielsenwire/online_mobile/americans-watching-more-tv-than-ever
Nihalani, P. (2010). Globalization and international intelligibility. In M. Saxena and T. Omoniyi (eds.), *Contending with globalization in world Englishes* (23–44). Bristol, UK: Multilingual Matters.
Nikolov, M. (2000). The *Critical Period Hypothesis* reconsidered: Successful adult learners of Hungarian and English. *IRAL*, 38, 109–24.
Noels, K. (2005). Orientations to learning German: Heritage language learning and motivational substrates. *The Canadian Modern Language Review*, 62, 285–312.
Noels, K. and Clément, R. (1989). Orientation to learning German: The effects of language heritage on second language acquisition. *Canadian Modern Language Review*, 45, 245–57.
Norton Pierce, B. (1995). Social identity, investment and language learning. *TESOL Quarterly*, 29, 9–31.
Nowacka, M. (2011). The productive and receptive acquisition of consonants and connected speech by Polish students of English. In J. Arabski and A. Wojtaszek (eds.), *The acquisition of L2 phonology* (59–73). Clevedon, UK: Multilingual Matters.
O'Grady, W. (2003). The radical middle: Nativism without universal grammar. In C. Doughty and M. Long (eds.), *The handbook of second language acquisition* (43–62). Malden, MA: Blackwell.
O'Malley, J. and Chamot, A. (1990). *Learning strategies in second language acquisition*. Cambridge, UK: Cambridge University Press.
Obler, L. (1989). Exceptional second language learners. In S. Gass, C. Madden, D. Preston, and L. Selinker (eds.), *Variation in second language acquisition, Vol. II: Psycholinguistic issues* (141–59). Clevedon, UK: Multilingual Matters.
  (1993). Neurolinguistic aspects of second language development and attrition. In K. Hyltenstam and A. Viberg (eds.), *Progression and regression in language: Sociocultural, neuropsychological and linguistic perspectives* (178–95). Cambridge, UK: Cambridge University Press.
Obler, L. and Gjerlow, K. (1999). *Language and the brain*. Cambridge, UK: Cambridge University Press.
Odlin, T. (1989). *Language transfer: Cross-linguistic influence in language learning*. Cambridge, UK: Cambridge University Press.

Olson, L. and Samuels, S. (1982) The relationship between age and accuracy of foreign language pronunciation. In S. Krashen, R. Scarcella, and M. Long (eds), *Child–adult differences in second language acquisition* (67–75). Rowley, MA: Newbury House.

Olson, W. (1997). Say what? *Reason*, 29, 54–5. Retrieved from http://web.ebscohost.com

Oppliger, P. (2007). Effects of gender stereotyping on socialization. In R. Preiss, B. Gayle, N. Burrell, M. Allen, and J. Bryant (eds.), *Mass media effects research* (199–214). Mahwah, NJ: Lawrence Erlbaum.

Orth, J. (1982). Evaluational reactions to spoken language: A dilemma for the teaching and testing of speaking proficiency. *Journal of the Linguistic Association of the Southwest*, 5, 216–33.

Ortmeyer, C. and Boyle, J. (1985). The effect of accent differences on comprehension. *RELC Journal*, 16, 48–53.

Osburne, A. (2003). Pronunciation strategies of advanced ESOL learners. *IRAL*, 41, 131–43.

Oxford, R. (1990.) *Language learning strategies*. Boston, MA: Heinle & Heinle.

Oyama, S. (1976). A sensitive period for the acquisition of a non-native phonological system. *Journal of Psycholinguistic Research*, 5, 261–83.

Paradis, M. (1997). The cognitive neuropsychology of bilingualism. In A. DeGroot and J. Kroll (eds.), *Tutorials in bilingualism: Psycholinguistic perspectives* (331–54). Mahwah, NJ: Erlbaum.

(2007). L1 attrition features predicted by a neurolinguistic theory of bilingualism. In B. Köpke, M. Schmid, M. Keijzer, and S. Dostert (eds.), *Language attrition: Theoretical perspectives* (121–33). Amsterdam: John Benjamins.

Pardo, J. (2006). On phonetic convergence during conversational interaction. *Journal of the Acoustical Society of America*, 119, 2382–93.

Parrino, A. (1998). The politics of pronunciation and the adult learner. In T. Smoke (ed.), *Adult ESL: Politics, pedagogy, and participation in classroom and community programs* (171–84). Mahwah, NJ: Lawrence Erlbaum.

Pavlenko, A. and Lantolf, J. (2000). Second language learning as participation and the (re)construction of selves. In J. Lantolf (ed.), *Sociocultural theory and second language learning* (155–78). Oxford, UK: Oxford University Press.

Pawlak, M. (2011). Students' successes and failures in learning foreign language pronunciation: Insights from diary data. In J. Arabski and A. Wojtaszek (eds.), *The acquisition of L2 phonology* (165–82). Clevedon, UK: Multilingual Matters.

Pennington, M. (1989). Teaching pronunciation from the top down. *RELC Journal*, 20, 20–38.

(1999). Computer-aided pronunciation pedagogy: Promise, limitations, directions. *Computer Assisted Language Learning*, 12, 427–40.

Pennington, M. and Richards, J. (1986). Pronunciation revisited. *TESOL Quarterly*, 20, 207–25.

Perani, D., Paulesu, E., Sebastián-Gallés, N., Dupoux, E., Dehaene, S., Bettinardi, V., Cappa, S., Fazio, F., and Mehler, J. (1998). The bilingual brain. Proficiency and age of acquisition of the second language. *Brain*, 121, 1841–52.

Perfetti, C. and Bolger, D. (2004). The brain might read that way. *Scientific Studies of Reading*, 8, 293–304.

Perfetti, C. and Liu, Y. (2005). Orthography to phonology and meaning: Comparisons across and within writing systems. *Reading and Writing*, 18, 193–210.
Perry, G. and Harris, C. (2002). Linguistically sensitive periods for second language acquisition. *Proceedings of the Annual Boston University Conference on Language Development*. Somerville, MA: Cascadilla Press.
Piatt, B. (1993). *Language on the job: Balancing business needs and employee rights*. Albuquerque, NM: University of New Mexico Press.
Pickering, L. (2001). The role of tone choice in improving ITA communication in the classroom. *TESOL Quarterly*, 35, 233–55.
  (2006). Current research on intelligibility in English as a lingua franca. *Annual Review of Applied Linguistics*, 26, 219–33.
  (2009). Intonation as a pragmatic resource in ELF interaction. *Intercultural Pragmatics*, 6, 235–55.
Piller, I. (2002). Passing for a native speaker: Identity and success in second language learning. *Journal of Sociolinguistics*, 6, 179–206.
Piper, T. (1987). On the difference between L1 and L2 acquisition of phonology. *The Canadian Journal of Linguistics*, 32, 245–59.
Piske, T. (2007). Implications of James E. Flege's research for the foreign language classroom. In O. Bohn and M. Munro (eds.), *Language experience in second language speech learning* (301–30). Amsterdam: John Benjamins.
  (2008). Phonetic awareness, phonetic sensitivity and the second language learner. In J. Cenoz and N. Hornberger (eds.), *Encyclopedia of language and education*, 2nd edn., Vol. 6: *Knowledge about language* (155–66). New York: Springer.
Piske, T., MacKay, I., and Flege, J. (2001). Factors affecting degree of foreign accent in an L2: A review. *Journal of Phonetics* 29, 191–215.
Plante, E., Schmithorst, V., Holland, S., and Byars, A. (2006). Sex differences in the activation of language cortex during childhood. *Neuropsychologia*, 44, 1210–21.
Polat, N. and Mahalingappa, L. (2010). Gender differences in identity and acculturation patterns in L2 accent attainment. *Journal of Language, Identity and Education*, 9, 17–35.
Polka, L. (1995). Linguistic influences in adult perception of non-native vowel contrasts. *Journal of the Acoustical Society of America*, 97, 1286–96.
Polka, L. and Werker, J. (1994). Developmental changes in perception of nonnative vowel contrasts. *Journal of Experimental Psychology*, 20, 421–35.
Prescher, P. (2007). Identity, immigration and first language attrition. In B. Köpke, M. Schmid, M. Keijzer, and S. Dostert (eds.), *Language attrition: Theoretical perspectives* (189–204). Amsterdam: John Benjamins.
Preston, D. (1999). *Handbook of perceptual dialectology*. Amsterdam: John Benjamins.
Preston, D. and Yamagata, A. (2004). Katakana representation of English loanwords: Mora conservation and variable learner strategies. *Journal of Sociolinguistics*, 8, 359–79.
Purcell, E. and Suter, R. (1980). Predictors of pronunciation accuracy: A re-examination. *Language Learning*, 30, 271–87.
Purnell, T., Idsardi, W., and Baugh, J. (1999). Perceptual and phonetic experiments on American English dialect identification. *Journal of Language and Social Psychology*, 18, 10–30.
Rahman, T. (2009). Language ideology, identity and the commodification of language in the call centers of Pakistan. *Language in Society*, 38, 233–58.

References

Ramirez Verdugo, D. (2006). A study of intonation awareness and learning in non-native speakers of English. *Language Awareness*, 15, 141–59.

Reiterer, S. (2009). Brain and language talent: A synopsis. In G. Dogil and S. Reiterer (eds.), *Language talent and brain activity* (155–91). Berlin: Mouton de Gruyter.

Reves, R. (1978, August). The ability to imitate as a characteristic of the good language learner. Paper presented to Fifth International Congress of Applied Linguistics (AILA), Montreal.

Rey, A. (1977). Accent and employability: Language attitudes. *Language Sciences*, 47, 7–12.

Rindal, U. (2010). Constructing identity with L2: Pronunciation and attitudes among Norwegian learners of English. *Journal of Sociolinguistics*, 14, 240–61.

Riney, T. and Takagi, N. (1999). Global foreign accent and voice onset time among Japanese EFL speakers. *Language Learning*, 49, 275–302.

Riney, T., Takagi, N., and Inutsuka, K. (2005). Phonetic parameters and perceptual judgments of accent in English by American and Japanese listeners. *TESOL Quarterly*, 39, 441–66.

Robinson, P. (2003). Attention and memory during SLA. In C. Doughty and M. Long (eds.), *The handbook of second language acquisition* (631–78). Malden, MA: Blackwell.

Robinson, W. P. (1979). Speech markers and social class. In K. R. Scherer and H. Giles (eds.), *Social markers in speech* (211–50). Cambridge, UK: Cambridge University Press.

Rogers, C., Dalby, J., and Nishi, K. (2004). Effects of noise and proficiency on intelligibility of Chinese-accented English. *Language and Speech*, 47, 139–54.

Rojczyk, A. (2011). Perception of English voice onset time continuum by Polish learners. In J. Arabski and A. Wojtaszek (eds.), *The acquisition of L2 phonology* (37–58). Clevedon, UK: Multilingual Matters.

Ross, E. and Monnot, M. (2008). Neurology of affective prosody and its functional–anatomic organization in right hemisphere. *Brain and Language*, 104, 51–74.

Rota, G. and Reiterer, S. (2009). Cognitive aspects of pronunciation talent. In G. Dogil and S. Reiterer (eds.), *Language talent and brain activity* (67–96). Berlin: Mouton de Gruyter.

Rubin, D. (1992). Nonlanguage factors affecting undergraduates' judgments of non-native English-speaking teaching assistants. *Research in Higher Education*, 33, 511–31.

Rubin, D., DeHart, J., and Heintzman, M. (1991). Effects of accented speech and culture-typical compliance-gaining style on subordinates' impressions of managers. *International Journal of Intercultural Relations*, 15, 267–83.

Rubin, D. and Smith, K. (1990). Effects of accent, ethnicity and lecture topic on undergraduates' perceptions of nonnative English-speaking teaching assistants. *International Journal of Intercultural Relations*, 14, 337–53.

Rubio-Marin, R. (2003). Language rights: Exploring the competing rationales. In W. Kymlicka and A. Patten, *Language rights and political theory* (52–79). Oxford, UK: Oxford University Press.

Russell, J. and Spada, N. (2006). The effectiveness of corrective feedback for the acquisition of L2 grammar. In J. Norris and L. Ortega (eds.), *Synthesizing research on language learning and teaching* (133–64). Amsterdam: John Benjamins.

Ryan, E., Carranza, M., and Moffie, R. (1975). Mexican American reactions to accented English. In J. Berry and W. Lonner (eds.), *Applied cross-cultural psychology: Selected papers from the Second International Conference of the IACCP.* Amsterdam: Swets and Zeitlinger.

(1977). Reactions toward varying degrees of accentedness in the speech of Spanish–English bilinguals. *Language and Speech*, 20, 267–73.

Rymarczyk, K. and Grabowska, A. (2007). Sex differences in brain control of prosody. *Neuropsychologia*, 45, 921–30.

Rysiewicz, J. (2008). Cognitive profiles of (un)successful FL learners: A cluster analytical study. *Modern Language Journal*, 92, 87–99.

Safar, A. and Kormos, J. (2008). Revisiting problems with foreign language aptitude. *IRAL*, 46, 113–36.

Saito, K. (2011). Examining the role of explicit phonetic instruction in native-like and comprehensible pronunciation development: An instructed SLA approach to L2 phonology. *Language Awareness*, 20, 45–61.

Sanchez, K. (1995). For want of the standard educated variety of Spanish … a German accent: A sociolinguistic study. *International Journal of the Sociology of Language*, 116, 5–16.

Sanz, C. and Morgan-Short, K. (2005). Explicitness in pedagogical interventions: Input, practice and feedback. In C. Sanz (ed.), *Mind and context in adult second language acquisition: Methods, theory and practice* (234–63). Washington, DC: Georgetown University Press.

Sato, C. (1987). Phonological processes in second language acquisition: Another look at interlanguage syllable structure. In G. Ioup and S. Weinberger (eds.), *Interlanguage phonology* (248–60). Cambridge, MA: Newbury House.

Sawyer, M. and Ranta, L. (2001). Aptitude, individual differences, and instructional design. In P. Robinson (ed.), *Cognition and second language instruction* (319–53). Cambridge, UK: Cambridge University Press.

Scales, J., Wennerstrom, A., Richard, D., and Wu, S. (2006). Language learners' perceptions of accent. *TESOL Quarterly*, 40, 715–38.

Schairer, K. (1992). Native speaker reaction to non-native speech. *Modern Language Journal*, 76, 309–19.

Schiappa, E. (2008). *Beyond representational correctness: Rethinking criticism of popular media.* Albany, NY: State University of New York.

Schiffler, L. (2001). Recent neurophysiological studies of the brain and their relation to foreign language learning. *IRAL*, 39, 327–32.

Schmid, M. and Köpke, B. (2007). Bilingualism and attrition. In B. Köpke, M. Schmid, M. Keijzer, and S. Dostert (eds.), *Language attrition: Theoretical perspectives* (1–8). Amsterdam: John Benjamins.

Schmid, P. and Yeni-Komshian, G. (1999). The effects of speaker accent and target predictability on perception of mispronunciations. *Journal of Speech, Language and Hearing Research*, 42, 56–64.

Schmidt, R. (1992). Psychological mechanisms underlying second language fluency. *Studies in Second Language Acquisition*, 14, 357–85.

Schneiderman, E., Bourdages, J., and Champagne, C. (1988). Second-language accent: The relationship between discrimination and perception in acquisition. *Language Learning*, 38, 1–19.

References

Schneiderman, E. and Desmarais, C. (1988). A neuropsychological substrate for talent in second-language acquisition. In L. Obler and D. Fein (eds.), *The exceptional brain: The neuropsychology of talent and special abilities* (103–26). New York: Guilford Press.

Schumann, J. (1975). Affective factors and the problem of age in second language acquisition. *Language Learning*, 25, 209–35.

(1978). *The pidginization process: A model for second language acquisition*. Rowley, MA: Newbury House.

(1994). Where is cognition? Emotion and cognition in second language acquisition. *Studies in Second Language Acquisition*, 16, 231–42.

Scovel, T. (1981). The effects of neurological age on nonprimary language acquisition. In R. Andersen (ed.), *New dimensions in second language acquisition research* (33–42). Rowley, MA: Newbury House.

(1988). *A time to speak: A psycholinguistic inquiry into the critical period for human speech*. New York: Newbury House.

(2000). A critical review of the Critical Period research. *Annual Review of Applied Linguistics*, 20, 213–23.

Seferoglu, G. (2005). Improving students' pronunciation through accent reduction software. *British Journal of Educational Technology*, 36, 303–16.

Segalowitz, N. (2003). Automaticity and second languages. In C. Doughty and M. Long (eds.), *The handbook of second language acquisition* (382–408). Malden, MA: Blackwell.

Segalowitz, N. and Freed, B. (2004). Context, contact, and cognition in oral fluency acquisition: Learning Spanish in at home and study abroad contexts. *Studies in Second Language Acquisition*, 26, 173–99.

Seggie, I. (1983). Attribution of guilt as a function of ethnic attitude and type of crime. *Journal of Multicultural and Multilingual Development*, 4, 197–206.

Seidlhofer, B. (2004). Research perspectives on teaching English as a lingua franca. *Annual Review of Applied Linguistics*, 24, 209–39.

Seidlhofer, B., Breitender, A., and Pitzl, M. (2006). English as a lingua franca in Europe: Challenges for applied linguistics. *Annual Review of Applied Linguistics*, 26, 3–34.

Selinker, L. (1972). Interlanguage. *IRAL*, 10, 209–31.

Sengstock, M. (2009). *Voices of diversity: Multiculturalism in America*. New York: Springer Science+Business Media.

Sereno, J. and Wang, Y. (2007). Behavioral and cortical effects of learning a second language. In O. Bohn and M. Munro (eds.), *Language experience in second language speech learning* (239–58). Amsterdam: John Benjamins.

Setter, J. (2006). Speech rhythm in World Englishes: The case of Hong Kong. *TESOL Quarterly*, 40, 763–82.

Sharma, D. (2005). Dialect stabilization and speaker awareness in non-native varieties of English. *Journal of Sociolinguistics*, 9, 194–224.

Sharwood-Smith, M. (1991). Speaking to many minds: On the relevance of different types of language information for the L2 learner. *Second Language Research*, 7, 118–32.

Sheen, Y. (2006). Exploring the relationship between characteristics of recasts and learner uptake. *Language Teaching Research*, 10, 361–92.

Shen, X. (1990). Ability of learning the prosody of an intonational language by speakers of a tonal language: Chinese speakers learning French prosody. *IRAL*, 28, 119–34.

Shockey, L. (1984). All in a flap: Long-term accommodation in phonology. *International Journal of the Sociology of Language*, 46, 87–95.
Shuy, R. (2008). *Fighting over words. Language and civil law cases.* Oxford, UK: Oxford University Press.
Sifakis, N. and Sougari, A. (2005). Pronunciation issues and EIL pedagogy in the periphery: A survey of Greek state school teachers' beliefs. *TESOL Quarterly*, 39, 467–88.
Simon, E. (2005). How native-like do you want to sound? A study of the pronunciation target of advanced learners of English in Flanders. *Moderna Sprak*, 99, 12–21.
Singleton, D. (2005). The *Critical Period Hypothesis*: A coat of many colors. *IRAL*, 43, 269–85.
Singleton, D. and Ryan, L. (2004). *Language acquisition: The age factor*, 2nd ed. Clevedon, UK: Multilingual Matters.
Skehan, P. (1998). *A cognitive approach to language learning.* Oxford, UK: Oxford University Press.
Smit, U. (2002). The interaction of motivation and achievement in advanced EFL pronunciation learners. *IRAL*, 40, 89–116.
Smith, G. (2005). I want to speak like a native speaker: The case for lowering the plaintiff's burden of proof in Title VII accent discrimination cases. *Ohio State Law Journal*, 66, 231–67.
Smith, J. and Beckmann, B. (2010). Noticing-reformulation tasks as a stimulus towards continued autonomous phonological development. *New Zealand Studies in Applied Linguistics*, 16, 35–50.
Smith, L. and Bisazza, J. (1982). The comprehensibility of three varieties of English for college students in seven countries. *Language Learning*, 32, 259–69.
Smith, L. and Rafiqzad, K. (1979). English for cross-cultural communication: The question of intelligibility. *TESOL Quarterly*, 13, 371–80.
Smith, Z. (2009, Feb. 26). Speaking in tongues. *New York Review of Books*, 56(3), 41–4.
Snow, C. and Hoefnagel-Höhle, M. (1982). The critical period for language acquisition: Evidence from second language learning. In S. Krashen, R. Scarcella, and M. Long (eds.), *Child–adult differences in second language acquisition* (93–111). Rowley, MA: Newbury House.
Solan, L. and Tiersma, P. (2004). Author identification in American courts. *Applied Linguistics*, 25, 448–65.
Sommer, I., Aleman, A., Somers, M., Boks, M., and Kahn, R. (2008). Sex differences in handedness, asymmetry of the planum temporale and functional language lateralization. *Brain Research*, 24, 76–88.
Spada, N. (2011). SLA research and L2 pedagogy. Misapplications and questions of relevance. Presentation to Second Language Research Forum, Iowa State University, Ames, IA.
Spezzini, S. (2004). English immersion in Paraguay: Individual and sociocultural dimensions of language learning and use. *International Journal of Bilingual Education and Bilingualism*, 7, 412–31.
Spoelders, M., Guiora, A., VanLeeuwen, K., Meuleman, C., VanBesien, F., Vyt, A., and DeSoete, G. (1996). A psycholinguistic study of pronunciation of bilinguals: The case of Belgium. In T. Hickey and J. Williams (eds.), *Language, education and society in a changing world* (117–26). Clevedon, UK: Multilingual Matters.

References

Steinhauer, K., White, E., and Drury, J. (2009). Temporal dynamics of late second language acquisition: Evidence from event-related potentials. *Second Language Research*, 25, 13–41.

Stern, H. (1975). What can we learn from the good language learner? *Canadian Modern Language Review*, 31, 304–18.

Stowe, L. and Sabourin, L. (2005). Imaging the processing of a second language: Effects of maturation and proficiency on the neural processes involved. *IRAL*, 43, 329–53.

Strange, W. (1995). Cross-language study of speech perception: A historical review. In W. Strange (ed.), *Speech perception and linguistic experience: Issues in cross-language research* (3–45). Baltimore, MD: York Press.

  (2002). Speech perception and language learning: Wode's developmental model of speech perception revisited. In P. Burmeister, T. Piske, and A. Rohde (eds.), *An integrated view of language development: Papers in honor of Henning Wode* (245–61). Trier, Germany: Wissenschaftlicher Verlag Trier.

  (2007). Cross-language phonetic similarity of vowels. In O. Bohn and M. Munro (eds.), *Language experience in second language speech learning* (35–55). Amsterdam: John Benjamins.

Strange, W. and Shafer, V. (2008). Speech perception in second language learners. the re-education of selective perception. In J. Hansen-Edwards and M. Zampini (eds.), *Phonology and second language acquisition* (153–191). Amsterdam: John Benjamins.

Suter, R. (1976). Predictors of pronunciation accuracy in second language learning. *Language Learning*, 26, 233–53.

Swain, M. (1998). Focus on form through conscious reflection. In C. Doughty and J. Williams (eds.), *Focus on form in classroom second language acquisition* (64–81). Cambridge, UK: Cambridge University Press.

Tabouret-Keller, A. (1997). Language and identity. In F. Coulmas (ed.), *The handbook of sociolinguistics* (315–26). Malden, MA: Blackwell.

Tahta, S., Wood, M., and Loewenthal, K. (1981). Foreign accents: Factors relating to transfer of accent from the first language to the second language. *Language and Speech*, 24, 265–72.

Tajfel, H. and Turner, J. (1979). An integrative theory of intergroup conflict. In W. Austin and S. Worschel (eds.), *The social psychology of intergroup relations* (33–47). Monterey, CA: Brooks/Cole.

Tanner, M. and Landon, M. (2009). The effects of computer-assisted pronunciation readings on ESL learners' use of pausing, stress, intonation, and overall comprehensibility. *Language Learning and Technology*, 13, 51–65.

Tarone, E. (1982). Systematicity and attention in interlanguage. *Language Learning*, 32, 69–82.

  (1987). The phonology of interlanguage. In G. Ioup and S. Weinberger (eds.), *Interlanguage phonology* (70–85). Cambridge, MA: Newbury House.

Taylor, D. (1977). Bilingualism and intergroup relations. In P. Hornby (ed.), *Bilingualism: Psychological, social and educational implications* (67–75). New York: Academic Press.

Tees, R. and Werker, J. (1984). Perceptual flexibility: Maintenance or recovery of the ability to discriminate non-native speech sounds. *Canadian Journal of Psychology*, 38, 579–90.

Thakerer, J., Giles, H., and Cheshire, J. (1982). Speech accommodation theory. In C. Fraser and K. Scherer (eds.), *Advances in the social psychology of language* (205–55). Cambridge, UK: Cambridge University Press.

Thiederman, S. (1991). *Bridging cultural barriers for corporate success: How to manage the multicultural work force*. Lexington, MA: Lexington Books.

Thompson, I. (1991). Foreign accents revisited: The English pronunciation of Russian immigrants. *Language Learning*, 41, 177–204.

Tiersma, P. and Solan, L. (2002). The linguist on the witness stand: Forensic linguistics in American courts. *Language*, 78, 221–39.

Tokuhama-Espinosa, T. (2003). The relationship between musical ability and foreign languages. In T. Tokuhama-Espinosa (ed.), *The multilingual mind* (65–80). Westport, CT: Praeger.

Tomlin, R. and Villa, V. (1994). Attention in cognitive science and second language acquisition. *Studies in Second Language Acquisition*, 16, 183–203.

Trofimovich, P. and Baker, W. (2006). Learning second language suprasegmentals: Effect of L2 experience on prosody and fluency characteristics of L2 speech. *Studies in Second Language Acquisition*, 28, 1–30.

Trofimovich, P., Baker, W., and Mack, M. (2001). Context and experience-based effects on the learning of vowels in a second language. *Studies in the Linguistic Sciences*, 31, 167–86.

Troutt, D. (2005). Defining who we are in society. In K. Walters and M. Brody (eds.), *What's language got to do with it?* (289–93). New York: Norton.

Trudgill, P. (1999). Standard English: What it isn't. In T. Bex and R. Watts (eds.), *Standard English: The widening debate* (117–28). Routledge: London.

Trudgill, P. and Hannah, J. (2008). *International English. A guide to the varieties of Standard English*, 5th edn. London: Hodder Education.

Tse, L. (2001). *Why don't they learn English? Separating fact from fallacy in the US language debate*. New York: Teachers College Press, Columbia University.

Ullman, M. (2005). A cognitive neuroscience perspective on second language acquisition: The Declarative/Procedural Model. In C. Sanz (ed.), *Mind and context in adult second language acquisition. Methods, theory and practice* (141–78). Washington, DC: Georgetown University Press.

University of Iowa (2000). Accents: Problem or opportunity to learn? *Parent Times Online*, 43, 3, retrieved from www.uiowa.edu/~ptimes/issues99–00/spr99-00/accents.html

Van Els, T. and DeBot, K. (1987). The role of intonation in foreign accent. *Modern Language Journal*, 71, 147–55.

Van Geert, P. (2009). A comprehensive dynamic systems theory of language development. In K. DeBot and R. Schrauf (eds.), *Language development over the lifespan* (60–104). New York: Routledge.

Van Wijngaarden, S., Steeneken, H., and Houtgast, T. (2002). Quantifying the intelligibility of speech in noise for non-native talkers. *Journal of the Acoustical Society of America*, 112, 3004–13.

VanPatten, B. and Cadierno, T. (1993). Explicit instruction and input processing. *Studies in Second Language Acquisition*, 15, 225–43.

Verhoeven, L. (2007). Early bilingualism, language transfer and phonological awareness. *Applied Psycholinguistics*, 28, 425–39.

Victori, M. and Tragant, E. (2003). Learner strategies: A cross-sectional and longitudinal study of primary and high school EFL learners. In M. Garcia Mayo and M. Garcia Lecumberri (eds.), *Age and the acquisition of English as a foreign language* (182–209). Clevedon, UK: Multilingual Matters.

Vornik, L., Sharman, S., and Garry, M. (2003). The power of the spoken word: Sociolinguistic cues influence the misinformation effect. *Memory*, 11, 101–9.

Vygotsky, L. (1987). *The collected works of L. S. Vygotsky. Vol. 1. Thinking and speaking*. New York: Plenum Press.

Wallentin, M. (2009). Putative sex differences in verbal abilities and language cortex: A critical review. *Brain and Language*, 108, 175–83.

Walsh, T. and Diller, K. (1981). Neurolinguistic considerations on the optimum age for second language learning. In K. Diller (ed.), *Individual differences and universals in language learning aptitude* (3–21). Rowley, MA: Newbury House.

Wang, X. and Munro, M. (2004). Computer-based training for learning English vowel contrasts. *System*, 32, 539–52.

Wardhaugh, R. (1999). *Proper English: Myths and misunderstandings about language*. Malden, MA: Blackwell.

Wardhaugh, R. (2010). *An introduction to sociolinguistics*, 6th edn. Malden, MA: Wiley-Blackwell.

Wattendorf, E. and Festman, J. (2008). Images of the multilingual brain: The effect of age of second language acquisition. *Annual Review of Applied Linguistics*, 28, 3–24.

Weber-Fox, C. and Neville, H. (1996). Maturational constraints on functional specializations for language processing: ERP and behavioral evidence in bilingual speakers. *Journal of Cognitive Neuroscience*, 8, 231–56.

Webster, N. (1789). *An American selection of lessons in reading and speaking: Calculated to improve the minds and refine the taste of youth*. Hartford, CT: Hudson and Goodwin.

Wennerstrom, A. (1994). Intonational meaning in English discourse: A study of non-native speakers. *Applied Linguistics*, 15, 399–420.

  (1998). Intonation as cohesion in academic discourse: A study of Chinese speakers of English. *Studies in Second Language Acquisition*, 20, 1–25.

  (2001). *The music of everyday speech: Prosody and discourse analysis*. Oxford, UK: Oxford University Press.

Werker, J. and Pegg, J. (1992). Infant speech perception and phonological acquisition. In C. Ferguson, L. Menn, and C. Stoel-Gammon (eds.), *Phonological development: Models, research, implications* (285–311). Timonium, MD: York Press.

Werker, J. and Tees, R. (2005). Speech perception as a window for understanding plasticity and commitment in language systems of the brain. *Developmental Psychobiology*, 46, 233–51.

White, L. (2003). On the nature of interlanguage representation: Universal grammar in the second language. In C. Doughty and M. Long (eds.), *The handbook of second language acquisition* (19–42). Malden, MA: Blackwell.

Wilkerson, M. and Salmons, J. (2008). "Good old immigrants of yesteryear" who didn't learn English: Germans in Wisconsin. *American Speech*, 83, 259–83.

Willemyns, M., Gallois, D., Callan, V., and Pittam, J. (1997). Accent accommodation in the job interview. *Journal of Language and Social Psychology*, 16, 3–22.

Williams, G. (2011). Examining classroom negotiation strategies of international teaching assistants. *International Journal for the Scholarship of Teaching and Learning*, 5, 1–16.
Wode, H. (1983). The beginnings of non-school room L2 phonological acquisition. A survey of problems and issues based on data from English as L2 with German as L1. In H. Wode (ed.), *Papers on language acquisition, language learning and language teaching* (150–65). Heidelberg, Germany: Julius Groos Verlag.
  (1992). Categorical perception and segmental coding in the ontogeny of sound systems. In C. Ferguson, L. Menn, and C. Stoehl-Gammon (eds.), *Phonological development: Models, research, implications* (605–31). Timonium, MD: York Press.
Wong, R. (1985). Does pronunciation teaching have a place in the communicative classroom? *Georgetown University Roundtable on Languages and Linguistics*, http://search.proquest.com/docview/85471387?accountid=14696
Yabukoshi, T. and Takeuchi, O. (2009). Language learning strategies used by lower secondary school learners in a Japanese EFL context. *International Journal of Applied Linguistics*, 19, 136–72.
Young-Scholten, M. (2002). Orthographic input in L2 phonological development. In P. Burmeister, T. Piske, and A. Rohde (eds.), *An integrated view of language development. Papers in honor of Henning Wode* (263–79). Trier, Germany: Wissenschaftlicher Verlag Trier.
Young-Scholten, M. and Archibald, J. (2000). Second language syllable structure. In J. Archibald (ed.), *Second language acquisition and linguistic theory* (64–101). Malden, MA: Blackwell.
Yule, G., Hoffman, P., and Damico, J. (1987). Paying attention to pronunciation: The role of self-monitoring in perception. *TESOL Quarterly*, 21, 765–68.
Yuracko, K. (2006). Trait discrimination as race discrimination: An argument about assimilation. *George Washington Law Review*, 74, 365–438.
Zampini, M. (2008). L2 speech production research. In J. Hansen Edwards and M. Zampini (eds.), *Phonology and second language acquisition* (219–49). Amsterdam: John Benjamins.
Zatorre, R. and Samson, S. (1991). Role of the right temporal neocortex in retention of pitch in auditory short-term memory. *Brain*, 114, 2403–17.
Zhang, L. (2004). Awareness-raising in the TEFL phonology classroom: Student voices and sociocultural and psychological considerations. *ITL, Review of Applied Linguistics*, 145(1), 219–68.
Zuengler, J. (1982). Applying accommodation theory to variable performance data in L2. *Studies in Second Language Acquisition*, 4, 181–92.
  (1988). Identity markers and L2 pronunciation. *Studies in Second Language Acquisition*, 10, 33–49.

Index

accent (definition; significance of) 2, 3, 9, 10–12, 19–20, 85, 148, 171
acceptability 5, 6, 14, 175
accommodation 3, 5, 8, 99–101, 122, 147, 172, 174, 179
acculturation 63–4, 175, 179
ACTFL guidelines (*see* ILR)
Activation Threshold Hypothesis 79
affect (*see* socio-psychological factors)
age of onset (AO)/age effects 1, 12–13, 21–4, 26, 36, 43, 44, 46–8, 50, 58, 59, 76, 77, 84, 176–7, 179
age vs. 'stage' issue 29, 44, 47, 173
agency 41, 58, 64, 66, 69, 70, 71, 84, 173, 174, 175
anchoring hypothesis 44
aptitude 12, 22, 23, 27, 39, 44, 52–3, 55, 57, 84
assimilation 50, 67, 70, 81, 84, 89, 90, 123–4, 131, 144, 145
asymmetrical abilities (perception vs. production) 4, 30, 37, 38
attention 31, 33, 48, 56, 60, 152–4, 155, 158, 160, 167, 172, 173, 174, 179
attitudes 14–15, 19, 60, 61, 70–2, 91, 93, 99, 102–9, 116, 117–18, 120, 121, 125, 172, 173, 174–5 (*see also* stereotypes, prestige, discrimination)
attrition (L1) 78–9, 176 (*see also* language dominance)
authenticity 2, 7, 18, 22, 27, 58, 147, 167, 168, 180
Automated Speech Recognition (ASR) 156–7, 159

belonging (*see* identity)
bilingualism (advantages for phonology) 4, 36, 42–6, 48, 76, 78, 154

categorical perception 3, 31–7, 42
cognitive–affective interface 31, 56, 173, 174
cognitive style/strategies 52, 57, 60, 69, 81, 83, 173, 174

Common European Framework 164
communicative burden 15, 107, 122, 140, 172–7
communicative competence 7, 138, 149
communicative impact of foreign accent 92–102, 107–8, 170
comprehensibility (*see also* intelligibility) 5, 7, 15, 92, 93–5, 99, 104–5, 117, 118–22, 130, 131, 136, 140, 144, 151, 155, 167, 171, 172, 173, 174, 180
computer-assisted pronunciation training (CAPT) 7, 155, 157, 158–61, 168
concern for pronunciation accuracy 19, 23, 51, 60, 70, 80, 82, 168 (*see also* desire to sound native)
contrastive analysis 37
critical period/Critical Period Hypothesis (CPH) 2, 4, 13, 19, 23, 24, 25–7, 42, 47, 48, 74, 180
cue weighting 32, 36, 55, 158, 161–3

declarative vs. procedural knowledge 31, 180
desire to sound native 52, 60, 70, 78, 82
    (*see also* concern for pronunciation accuracy)
developmental processes 15–18, 32, 39, 40–1, 47
dialect 10–11, 90, 100, 127 (*see also* variation – sociolinguistic)
discrimination 6, 86, 89, 110, 113, 126, 128–30, 131–45, 172 (*see also* stereotypes)
dynamic systems theory 49

empathy 56, 63, 80, 101, 174
exceptional learning 5, 18, 50, 51, 69, 80–2, 178
experience (impact on phonology) 12, 24, 36, 44, 47, 48, 51, 72–80, 82, 84, 154, 175–7

Feature Competition Model 34
feedback (corrective) 7, 54, 74, 148, 150, 152, 153, 156–8, 168
fluency 3, 7, 11, 15, 57, 74, 120, 139, 147, 167, 168, 169, 172, 173, 177, 180
foreigner talk 99
forensic linguistics 141

217

Index

gender differences 4, 58–61, 107, 173, 174

identity 1, 10, 11, 19, 62–7, 76, 78, 79, 99, 115, 125, 163, 175, 178
ILR (Interagency Language Roundtable) 164–5
immigrant language acquisition 4, 19, 21, 64, 91, 122–4, 131, 144, 175, 176
individual differences/individual factors 2, 4–5, 49–84, 147, 173, 174
input 18, 19, 26, 27, 31, 32, 34, 36, 39, 41, 47, 51, 71, 72, 83, 152, 175, 176
instruction (*see also* computer-assisted pronunciation training) 2, 7, 23, 60, 74, 81, 120, 139, 146–70, 173, 174, 177
intelligibility 1, 2, 5, 7, 89, 92, 93–8, 117, 121–2, 133, 147, 151, 158, 160, 169, 171, 180
interaction (impact on phonology) 4, 13, 36–7, 61, 64, 74, 75, 80, 81, 82, 84, 174, 177
interference (*see* transfer)
investment/intention toward target language 48, 58, 70–2, 75, 84, 173, 174, 176, 178

L2 accent features/L1-L2 contrasts 15–18, 33–6
L2 use/contact 4, 18, 31, 75–6, 77, 79, 80, 81, 82, 84, 156, 173, 174, 176
(*see also* experience)
language dominance 76–8, 124
language ego 44, 62, 64, 80
lateralization (*see also* plasticity) 26, 28
learning styles/strategies 56–8, 167
length of residence 18, 23, 60, 73–5, 76
linguistic profiling 6, 126–8, 141, 143

markedness 40–1, 162
matched guise 14, 103, 108, 141, 181
memory 53–4, 60, 167
methodological issues in L2 phonology 23, 27, 60, 61, 67, 77, 84, 98, 108–9, 158, 162, 172–7
motivation 52, 63, 67–9, 81, 172, 173, 174
musical talent (related to pronunciation) 54–5

Native Language Perceptual Magnet 32
nativeness 2, 7, 18, 50, 91, 122, 147, 171, 174, 181
noticing (*see* attention)

Ontogeny–Phylogeny Model 40
Optimality Theoretic Model 35
orientation (learner) 4, 51, 70, 82, 83, 174
orthographic input/interference 158, 161–3
overhearing (passive exposure) 45–6

passing 5, 65–6, 84, 174, 176, 181

perception/perceptual abilities 15, 32, 36, 38, 83, 163, 172, 173, 174–5
Perceptual Assimilation Model 34
phonological awareness 42
phonology (uniqueness of) 3, 12, 62
phonology/phonetics (definitions) 10, 181
plasticity (*see also* lateralization) 25, 26, 27–30, 44, 82, 182
prescriptivism 5, 87–9, 104, 116, 182
prestige 14, 87, 91, 99, 102–6, 113, 130
processing 3–4, 22, 25, 27–8, 29–30, 31, 44, 45, 53, 54–6, 59, 98, 172, 173, 176, 182
profiling (*see* linguistic profiling)
pronunciation (definition) 10

recasts 156–7, 159
received pronunciation (RP) 89, 91, 102

self-monitoring 7, 47, 48, 56, 152, 154–6, 167, 175
self-regulation; self-efficacy; self-determination (*see* agency)
simplification (*see also* developmental processes) 11, 15, 39
social identity theory 110
social-psychological factors 5, 13, 19, 24, 57, 61, 62–72, 74, 101, 172, 173, 174–5
Speech Learning Model 35, 41
standards for accent 8, 14, 60, 84, 86, 87–92, 125–6, 163–7, 171
stereotypes 91, 104, 107, 109–21, 130, 143 (*see also* discrimination)
strategies for improving pronunciation 56, 84, 174
style-shifting 3, 13–14, 122, 147, 183
successful learners (*see* exceptional learning)
suprasegmental features/fluency 7, 18, 23, 27, 37, 56, 57, 73, 85, 95–6, 99, 118, 119, 150, 151, 165, 168, 170, 173, 174, 183

task differences 12, 22, 23, 27, 39, 44, 46, 155
Title VII 6, 134–7, 144, 145
transfer 15–17, 34, 37–8, 40, 41, 43, 47

ultimate attainment 5, 18, 22, 26, 27, 183
underlying representations 43–4, 47, 78, 82
universal processes 16, 31, 34, 39–40, 46, 158, 162 (*see also* developmental processes; markedness)
uptake 157, 158–61

variation – individual abilities 4, 12, 26, 41, 47
variation – sociolinguistic 7, 13–14, 46, 60, 88, 100, 102, 116, 130, 135 (*see also* dialect)

World Englishes 91–2, 95, 98, 169